W9-CDL-879

EARNED

IN

BLOOD

EARNED
IN
BLOOD

My Journey from Old-Breed Marine to
the Most Dangerous Job in America

THURMAN MILLER

ST. MARTIN'S PRESS
NEW YORK

EARNED IN BLOOD. Copyright © 2013 by Thurman Miller. Foreword copyright © 2013 by Richard Frank. All rights reserved. Printed in the United States of America. For information, address St. Martin's Press, 175 Fifth Avenue, New York, N.Y. 10010.

www.stmartins.com
Maps by Paul J. Pugliese

Library of Congress Cataloging-in-Publication Data

Miller, Thurman I., 1919–
    Earned in blood : my journey from Old-Breed Marine to the most dangerous job in America / Thurman Miller.—First edition.
        p. cm.
    Includes bibliographical references and index.
    ISBN 978-1-250-00499-4 (hardcover)
    ISBN 978-1-250-02126-7 (e-book)
    1. Miller, Thurman I., 1919– 2. United States. Marine Corps. Marine Regiment, 5th. Battalion, 3rd. Company K.   3. Marines—United States—Biography.   4. Coal miners—West Virginia—Biography.   5. World War, 1939–1945—Campaigns—Solomon Islands—Guadalcanal.   6. World War, 1939–1945—Campaigns—Papua New Guinea—New Britain Island.   7. World War, 1939–1945—Personal narratives, American.   8. Appalachian Region—Social life and customs—20th century.   9. Rural poor—West Virginia—Biography.   10. West Virginia—Biography.   I. Title.   II. Title: My journey from Old-Breed Marine to the most dangerous job in America.
    D767.99.P4M55 2013
    940.54'265933092—dc23
    [B]
                                                                    2013004028

St. Martin's Press books may be purchased for educational, business, or promotional use. For information on bulk purchases, please contact Macmillan Corporate and Premium Sales Department at 1-800-221-7945 extension 5442 or write specialmarkets@macmillan.com.

First Edition: May 2013

10 9 8 7 6 5 4 3 2 1

This book is dedicated to the men of K Company.
Semper Fi.

Contents

FOREWORD

W HEN I FINISHED READING THIS compelling work, my mind reflected not only on what I had just experienced, but also on how it fits both into the long sweep of writing on war and in the American literature on World War II. Classic works by the Greeks Herodotus and Thucydides created the template in Western Civilization of the master narrative we label "history" and the role of the "historian." But the past refuses to anoint only one legitimate mode or one set of scribes. Side by side with the rise of the master narrative another enduring method, the memoir, rose and flourished. While the aperture through which a memoir retells the past is narrow, a quality memoir rewards us with an intimate physical and psychological sense of the past.

The riveting story of World War II as retold in the United States emerged in part as a competition between master narratives and memoirs. In the first and largest wave from the end of the war to roughly about four or five decades thereafter, classic narratives exercised an overall ascendency. These master narratives owed their dominance to the urge to make sense of such huge and transformative events. Historians culled archival holdings and aimed to displace the voids or misapprehensions of wartime accounts with an orderly and richly sourced work. The opening of new troves of records triggered new cycles of this process. Since at least about the mid-1990s, however, the quantum of fresh and important American archival material or private records entering the public domain yearly has slowed. On the other hand, we have witnessed an encouraging surge of narratives based on previously untapped archival material from the former Soviet Union and Japan—and we have just barely begun this process for China. The master narrative will by no means disappear, but presumably we are looking forward to an era in which a more international approach, exploiting records from multiple nations, will prove the cutting edge of these publications.

This is not to say that during this earlier phase no memoirs appeared or that they failed to enjoy critical and public success. On the contrary, publishers rushed out scores of memoirs shortly after the end of the war. These overwhelmingly comprised the stories of those who held consequential positions of one variety or another. Numerically and especially proportionately, the memoirs of those serving in capacities both more modest and usually more dangerous proved slower to appear. Even when the memoirs of those manning the frontline positions began to emerge in numbers, they skewed toward veterans of air or sea units. Relatively few such memoirs emerged from those who engaged in ground combat. Partly this stemmed from the fact that air and sea combat environments often permitted the maintenance of personal notes, a privilege usually unavailable to those in ground combat units. Moreover, given public conventions of the times, reinforced in many instances by self-censorship, the early generations of frontline memoirs now sometimes seem stilted.

It is commonplace to attribute to the generation that fought World War II a reticence compared to later American cultural conventions. This is certainly true to an important degree, but by no means the whole story. The most important factor is that those who served in frontline positions were young men who took off their uniforms and eagerly turned to the tasks of work and raising families, leaving little time for the hard work of writing. Another complex factor involved issues that gnawed at many veterans: Was my contribution that significant or my sacrifice that singular? Service in uniform was the common coin of that generation. In the first decades after the war, many veterans regarded their personal contribution as modest. Those who witnessed the wholesale death or maiming of comrades often felt a humbling sense of good or even unmerited fortune in war's random lottery of survival. These factors suppressed in many cases any urge to record personal experiences. It was only when the generation that fought the war reached later years and they had the time and often the impetus of recording their experiences for their own families that we witnessed a large upswing in memoirs of genuine combatants and particularly those who served in the infantry.

About the same time the memoir industry slipped into a surge of production, public taste in World War II history underwent a shift. The master narrative did not disappear, but the reality or the perception that archives had been thoroughly mined coupled with the diversion of work into the great events of the decades following World War II thinned the ranks of historians working the period. At the same time, a numerical and qualitative rival to the classic narrative pressed forward. This was the journalistic account perhaps best exemplified by the works of Cornelius Ryan's, including *The Longest Day, The Last Battle,* and *A Bridge Too Far.* Ryan and his peers deftly merged a narrative framework with dozens of highly colorful and detailed individual vignettes. In a sense, these works combined the classic master narrative with the memoir to provide both the form and sense of events. In my view, this type of work has now eclipsed the older-style master narrative in public taste with respect to works published in the United States about World War II. Even journalistic accounts now are challenged if not overtaken by an eager public hunger for memoirs heightened by the knowledge of the mortality of the World War II generation.

All of this background is important in understanding the virtues and significance of *Earned in Blood.* Broadly, it appears as one of a wave of memoirs of actual ground combatants produced in later life. Even within this now much enlarged category, it contains important features that set it apart. The book begins with a very engaging and insightful evocation of growing up in West Virginia amid the Great Depression. This section is lyrical about the beauty and entertainment produced by nature, but does not overlook nature's trials, like drought and forest fires. The opening section is also quite gritty and clear-eyed about the often baleful nature of the coal industry and the grinding burdens of poverty. Thurman Miller's home was in a "holler," one of those tiny valleys tucked into the steep uplands of his state. His youth featured places like churches, schools, swimming holes, and lumber company railroad tracks. Much of his daily life was consumed by domestic tasks like gathering wood and repairing clothes and shoes, not all that common in the era and rare today. Thurman was a high school graduate, a major achievement in that period that was even more impressive in West Virginia, where many boys left school to work from about middle school.

Another facet setting this memoir apart is that, unlike the great majority of American World War II veterans, Thurman joined the Marine Corps pre–Pearl Harbor. He finds that his rugged upbringing, where food and sleep were short and outdoor hours long, empowered him to negotiate the rigors of marine Boot Camp with comparative ease. He then is assigned to Company K, 3rd Battalion, 5th Regiment, 1st Marine Brigade. The brigade later becomes the 1st Marine Division. K/3/5 ("K-3-5" in marine jargon) would become perhaps the most famous marine rifle company in the war, primarily due to Eugene Sledge's fabled *With the Old Breed at Peleliu and Okinawa*. Many critics regard Sledge's work as one of the greatest American combat memoirs of the war, if not the greatest. That fame and those campaigns were far in the future when Thurman joins the company. They train relentlessly for amphibious operations and jungle warfare, most notably in Cuba. Thurman mentions his rise to the position of platoon guide, an event that demonstrates his superiors noted his leadership ability very quickly. Then, in the rapidly expanding but still small Marine Corps, Thurman makes sergeant before Pearl Harbor.

The heart of the book covers World War II. Thurman's unit, the soon legendary 1st Marine Division, hastily mounts and executes the first American offensive of the war by landing on

Guadalcanal on August 7, 1942. While the landing proved an-
ticlimactic on Guadalcanal, the next four months constituted
an epic ordeal. Thurman relates with equal attention the dangers posed by the Japanese on land, sea, and in the air, and the
trials of the weather ("two settings: Wet and Less Wet"), the
lack of food (he joined the marines at 160 pounds and weighed
115 on leaving the island) and the want of rest that tested the
marines to the limit. He is particularly vivid about malaria and
its effects, although he personally escaped its grip on Guadalcanal. Like other rifle units, his company spent endless hours and
days on patrol self-schooling themselves in the finer points of
that duty. He devotes lengthy attention to his comrades, both
those who survived and those who did not.

From Guadalcanal, Thurman goes to Australia. He is now a
platoon sergeant, a testament to his excellent performance on
Guadalcanal. Australia provides an idyllic interlude in which
he and his comrades can refurbish themselves in mind and body.
From there the next operation is Cape Gloucester on the island
of New Britain. Thurman lists the charms of Cape Gloucester as
"the rain, the snakes, the heat, fungus, dysentery, and malaria."
If K/3/5 experienced perhaps less major action "on the line"
than some other units on Guadalcanal by luck of the draw, it
more than made up for this in the utterly miserable rain forest
of Cape Gloucester. There are ferocious fights at places called
Suicide Creek and Walt's Ridge. Thurman describes the excru-
ciating experience of ordering a friend, a squad leader, into an
assault:

> He told me it was a suicide mission. I told him it was an order.
> Without another word he turned, gathered his squad and left.

That was the last I ever saw of him. Our lines were so close I heard him engage the enemy. I heard him cry out when he got hit. I heard him dying, and in the din of the battle, the rattle of his breathing was sharp and unnatural. He had been shot in the throat, and the air sucked into the hole made the sound of snoring. He was about fifteen minutes dying.

After Cape Gloucester, Thurman's overseas service has earned him the points to qualify for a program of rotation back to the States. By now, the Marine Corps has elevated him to the exalted rank of gunnery sergeant. This is a position occupied only by men deemed to epitomize the highest qualities of field leadership and savvy. Captain Andrew Haldane offers Thurman the job of top sergeant of K/3/5 if he would go on to what proves to be Peleliu. Thurman—who admits a powerful sense that his luck is running out—turns down that much-respected officer.

On reaching the States, he marries the girl who waited for him, the beautiful Recie Marshall. They start their life together as Thurman, after a brief taste of other duty, turns to the assignment of officer training. He understands the life-or-death importance of good officers and tries his best to make sure he only passes those he thinks can pass the test of combat leadership.

By now, malaria has a grip on Thurman that it will not release for years. It appears in relapses that incapacitate even a man of his great strength, but it's not just his body that retains residuals of his experiences. He is plagued by a symptom complex he vividly describes, manifested prominently by recurrent, disordered, and often disturbing dreams. *Earned in Blood* tenders a great deal of insight into what now goes under the label of post-traumatic stress disorder. The book is of particular value because it honestly confronts a condition found all too frequently among combat veterans and illustrates that it is not some recent phenomenon. He will experience many occasions where he is torn, as he puts it, between "the desire to end it all or [to] fight it out." In the end, he fights it out with the indispensable help of his wife.

When the war ends, Thurman elects to be discharged and returns to West Virginia. Here again is another distinctive feature of this memoir. Unlike most such works, Thurman gives extended coverage of his postwar life. That life starts very hard. He leaves the Marine Corps and two tough campaigns and goes into West Virginia's staple employment: coal mining, the most dangerous of civilian occupations. He provides a primer on just how demanding and miserable is the labor of separating coal from the earth. The recurrent bouts of malaria and the dreams make this passage even more challenging. With time, much support, and his own inner strength, Thurman forges a life of dignity and achievement.

Beyond the merits of Thurman's descriptions of his wartime service, *Earned in Blood* makes two distinctive contributions to the American memoir library from World War II. As noted, it stands apart from the general run of memoirs because of the extent and quality of its coverage of prewar and postwar events. Thus, it takes the reader back not just to the turmoil of the war, but to the rigors and pleasures of youth in Appalachia and the long challenges and eventual satisfactions of over six decades of postwar adjustment. It is thus the memoir not only of a war, but also of a generation. Moreover, it stands out because it meshes with other landmarks in the memoir literature. One can now read Thurman Miller's book and follow K/3/5 from prewar to Cape Gloucester. Sledge's book takes up the story for the last two campaigns of the company at Peleliu and Okinawa. Further enriching this unique situation, R. V. Burgin's *Islands of the Damned* provides a vivid portrait of K/3/5 from Cape Gloucester to Okinawa. These memoirs provide an opportunity to see the 1st Marine Division's four campaigns through the eyes of veterans of a single rifle company.

In sum, *Earned in Blood* provides the reader with a vivid panorama, painted with directness and honesty, of an exceptional personal journey through peace and war—a peace and war both without and within.

—RICHARD FRANK

Greater love hath no man than this,
that a man lay down his life for his friends.

—JOHN 15:13

Humility must always be the portion of any man
who receives acclaim earned in blood of his followers
and sacrifices of his friends.

—GEN. DWIGHT D. EISENHOWER

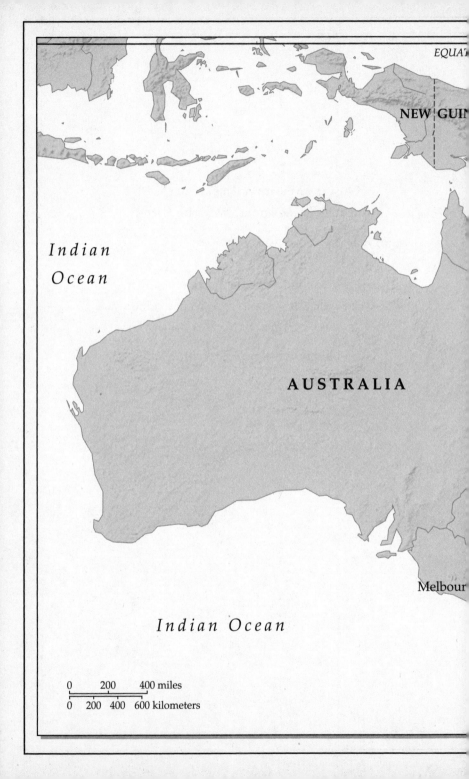

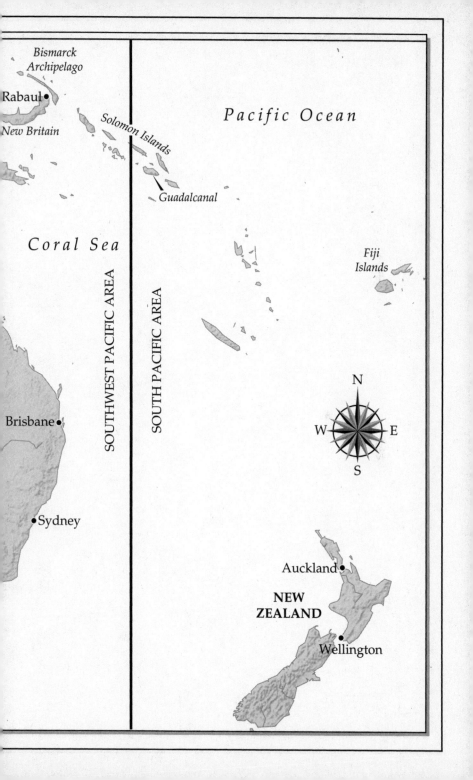

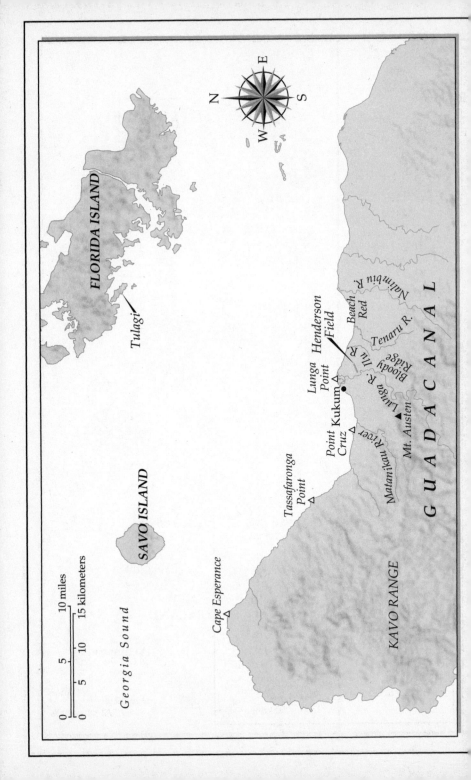

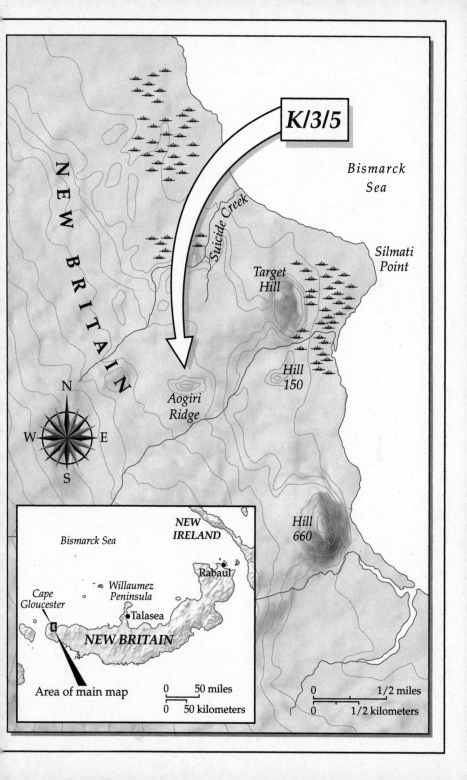

EARNED
IN
BLOOD

PROLOGUE

I AM NO SCHOLAR OF WAR. When I returned from the South Pacific I wanted nothing more to do with jungles or killing; the recurring malaria and tropical diseases I brought home with me were more than sufficient reminders of my time in service to this country I love.

Soldiers on the ground never see the strategic importance of their deployment, never understand, at the time, why they are sent where they are sent. We do as ordered. It was only in the years after the war, as my family life stabilized and my health began to improve, that I began to study the small but pivotal role my outfit played in the war. I understood very well why many men never want to discuss the things they did, and still must do, to fight a war; yet I have always been curious by nature, and no subject could be more intriguing to a man than the minor part he played in such a momentous event.

Having said this, I lay no claim to expertise in anything but my own life. There is no shortage of exhaustive research on Guadalcanal, New Britain, and the war in general, with more being added daily, and I will leave to others the painstaking work of recording the details of troop movements, how battle plans succeeded or went awry, and so on. Here I supply only what interests me and is necessary to tell my story as honestly as I can within the larger context of the war. After the passage of so many years, I hope the reader will forgive me for any instance where my own memory diverges from a more formal accounting.

As the wounds of the hard years of war began to heal I found that although I had the love of a good woman, and a beautiful family, and a job that would permit our rise from Appalachian poverty into the American middle class, I was also lacking something. I did not know what that was until years later when I again met my friend "Mo" Darsey and the other men of K Company, and we began to talk about our shared experience. I realized I missed the brothers who would understand the journey I had taken. I come from a very large family, and we were all very close; but in the Marine Corps I made a new family, new brothers, a kinship that can only arise among a group of young men with nothing in common, thrown together, broken down, and built back up into a cohesive unit much greater than the sum of our members.

Therefore, this is my story, but it is unavoidably also the story of the 172 men of K Company, the men who took their places as they fell, and the 1st Marine Division of which we were a part. In time, 25 members of our original company would be killed in action, 54 others seriously wounded. Thirty-one more would develop malaria severely enough to be sent home, while others fell to the disease months or years later. Our members earned the Silver Star, the Navy Cross, and many other decorations, but all of us who survived carry some scar by which we recognize each other, whether the systemic weakness of malaria or wounds that drained us of our youth. The men of K Company shared their stories with me, and I am honored to weave them into my own. Some went on to other battles after Cape Gloucester, while I returned stateside to teach future officers the lessons we had learned on those obscure islands in the South Pacific, to prepare men barely out of their teens to lead other young men into a war against an enemy of unprecedented ruthlessness.

Every war is in reality thousands of individual wars, as each soldier battles both his own fear and the man directly in front of him, equally convinced of the rightness of his cause. Every peace, for a veteran, is a separate peace, constructed by the hard work of coming to terms with what he has seen. This is the story of the war I fought and the peace I found.

1

West Virginia, America, 1940

Carving a life

Being a United States Marine came to define my life, but Appalachia defined me first. My family has deep roots in southern West Virginia. My great-grandfather on my father's side, Franklin Sizemore, was one of the earliest settlers here, part of a large migration from North Carolina in the mid-nineteenth century. He cleared the land that eventually became my hometown of Otsego. He was born in North Carolina in 1817 and migrated to Virginia about 1840. He became a postmaster and started a one-room log-cabin school near the mouth of Cedar Creek in 1874 and raised a very large family, including a son, William, my grandfather.[1] My father, Eli Center Miller, was one of William's many sons.

I come from a very large family, both my parents having been married and widowed with several children before finding each other. My mother, Elvira Rinehart, lost her first husband to malaria around 1915, the same disease that would play such a large role in my own life. His death left her alone and penniless, with seven children between the ages of one and twelve and still another on the way. My father lost his first wife at about the same time, probably to influenza, leaving him to care for their five surviving children alone. Perhaps mutual loneliness drew my father and mother together after each of their spouses passed away. They proceeded to add children of their own, four of us surviving to adulthood. I was fortunate to have had the joy of so many brothers and sisters.

Not all of us lived in the cabin on Cedar Creek, of course. As often happened in those days, relatives stepped in to take care of some of my mother's children; there were just too many to feed and care for. Even with those who remained, my parents' oft-repeated lament was "Your kids and my kids are beating the hell out of our kids!"

I was born on November 26, 1919, in a time of great upheaval. The world had just endured a war designed to make the world safe for democracy—a war, it was said, to end all war. The Roaring 20s were not so loud for us, for although nature provided plenty of fruit and fish during the warmer months, how much food we would have during the winter months was left up to us, as money was scarce and what we ate we had to grow. We were, after all, just simple farm folk and lived mostly from the hillside plots and a small amount of bottomland, with plantings of corn, potatoes, and other staples.

One of my earliest memories is of my grandfather hoeing corn; his arms, long and powerful, drove the hoe forward, upward, and back again in one smooth motion, shoulders broad and rippling, tireless muscles moving with precision. Before I was old enough to help, I played among the cornstalks as I watched him. Grandfather's gnarled hands would wrap around the handle of the hoe as he worked along the row, the six-feet-plus of man blending perfectly with his tool, defining economy of motion as his hoe cut its way smoothly through the dirt and replaced it without leaving weeds or piles. He was a giant to me, a crease in his brow, a handlebar mustache curling about his lips. He knew how to carve a living from the land and preserve it for coming generations. When he spoke, which wasn't that often, I hung on his every word. I wish I had more of them to recall.

There were so many mouths to feed that children were put to work early then. I was eight years old when my father gave me my own hoe. I took my place at the end of the line, because hoeing in the mountainside was truly an adventure. My dad was first to start a row, and then the next best worker and so on down the line. The work was difficult, and it made my hands hard and rough and my back stiff. My mother worked the fields alongside us. We stored up corn for the winter to feed the livestock and poultry.

My father was a carpenter and a subsistence farmer; my mother would can and pickle and dry-preserve the garden's produce. We sat down to a table full of food we had raised ourselves, by the grace of God. We didn't go hungry, but we didn't get fat either, and we knew of many who had much less than we did. It was a life that was echoed throughout West Virginia, throughout all Appalachia. My Dad never prayed aloud much in church, but he said thanks at the table. I will never forget the humility and sincerity of his blessing, "Dear Lord, we thank Thee for this food as a nourishment for our bodies." Sometimes the larder would be empty of almost anything except the corn before the long winter months ended, but Mother would take the corn and turn it into some kind of meal.

Despite having no money, my parents had a deep sense of dignity. My mother's last-born child, a boy, lived only a few hours. My father and uncle took a large poplar board from the fence to make a tiny coffin. We couldn't afford sandpaper, so my father used bits of broken glass to smooth the wood down. My mother took a pillow from the bed to make a pad for the bottom and sewed tiny, perfect pleats around the border of a scrap of white cloth for the lining.

Although my family had been in West Virginia for a century and a half, like a lot of Appalachian families we never owned the land on which we lived. We were raised on a leasehold; large coal or timber companies owned all the land in our part of the state, and I lived on our leased land until I had a family of my own.[2] For now, we lived peacefully with the land and it sustained us. There were moonshine stills in the dense forests above our home, and as I explored the woods one day looking for straight weeds to make arrows I stumbled on a sack full of half-gallon fruit jars. I took the sack home and gave it to my mother, not realizing the jars belonged to moonshiners. We couldn't afford to ignore anything of value, but I soon learned that moonshiners weren't shy about defending their property, and I never again disturbed their stills.

Houses back then were mostly plain lumber, many of the "Jenny Lind" design, with the walls consisting of wide boards nailed to two-by-sixes and narrow boards covering the seams. The insides usually had no studs, and as the vertical boards began to cure, gaps would appear. These were covered with whatever people could find to keep out the cold wind. My mother, after lining the walls with large pasteboard boxes or scraps of fabric, would carefully tear up old magazines and, after making her own paste from flour and starch, would "wallpaper" entire rooms, including the ceiling. As we grew up and had nothing much else to do, we would start reading different articles on the walls. Some were incomplete and we would have to search for the rest of the article. We would pencil "continued in the kitchen" for the next reader. In addition to the comics and casual articles, our walls told a broken but engaging story of a world in the grip of economic malaise, with war and rumors of war in faraway places with names we could not pronounce.

During the twenties and thirties, we had no electricity, no heating system, no plumbing or running water in the house. All heating and cooking were done on either coal or wood stoves. As a small child I found refuge behind our large cookstove and lay there and napped when it was cold. As the youngest boy in the family, I was given the chore of building all the fires in the morning. In winter this was a hard job because of the number of fires I had to build. We had two heaters, one for the living room and another on the other end of the house in the big room that served as both a sitting room and bedroom. I had to get a good fire started in the cookstove first, because my mother was an early riser and always had breakfast on the table before daybreak. My mother told me I would have to build the morning fires only until we heard the first whippoorwill of spring.

Poor as we were, and with so many of our own mouths to feed, I never knew of our mother turning anyone away from our door. She fed them all, whether a relative or just some old man without a home. Our family would let them stay in a little shed close by, and when Mom got a meal on the table they always had a place and were treated like family. Many itinerant preachers would visit our town and sometimes stay with us, and occasionally they would organize an all-day revival with music and "dinner on the ground." We children loved these because we could eat our fill.

We bathed using a big pot of water on the kitchen stove, a washpan, and some soap. We washed our upper body and then closed the door and warned everybody we were washing the rest. We'd brush our teeth with baking soda or with just plain soap and a rag. In the summer months, we usually had a small swimming hole nearby and would take along some soap and bathe while swimming.

By the age of ten, I had begun tending our cows, and this chore kept me close to nature year-round. I grew up under the old rule that children should be seen and not heard, so while around adults I kept silent, but while I tended the cows I sang, loud and long, and some say they heard me all over the mountains. Singing as I drove in the cattle, I was sometimes lost in a dream world, and these times were carefree and simple.

When early spring brought new life to the land, everything began to bud and bloom. Sap began to rise in the maple trees, and my father would begin to plan for that year's crops. Here in Appalachia, there was little or no bottomland on leased farms where families such as ours lived, so the mountainsides became our cornfields. (A friend from another part of the country described us as farming "land you could fall off of.") Clearing tillable acreage was arduous, backbreaking work. To make a plot suitable for farming, the trees had to be cut down, eventually to be turned into fence posts, and the stumps removed. All the underbrush was grubbed out with a mattock and hoe. The brush and small saplings were piled in several stacks throughout the field to be burned after they had dried out. Rocks also had to be cleared and piled. The entire process of clearing new ground took about a year from start to finish.

When new life burst forth in the spring, it meant fishing in Cedar Creek and an abundance of small game. There were rabbits, groundhogs, coons, foxes, and all manner of wildlife. Maybe it was my imagination, but they never seemed afraid of me in the woods. The squirrels kept their distance but were not disturbed by my presence. I guess this may have had some bearing on why I never hunted much as I grew up. My dad told of bigger game when he was a boy, plenty of bear and wildcat. Whatever nature could provide us to eat, or trade for something to eat, we didn't have the luxury of turning down. We saved seeds year to year because we couldn't afford to buy new; we made medicine from catnip and sassafras and crushed jewelweed; we harvested wild blueberries and blackberries and huckleberries.

Though hillsides were hard to till, the ground was fertile, and paid off in the fall with an abundant corn crop. Fall was kicking my bare feet in a pile of leaves and eating the wild nuts of the woods, a time to gather the fruits of our labor. We wore no shoes until very late in the year, and on frosty fall mornings I would run the cows up and stand where they had lain all night to warm my feet. I hasten to say this was not cruelty on the part of my parents but rather was a way of life for many.

The mountain also gave us heat for the winter. Coal was so abundant that many dark outcroppings of it—coal blooms—could be seen along creek beds and hillsides. Just in front of our house a seam of coal was sometimes exposed when Cedar Creek was very low. We would all pitch in and shovel the dirt off a portion of the coal seam. My older brothers would obtain blasting powder—we didn't ask where they got such things—and blast the seam apart so we could shovel out the coal.

It's been said that those of us from Appalachia were "born fighting."[3] I'm not sure about everybody else, but it certainly worked for me. Fighting, and playing, and hiding in the hills. Appalachia is not just a region: It's a culture, a frame of mind, a history, a family, a being. For over a hundred and fifty years my family has lived in the same villages—and even the same cabins—as our grandparents, great-grandparents, and great-greats. The land is dense and steep and impenetrably wooded with oak and hickory, with maple and pine and locust. The mountains seem to muscle in upon one another. Cabins are built on whatever flat land can be found, almost always alongside a creek, which carries the runoff at the base of the mountain. If five or six cabins will fit, we'll call it a town and give it a name. Our homestead on Cedar Creek, where I was born and raised, was a holler, which is essentially a valley, a valley only yards wide.

Even in the chaos of our busy house, it was a glorious time to be a boy in the mountains. I often played in Cedar Creek. Naked or clothed, it didn't matter to me. They say I once clad myself in only a necktie. The railroad men must have found this very amusing, because the tale has followed me down to the time of this writing. The railroad was installed along Cedar Creek for timbering up the mountain, so track was laid up by where we lived. As small children, we all enjoyed watching the log trains come and go and waved at the men working on them. After the logging was completed, the lumber company left the track for a few years. They also left some little flatcars they had used for hauling supplies. When I got older, we would push these cars to about a mile above our home, load them with wood, and ride them back down.

A small boy remembers small-boy things. I was an imaginative child. Sometimes I was a cowboy. Sometimes I was a soldier and went off to war. I remember visiting my much older brother-in-law, Fountain Sumner, and seeing his World War I doughboy uniform hanging up in the closet. I was always in awe of it. I realized even then that he belonged to an exclusive club, one in which membership is paid not in money but in the price asked of those who must seek out another human and cause him to die. He was a coal miner after the war, and I would study Fountain's face and try to look beyond the coal grime. Coal miners acquire a ring of black around their eyes, and Fountain's seemed magnified, so one could look deep into his soul. In church I would steal glances from the shaped-note hymnal back to him, wondering what was in his mind. From time to time, I would catch a bleakness, a despair, and I could only imagine what he must have been thinking. Now I know, for only those who have been similarly tried can truly understand.

In 1931, when I was twelve, a great drought swept across the land, although knowledge of what was happening outside our hills came to me only years later, for we had no radio or newspaper. The great Dust Bowl movement in the West had begun. The nation's breadbasket dried up, and the wind began to

destroy the land on which people depended. The drought began slowly, scorching farms and everything else in its path from
Mexico to the far North. It brought an end to many small
farms in the Appalachians and along the Blue Ridge. Water
became scarce; streams dried up and became dusty troughs
smelling of dead fish. There was no corn, no wheat, no rye, no
feed for the livestock. Our cattle began to die, so there was no
fresh beef or milk. The horses began to die. There were no pen-
nies, nickels, and dimes lying around unclaimed as there are
today; money simply went away.

This was a war for which there were no weapons, only prayer.
The churches filled up, as the fulfillment of the Bible's prophecy
of "famine and pestilence in the land" appeared imminent. Depression and drought were the Axis powers of our first war, for
we were to fight it alongside our parents. The elements themselves had become the enemy. The harsh rays of the sun beat
down to wither anything green. Even the ground dried up and
blew away on winds created by the terrible heat. That year the
forest on Cedar Creek became tinder dry, and inevitably came
the fires. Every mountain seemed ablaze. For days thick smoke
filled the air and it was difficult to breathe. Even the roots of the
trees dried out and began to burn. Small game came out of the
woods in search of food and water, the different species no longer having the energy to prey on one another but rather searching for some mutual relief from the heat and thirst. I watched as
a groundhog ambled slowly by, completely unaware of anything
else around him. No fear even as I picked him up. Only fur and
bone. Nature's delicate balance had been upset, and as the year
went on, she failed to replenish herself.

I watched Cedar Creek become small pools of water here

and there. These filled with fish that flopped around until the water dropped even more, and finally Cedar Creek died. There were no victors in that war.

It just slowly came to an end as the rains returned, leaving the land scarred. One summer's drought was broken very dramatically. My brother Buck and I were standing by a creek near our home one day when the sky grew an angry purple and the wind picked up and the trees on the mountaintop began to sway crazily, as if they didn't know which way to bow. Then a small vortex seemed to gather all at once and came racing down into the valley, turning, twisting as it came. It hit bottom, swirled the waters in the creek, and continued across and up the other side. It suddenly turned to run along the hollow, and as it did it began twisting the trees and breaking them, large oaks and hickorys, as easily as a dry twig. Buck and I stood speechless. We turned to run, but the small storm raced after us. Buck was trailing me by a few yards, and as I looked back I heard an awful crack as a huge dead tree came crashing down between us. Buck emerged from the other side unhurt. Our wild run brought us safely out of the timberline, and we crossed a low bridge leading to an open field. Now the sky lit up and lightning surrounded us on all sides. Our hair began to crackle, and the storm seemed to concentrate over this one little spot. Lightning struck a wire fence just a few yards away and discharged into the earth. We lunged onto the safety of my sister's porch. When the storm subsided we went back, found our cattle, and started for home. The late-evening sun playing on the mountaintop seemed to spread its calm. The mountains slowly turned green again over that summer but were somehow never the same.

Perhaps our fight against the greatest of foes, nature,

tempered our generation for the great war to come. We learned the lessons of making do with whatever was at hand, or doing without.

I grew into my teens much the same as any boy. Girls began to be pretty instead of boring, and grown-ups seemed to get dumber as I became wise beyond all expectation. My grandfather began to falter, not quite as steady and broad shouldered as I had always known him.

I attended a little two-room schoolhouse in Otsego, down the valley from our Cedar Creek home. Otsego had about two hundred people, and in the sixth grade there were only two of us in my class. For seventh grade, which was considered high school, Otsego kids were bused into the town of Mullens, a big city to me with a population of several thousand spread out across a long and wide valley on the Guyandotte River. The first day I went to catch the bus to my new school, the driver wouldn't let me on. I was a scrawny kid, and he said I was too small to be going to high school. I should have agreed with him and just skipped it altogether, because when I did show up at Mullens, it was not to a warm welcome. Most in the school I attended looked down on the children who were bused in from the coal towns, much less those of us from the hills. A student who happened to be the child of a superintendent or foreman had it made, while plain coal miners' children were barely tolerated. I didn't even live in a coal town. We were "them kids from up the holler." As we walked up the street, we knew we were being sized up and our appearance compared to that of the kids from the towns.

Seventh grade was a big cultural change for me. That was the year I first used that mysterious object called the telephone.

I was summoned to the principal's office one day with the message that I was wanted on the phone. Well, by golly, that was something! Very timidly I picked up the phone and said hello, but there was no one there. Gently the secretary took the receiver from my hand and reversed the ends, and I heard the caller clearly.

The other students were mostly from Mullens, with parents who were merchants or trades people, and were far better dressers, and I always felt out of place. In grade school, we were for the most part all the same, children of farmers and coal miners. I decided it wasn't for me. I lied to the principal, told him I had the itch, and he was glad to get rid of me when I dropped out. My dad said nothing, but he introduced me to an array of farm tools and put me to work. I learned that year that I didn't want to be a subsistence farmer. I went back the next year and took the seventh grade over again, determined to graduate from high school, come hell or high water. Biology was the most interesting subject to me, for I grew up amid nature's bounty. I was very popular with girls when it came time to gather bugs and leaves for school.

During my high school years I had to buy my own books. There was no extra money, and I had to resort to whatever means I could in order to get them. I cut corn in the fall and dug potatoes and did anything else that came my way. For this I received a dollar a day. Believe it or not, this was considered good money for a boy. I cannot conceive of a modern boy doing this kind of work, tolerating the worms, or the big ears of corn banging you in the head. I once cut thirty-five regulation shocks of corn in a single day, and the man I worked for couldn't believe it. He raised my wages to a dollar and a half a day.

My brother Buck and I were appointed janitors for the school, a job our father had previously held. It paid eleven dollars a month. At the end of the month, we would get several large flour sacks and walk down to Mullens, to Shannon's General Store. We bought the entire eleven dollars in staples we couldn't raise at home. We didn't even ask our parents; we just took the money and bought the food we knew our family lacked. One of us carried a twenty-five-pound sack of meal and the other a twenty-four-pound sack of flour, and we filled our extra sack with salt and sugar and other items we knew our parents needed. We carried our sacks as we walked the several miles from Mullens to our home in Cedar Creek. During the spring and summer months we peddled fresh vegetables, eggs, and anything else we could sell to the people of the community. My primary job was to deliver the produce and collect a little money for Mom that she in turn used to purchase staples we could not raise. Sometimes I thought this beneath my dignity, but I did it, and later I was proud to have contributed to our family's survival in those hard years.

After three months in the eighth grade Buck decided he'd had enough of school and convinced my father to let him quit and get a job with the Works Progress Administration. The wages were small but did help the family. After a time, he went back to school, but our need was great, so he joined the Civilian Conservation Corps. He made $30 a month, $25 of which was automatically sent to our parents. The Corps gave him a uniform, and he looked good in it. The CCC fought fires and built roads and observation towers, and he stayed with the CCC for sixteen months.

Some teachers recognized that the kids from the hollers

needed special help. Once Buck stayed home from school and the teacher asked me where he was. I told her the truth, that he had no shoes to wear. She told me to tell *James* (she always insisted on his proper name) to come in the next day and wait in the hall. That morning, before school started, she gave him a pair of shoes that would do until my father could afford new ones. Kindness such as this helped dispel the feeling that everyone was against us.

One Christmas my dad came into a bit of extra cash. With it, he walked to Mullens and purchased each of us, boys and girls alike, a pair of boots with a knife scabbard on the side. All of us prized this gift very highly and wore them until they were completely worn out. I learned the art of "half-sole" at a very young age, and when my boots wore thin my dad would give me exactly enough money to buy leather, along with a box of brads, and I would resole my shoes. This was the norm in those days; we did what we had to do in order to live.

I made no great impression at school but did make good on my determination to pass. I also was determined to learn to use the typewriter, and this skill served me well over the years. (After the war I would develop the habit of carrying a notebook in my pocket and would jot notes to myself about my experiences and type them up as time permitted. I never intended for anyone else to read what I had written; it was just a kind of self-therapy, to give form to the ordeal I had experienced. Much of this book springs from those early writings.)

I borrowed a coat, dress shirt, and tie for my high school graduation and was proud to get my diploma. Now the big world was out there for me to conquer. Now I could be an active member of it. However, this was a world still in recovery from the

Depression. As I saw the many empty, expressionless faces I wondered, *What the hell will I do?* I began by clerking in the company store, but this job soon ended, and I went to work for a power company and then a construction company. When a big construction job was finished I was laid off, and that proved to be the last job I could find for a while, no matter how hard I looked.

That summer my grandfather took to his bed and passed on without my telling him I loved him, but it was understood. He had taught me to love the land and to respect it, to be in partnership with it as it provided sustenance, and to understand that we are to preserve it for our children.

The beginning of the new school year came down on me hard when I saw the others going back. Only then did it strike me that I was now for all practical purposes an adult. Unlearned, perhaps, but an adult nevertheless. When I began to view the world from that perspective, I didn't like what I saw. With the lack of jobs on our minds, one of my half brothers and I and a friend of ours decided to "go west, young man." We hopped a freight train and started out for California. Our trip was short. On the first leg of the journey we pulled into Dixon yards just out of Charleston, West Virginia, and were picked up by some railroad dicks. One detective took us on a "tour" of Riverside Boulevard, past the governor's mansion. He would always start his description the same dramatic way: "And this, gentlemen . . ."

The most impressive sight was the county courthouse. It contained many offices, including the place of confinement to which they brought offenders like us. The dick was still dramatic, "And this, gentlemen, is the county jail." There was a bounty on the head of every hobo they caught, and we were just one group among many. Among the three of us I was the first in line, but there were plenty of other vagrants ahead of me. I listened while the justice of the peace dealt out justice to those ahead of me. Guilty or not? "Not guilty," they replied. "Thirty days and costs," came the sentence. Well, I knew I was guilty and would plead so. I was both surprised and pleased at being sentenced to only ten days and costs. (I thought to myself, *I could do that standing on my head.*) My total confinement amounted to fourteen days, apparently because I couldn't pay the "costs"—even though it cost the county more to keep me there the extra days. It did me a lot of good to meet the seedy characters with whom I served my confinement. One guy paced and smacked his fist into his palm. "Hell," he said, "you got to buy 'em off or bump 'em off. And I've bumped off thousands of 'em." Pacing, back and forth. I learned the hard way not to put myself in situations where it would be necessary to be with these kinds of people, including some of my brothers.

It was an unexpected lesson, for between the ages of sixteen and twenty I had been the subject of much discussion in the community. During my high school years I had fallen under the influence of some of my older brothers who had become familiar with the local law enforcement agencies. I didn't have the ambition to be a true criminal but was curious and mischievous. Law enforcement agencies had more than once come to our home looking for one of my brothers, or for me; sometimes it was a case of guilt by association, but sometimes their suspicion of me was well founded. It was probably no surprise for any of them to hear I had been in jail in Charleston.

I finished up my sentence, returned home, and loafed about

with the other boys my age. By now, 1940, all of us were well aware of the gathering clouds of war and were discussing the probability of our being drafted. We had listened as our elders talked of Japan and Germany and, remembering Fountain, I wondered if there would be a time when I would be called to defend my country.

Five of us boys were playing cards one day in a railway tunnel near our homes, and talking about our futures, and we agreed we would join the Marine Corps together. Why the Corps? I'm not really sure. I don't recall seeing a particular movie that would have convinced me that it was the branch for me. I do know that the Marine Corps had a well-deserved reputation for being the elite branch, after its success at Belleau Wood and other battles. I also know that even though all the branches were seeking recruits, with the war just over the horizon, the marines had a special place in the armed services, the first to fight, capable of being sent anywhere (even, for example, the Halls of Montezuma, wherever they were). We made a pact: We would meet at eight o'clock Monday morning on the bridge that carried the main road over Cedar Creek and would go the nearly 100 miles to Charleston to join up.

I didn't think of it at the time, but Appalachia has paid more than its share of the nation's war debt. Our region continues to send our young people to the armed services at a very high rate, and I believe this is for two reasons. First, we tend to be a patriotic people, unashamed to demonstrate our love for our country. Perhaps this follows from our deep love of the land. Second, however, the armed services have offered a path out of the poverty that has marked both the perception and the reality of our most rural areas, a path that leads to a role commanding respect and rewarding hard work and self-discipline. Whether that promise is true for most young Appalachians is doubtful.[4]

My weekend was full of thought and soul-searching. I knew it would only be a matter of time until I would have to go into the service, and if I waited it would be on "their" terms. I decided I would enlist and go on my own terms.

Monday morning I found myself alone on the bridge. I decided I would go on by myself. I hitched a ride to Charleston—without getting into jail this time—and located the marine recruiting depot. The Marine Corps gave me a very stiff medical exam, finding only an overriding left little toe, which would have been enough to get me out of service, according to the doctor, but I wasn't looking to get out. They gave me a few days to go home and set my affairs, such as they were, in order. As I was not yet twenty-one my parents signed a form consenting to my enlistment and "relinquishing all claims" to my service to them; they certified my date of birth, that I had not been married nor served in the military, and that I had not been convicted of any felony. I presume there was a silent agreement on all our parts to ignore my adventure in the Kanawha County Jail, a misdemeanor.

Leaving home for a few days or weeks was one thing, but leaving for a more extended stay was something else. The full import of my decision came to me a few days later as I walked out of Cedar Creek. I felt a lump in the pit of my stomach. What lay in the future? What of the old folks? My brothers and sisters? I took a final look, avoiding any tearful good-byes, but I felt an immediate loneliness I would carry to the far reaches of the world. I felt my leaving was barely noticed by my peers. *He's gone* was all I imagined they would say. I had been a thorn in the side of some, but now I would trouble them no more.

I left home wanting the adventure that lay ahead and at the same time coveting the mountains of my childhood, with my secret caves and trees and hiding places. What of the girl I loved but had never really told? Would she remember me? Would I be a hero in her eyes, or would my absence cause her to find someone else?

The long walk to the Mullens bus stop to head back to the recruiting station and then on to boot camp gave me time to reflect. Once aboard the bus, I leaned back and rested my head on the seat and accepted what the future would hold. One thought gave me the determination to make good. My father had said, "Son, I'm afraid you'll spend all your time in a guardhouse." He was justified in thinking that. I had been pretty wild for a few years, and from my habit of just taking off and bumming my way here and there, I guess it was natural for my dad to think what he did. My reply came easily and naturally. "Dad, if I don't go, these people will make a criminal out of me anyway, so where I'm going will either make or break me. If I make good, I'll be back; if not, I'll stay away." I meant it. I loved my mother and father passionately, and the largest scar I carry is the guilt of causing them concern.

With these thoughts swelling in my breast, I checked in at the recruiting depot. I raised my right hand and they administered the Marine Corps oath. So help me God, I promised to defend these shores.

Then I shipped out to Parris Island to become a marine.

2

THE UNITED STATES MARINE CORPS

Humanity's reach

I HAD NO IDEA WHAT TO expect at boot camp. On the train trip to Parris Island, South Carolina, I wondered how I would take to the legendary discipline of the Corps, being an independent young man. The train trip was uneventful but not tranquil. The other recruits and I were escorted on the train by the ugliest, meanest man I had ever encountered: He stood over six feet tall, a livid scar beginning out of sight under his cap and running between his eyes, across his nose, mouth, and chin, and disappearing under his open shirt. His first words were *"All right, who told you bastards you were marines?"* All I could think was *What the hell have I let myself in for?* He belittled us all the way to the base, cursing us and telling us we were just farmers out of the hills and that they had scraped the bottom of the barrel to get us. *"You'll never make it!"* he swore. He uttered profanities I had never heard before. By the time we got to the base all of us had the desire to kill him, and truly, many of us would have been capable of it. He was right, however—we were mostly just kids out of the hills.

Looking back, I'm sure he was handpicked for the job of introducing recruits to Parris Island. Teach them to forget their loved ones at home. Teach them to hate. Give them a new vocabulary. Erase love, compassion, and decency. Rid them of any emotion that might retard their ability to kill, kill, kill. This man got us fighting mad. I was from a loving family and not used to being treated this way, but he was sowing the seeds of anger and resolve we would need to wage war. We were angry before we arrived at Parris Island, and we stayed that way through boot camp. The Marine Corps nurtured that hostility and kept it watered with the desire to strike out at something. Every second of a marine's training is geared toward one goal, the reminder that he is the best, most disciplined fighter in the world, always ready.

Our newly organized platoon was number 99 in the official book. Sergeant Strawarski and Corporal Edmonds were our drill instructors and took us all the way through boot camp. Our training, along with our being ridiculed, began very early each morning. The cry from the drill instructor was "Platoon 99, outside!" We learned to listen closely for this cry, for if he yelled it once and we didn't respond instantly we were made to run around the parade ground until we dropped.

Our daily training in Marine Corps history and military ranks and weaponry was supplemented by endless marching, on the parade ground and off. In between was work on the obstacle course, practice on cargo nets, and munitions training. Throughout, we were belittled and made to feel small. Every day was hard. We were given a 10-quart bucket, a brush, and soap, and with these we scrubbed down our barracks. We cleaned the cracks in the floor with a toothbrush. They broke us down to ground level; we soon realized we knew nothing except what the Corps had taught us. They erased all memories of our past lives, or tried to. It was drilled into us that nothing but strict and immediate obedience to orders given was acceptable.

We were becoming leathernecks, though marines hadn't worn leather neckpieces since the late 1800s. Our day started at dawn, with reveille. We'd jump out of bed, get dressed, head to the parade ground for roll call, then fall out to the chow hall. In those days, there was no cafeteria line; the food would be waiting on the table. We were required to stand at attention as the chaplain said grace, after which pandemonium ensued. I learned more cuss words at chow during boot camp than during all the rest of my life. If you didn't include at least three four-letter words in a sentence such as "Pass the potatoes," you didn't deserve to eat.

After chow, it was back to the parade ground for more marching. We wore the standard boots and dungarees, our field hats, a cartridge belt—no bullets—and a first aid pack and canteen filled with water on our belts. When the drill instructor ordered us to "Fall in!" he meant it, and we fell into formation immediately. We'd hop to our prearranged platoon formation and line up according to height: tallest on the extreme right, shortest on the extreme left. At 5'7", I tended to be in the middle. Then we'd do it again with a squad formation—and marching, always marching. We had one guy in the platoon, Williams, who was forever out of cadence and forever getting screamed at. One day, when the drill instructor was having a strangely good day, he stopped the march and ordered the platoon to match Williams's irregular rhythm. We were all flabbergasted, Williams most of all.

When we were in the field, our midday meal would be delivered in trucks and the containers set out on the tailgate. We'd file by with our mess kits. One day a hard summer rain hit just as they began serving. By the time I sat down to eat this "slum"—technically, vegetable soup—my mess kit was overflowing, but what little sustenance was there to begin with was diluted by the rain.

Our uniforms were identical, and our training soon shaped us into sixty pairs of heels clicking together in unison, sixty rifles slapping the manual of arms. The instructor now began referring to us as "his" platoon instead of "you bastards."

You will hear this tale over and over again from other marines; it is how the Marine Corps makes a man a marine—and it works. Parris Island to this day is synonymous with tough Marine Corps training. As one writer put it, "The training syllabus at the West Coast Recruit Depot in San Diego is identical, but Parris Island has the mystique" of the true Marine Corps spirit as compared to the "Hollywood marines" of the West Coast.[1]

One of the basic tenets of the Corps is that "every marine is a rifleman," down to cooks and clerks, and we learned that our rifle was our best friend, to be kept clean and at the ready at all times. We practiced on the rifle range for endless hours, and once we had mastered the rifle we learned the bayonet and hand-to-hand combat, how to first take away an enemy's rifle and then take away his life. We practiced tossing hand grenades into buckets from a distance. We used the .45 automatic pistol and resorted to Kentucky windage—throwing up a little dust to judge the wind—to aim our rifles. I only made marksman in the use of the rifle, but I knew enough about each firearm to use everything we'd been instructed in. I was also qualified as a combat swimmer, which requires swimming not just for endurance but as a matter of life and death; we trained to swim with full gear in case we had to disembark off the side of a boat into deep water and swim to the beach, in the days before amphibious landing boats had front ramps and tractor wheels. We even had training in riot duty.[2] The marines had to be ready for anything.

Much of the boot camp experience was less difficult for me than for the others, because I was used to having not quite enough to eat, roaming the hills for days on end, and going without sleep and working hard. In fact, those of us from the hills probably had a less difficult time in the military than many others. One historian, referring to Vietnam-era veterans, may just as well have been speaking of our generation when she wrote, "Appalachians were raised in an environment that necessitated the development of survival skills and when honed through a crash course in military combat tactics during boot camp, their potential to be good warriors often led to heroic actions on the battlefield. . . . Veterans who had grown up in rural areas indicated a better preparedness for the physical requirements of military service. Many Appalachian veterans credit their hunting and weapon skills, developed during childhood, in helping them to survive in combat."[3]

We were also schooled in what it meant to be not just a soldier but a marine. Both at Parris Island and later in Cuba we would occasionally be marched out to sit under a tree, where an officer would read the Articles of War to us. (After World War

II these would be subsumed into the Uniform Code of Military Justice.) We took the Articles seriously; I certainly did, wanting to present myself as a true marine and not just some hired killer. The importance of following the Articles was emphasized to us repeatedly; our conduct in war was to be governed by honor. Yet following such regulations regarding treatment of the enemy became more difficult in actual combat, as we would learn. The Articles covered virtually every situation we might be faced with—the treatment of prisoners, absences with and without leave, how courts-martial would be run, even down to the penalty for cowardice, for which "the crime, punishment, name, and place of abode of the delinquent shall be published in the newspapers in and about the camp and in the State from which the offender came or where he usually resides; and after such publication it shall be scandalous for an officer to associate with him."[4] I thought of my father's worry that I wouldn't have the discipline needed for the Corps.

We graduated from boot training into provisional companies. We were now full-fledged marines. We didn't know it at the time, but we were bound for the 1st Marine Brigade, the only unit in the country near to being ready for war. As we trained, world events kept edging the United States closer to war, and May 1940 saw the foundation of the entire Western world shatter. Hitler marched across Europe, subduing smaller countries, and sent his U-boats to harass South America and the Caribbean. We knew the marines were the only outfit that could be committed on a foreign shore without a formal declaration of war. Wherever Americans worked, lived, and had business interests, we could be landed for their protection. So they shipped us out to Guantánamo Bay, Cuba.

In 1898, the mysterious sinking of the battleship the USS *Maine* in the Havana harbor—and the resulting deaths of 258 American sailors and marines—transformed what had been the Spanish-Cuban War into the Spanish-American War. The same year, with cries of *"Remember the Maine!"* the United States had invaded the Spanish-controlled nation of Cuba, eventually putting an end to the four-hundred-year empire of Spain. In 1903 Theodore Roosevelt signed a treaty with the first president of the new Republic of Cuba, giving the United States a perpetual lease on the land and waters of Guantánamo Bay. There, a naval military and coaling station was built and manned. It is today the oldest military base outside our borders. For three decades a small American military presence had been garrisoned there, but as the war in Europe intensified, the American military stepped up its level of alert, and the brass decided to establish a Marine Corps presence at Guantánamo. My provisional company and I disembarked in Cuba on December 23, 1940, to join the existing nucleus of the 1st Marine Brigade. Little did I know when I set out for Cuba that the obscure naval base where I was to be stationed would someday become notorious as "Gitmo" and a prison for accused terrorists.

There were literally no structures when we landed. We carved our tent camp from the burning landscape of the desert. We broke rock and mixed and poured cement for the mess hall base, the head, and all other sanitation facilities. While the base was being built I walked guard duty with a fully loaded .30 caliber Springfield rifle and full ammo belt. Our camp was located on the desert slopes of the island and was barren except for lizards, cactus, and other forms of life that could survive in such a climate. We were told that if the lizards could take it, so could we. During the day the broiling sun burned us until we looked like the natives of Cuba.

We practiced the art of war during the next few months—landing on the beaches of the surrounding islands, assaulting hills, cutting through the jungles of the shoreline. We were taught to live, if we must, on bamboo shoots, grub worms dug from rotten logs, or anything else we could find. Hard and hungry we were, tough and ready for whatever we were asked to do. Again, my Appalachian boyhood of living off the land and making do prepared me for such privations better than most. One day we were given a potato and a couple of strips of raw bacon for our meal. The city boys couldn't figure out what to do with them, but I gathered pebbles from the beach and built a small firepit. I rested my mess kit over it and fried the bacon and sliced the potato into it. It was delicious, and the smell attracted some of the other guys. Before long small fires popped up all over the beach.

Meanwhile, the ambitions of the Rising Sun had begun to concern the entire world. Japanese aggression in China caused great unease to the United States, Australia, and the future Allied Powers who still had colonial enterprises in Asia. President Franklin Roosevelt committed economic aid and military support to China, including marines, and the War and Navy departments quietly began updating and revising their amphibious landing protocols and training. Colonel Earl "Pete" Ellis, an aide to Marine Corps Commandant John Lejeune, was the most vocal of these planners and eerily prescient:

Japan is a World Power and her army and navy will doubtless be up to date as to training and materiel. Considering our con-

THE UNITED STATES MARINE CORPS

sistent policy of nonaggression, she will probably initiate the war; which will indicate that, in her own mind, she believes that, considering her natural defensive position, she has sufficient military strength to defeat our fleet . . . In order to impose our will upon Japan, it will be necessary for us to project our fleet and land forces across the Pacific and wage war in Japanese waters. To effect this requires that we have sufficient bases to support the fleet, both during its projection and afterwards.[5]

Though amphibious landing operations have existed since the earliest times, they were historically inefficient at best and catastrophic at worst. Requiring coordination, good luck, and the willingness to sacrifice any number of troops, amphibious landings are always difficult. Lejeune instructed his men to begin creating a systematic plan to improve the corps amphibious landing operations. Published in 1934, the *Tentative Manual for Landing Operations* would become the blueprint for marine actions in the Pacific. Throughout the 1930s, a greatly reduced force began to put the new *Manual* through real-life tests. In 1934, Colonel A. A. Vandegrift took his men through the maneuvers in the Caribbean.

A scion of old-guard Virginians, Vandegrift was born in Charlottesville and joined the Marines in 1909, choosing the Corps only because at the time there was no army examination scheduled. Over the intervening years, Vandegrift moved up the ranks and from one Central American nation to another. In 1927, after completing stints in Panama, Nicaragua, and Venezuela, he and his marines were sent to China to protect Americans in Shanghai's International Settlement and to keep an eye on the Nationalist Army commander, Chiang Kai-shek. When he returned to Quantico, Vandegrift was assigned to the team polishing the *Manual's* text. This document was so important that marine classroom work was suspended to accommodate work on it. When it was done, the marines were ready, and the East and West Coast Expeditionary Forces were redesignated the Fleet Marine Force.

Refocusing Marine Corps training for amphibious assaults meant the Corps would not only have to coordinate the landing craft but also engineer a plan of support operations for naval gunfire and air support. If the landing was to succeed, all three components must be seamlessly interwoven. Getting the support of the other branches of the armed services—which jealously guarded their status and their funding—would remain an issue throughout the war.

Because of this emphasis, our training in Cuba was narrowly focused on amphibious landings and jungle warfare. Sailing between the tiny islands that lay off Cuba's shore, we went over the edge of our Higgins boats, stormed the beach, and pounded our way through the dense jungle. Two companies would go ashore abreast and immediately spread right and left, heading for the cover of the jungle. Each company would comprise three rifle platoons and a weapons platoon. Over and over we would do this, perfecting the art of amphibious landings.

The 1930s saw a lot of young men join the marines to escape the Depression, and those who joined in 1939 and '40 and earlier were called the "Regulars" because they were the first used to form the 1st Marine Division. They often are called the "Old Breed." Some members were relatively young, but all were "the Bearded First"—even if some could not yet grow a beard.[6] (On Guadalcanal a general would ask our Corporal Beltrami where his razor was. "I don't have one, sir; I don't shave." It's hard to believe how young we were.)

The other side of the coin was Sgt. Elmo "Pop" Haney, a 5th Marine veteran who'd served in France and kept coming back to the Corps even through the brutal Peleliu campaign; for men like him, the Corps was a life, not just a service to their country for a few years. I first became acquainted with Haney in Cuba while I was still a private. (I didn't make PFC until our return to the States.) Had I known at the time that he was a World War I marine I would have saluted him, whatever his rank. He had been discharged from the marines and had reportedly tried teaching school and selling vacuum cleaners before reenlisting in his old outfit.[7] I first noted how very GI he was. He never addressed anyone by his name but by his rank. He would, without orders, "Blanco" his gear with a khaki powder that when mixed with water and applied on gear would color it uniformly and form a protective coating, as he'd learned to do in World War I. He cleaned his gun constantly and kept his body as clean as conditions permitted. His readiness to kill was unquestionable. As Eugene Sledge wrote, "I felt that he was not a man born of woman, but that God had issued him to the Marine Corps."[8] Pop was platoon sergeant in Cuba and would stay with our company through the Canal and then Cape Gloucester.

The experience of the Old-Breed marines, the regulars, flowed out to the new recruits, the reserves. From the very first there was a camaraderie among the men in Cuba, both regulars and reserves, and it didn't make a bit of difference once we reached Guadalcanal and Cape Gloucester. In Cuba, all began to blend into one fighting unit. The importance of unity was stressed more and more by the officers and NCOs. I had a good platoon, men who would represent the Corps well in the South Pacific.

We were a motley crew in some ways, and an exotic bunch for a guy like me who had never been out of the hills. The platoon leader of our 1st Platoon was Arthur Lowell "Scoop" Adams from New York State, who had acquired his nickname while working on his college newspaper. Scoop would rise from second lieutenant to lieutenant colonel during his long career in the Corps. He was only average sized but had a strong marine bearing. We found in him the type of officer who recognizes that he can depend on those under his command, and we wanted to live up to that confidence. He was always ready to listen, already ready to dispense advice when just that was needed. He never flaunted his rank even as he moved his way up. I recognized his leadership immediately and was proud to serve under his command.

Maurice O. "Mo" Darsey would become platoon sergeant of the 1st Platoon, and as such was second in command. (He wasn't with us in Cuba but would join us at New River in 1941.) No one called him Maurice, not to his face. Mo was a Georgia man, an old-timer at the age of twenty-one because he had spent two years in China. He joined the Marine Corps in 1937 at age eighteen, wanting to make money and see the world. His family was too poor to send him to college, a familiar story. The navy was his first choice, but the marines called him first, so he joined up and after training at Parris Island guarded the embassy in China. Mo was a stout, strong man and may have looked overweight compared to the rest of us scrawny marines, but he was just large and sturdy, and the ravages of battle did not seem to affect him as much as they did others. Even when he was badly wounded he kept fighting. He was a very dedicated sergeant, and all the men of the platoon had great respect for him. For one thing, he had seen the Japanese atrocities in China, where the Japanese slaughtered a quarter-million civilians, and had a better idea of what we'd be facing than did any of the rest of us. Mo survived a lot of close calls during our time together, but his luck didn't begin with us—he had been stationed in Pearl Harbor but was pulled out of there the day before the Japanese attacked.[9]

I would become platoon guide, charged with assisting both the platoon leader and the sergeant, putting me third in its chain of command, and the three of us spent a lot of time together. Scoop, Mo, and I made up the platoon "headquarters unit," or platoon command post (CP). The CP would be located several yards in the rear of four squads, each consisting of twelve men plus the squad leader, so all would be in view of the CP. This command-post strategy started at the top, with the division command post, and on down to regimental, battalion, and company command-post level, as a matter of observing what was happening in front of us, and we could move another squad (or, higher up, a regiment or company) to plug any gap.

We were also fortunate to get a lot of good men assigned to our company, such as Charles "Slim" Somerville, a West Virginian like me, and Weldon DeLong, a Canadian by birth. I made good friends with Jim McEnery, squad leader of the platoon's 1st Squad. Jim stood about six feet and had a distinct Brooklyn accent. I had never been to New York City (or much of anywhere) then, and I always enjoyed listening to him no matter what he was saying, just for the accent. He had a colorful way of expressing himself, too, with a degree of drama. (He and I enlisted the same day, but because he took a boat from New York to Parris Island instead of a train I beat him there, so I was enrolled in Platoon 99 and he in 101.)

We spent Christmas of 1940 in Cuba, but it had lost its true meaning for us. Those of us from the hills could certainly never associate Christmas with sandy beaches and cactus. As the new year wore on we fell into a routine in Cuba and our training became more intense. We refined our methods, aimed a little straighter, bayoneted a little harder, and threw grenades into smaller holes from greater distances. We cohered as a fighting unit, and each of us sensed a growing need to be ready. Beneath the horseplay, which was natural for young men, there was an adult seriousness, an acknowledgment of the coming need. We studied the daily papers and speculated.

Liberty in "Gitmo" was a joke. There were no cities close by, so liberty was in Guantánamo City on a nearby island, which required riding on a bus, a train, and then a boat. The whole trip took about fifteen hours one way, and twenty-four hours was the limit for liberty. By the time we made the trip we were already late. In the long run it was better to frequent our own slop chutes and bug-infested movies.

During five months in Cuba, we had been parched by the intense heat, taught to survive on whatever nourishment could be gleaned from a hard environment, perfected amphibious landings, and been hardened into a fighting machine. We became leaner, more focused. We became the marines our country needed.

Then, abruptly, we were ordered to ship out. Our destination: New River, North Carolina.

New River, which would become Camp Lejeune in 1942, is the major Marine Corps training base on the East Coast. When we arrived, it was still officially Marine Barracks New River. It was home to the Fleet Marines, and it was brand-new. Earlier that year, the U.S. government, recognizing America's imminent entry into war and the coming strategic role of amphibious warfare, purchased 11,000 acres of land for Fleet Marine deployment and amphibious landing training facilities in Onslow County, North Carolina. When the 1st Marine Division landed in September 1941, all that stood at the base was farmhouses and a tobacco barn. A sprawling tent city was hastily thrown up in the sandy pine forest.

The Marine Corps' claim to those acres in Onslow County wasn't without grumbling from the locals, as the construction of the camp, beginning in the spring of 1941, displaced hundreds of families who had lived there for many generations. The new camp had an airfield, separate barracks for black marines, and immense training fields. It was renamed Lejeune because, for one thing, there was already a "New River" at the North Carolina/Virginia border, and a lot of shipments intended for our camp accidentally ended up there.

When we arrived—having gone totally native after months living among the scorpions, cactus, and live-fire exercises—the contrast between us Fleet Marines and those already on base was shocking. The base marine's clothing was neatly laundered and pressed, his boots shined to a high gloss. Even his high-and-tight haircut was meticulously barbered. That wasn't us. Our uniforms were worn and tattered, our boots still carrying sand from Cuba. We were men, ready to work, not examples of military precision and bearing. That was fine with us. We traveled in groups of twos and threes because we were the targets of all the sailors and base marines in Portsmouth as well as Norfolk, Virginia. They were amused and thought we were the misfits of the Corps. They started the fighting; we ended it.

The base marines rightly shied away from us, and the base commander was heard to yell, "Get those damned Fleet Marines the hell out of here." It was rumored that First Lady Eleanor Roosevelt said the Fleet Marines should not be allowed to mingle with the public for at least six months after being in the tropics. (Marines are also fond of repeating her apocryphal quote: "The marines I have seen around the world have the cleanest bodies, the filthiest minds, the highest morale, and the lowest morals of any group of animals I have ever seen. Thank God for the United States Marine Corps.")

Jacksonville, North Carolina, was the closest town to base. When our company first arrived in 1941, it was only a sleepy little hamlet with one place to eat and one movie house. The 5th and 1st regiments introduced the little town to the Corps. We swarmed down on the locals, who were at a loss as to what to do with so many marines. We had the occasional open-air movies, and the Division Service put up big circus tents and there were boxing matches. We traveled to the small towns nearby, following U.S. 17 to New Bern or Greenville or dances at East Carolina Teachers College. Even these towns were tiny, so there was little to look forward to on weekend liberty except going home to visit family.

We knew we were being prepared for war and would specialize in amphibious landings. The key to success for those was having the ability to put men and matériel right on the beach. The Higgins boat, as we came to know it—technically, a Landing Craft, Vehicle, Personnel (LCVP)—was the culmination of a long research effort by the navy to develop a flexible and fast beach landing craft for personnel and equipment, the type of craft that one general said "did more to win the war in the Pacific than any other single piece of equipment."[10] General Dwight D. Eisenhower went so far as to call its inventor "the man who won the war for us . . . If Higgins had not designed and built those LCVPs, we never could have landed over an open beach. The whole strategy of the war would have been different."[11] Adolf Hitler was reportedly aware of Higgins's accomplishment, calling him the "new Noah."[12] At its zenith Higgins Industries was supplying an astounding 92 percent of the ships in the U.S. fleet.[13]

The Japanese had been using beach landing craft with ramps in their bows since at least 1937, and the marines would eventually develop landing craft to match, but for now we would go over the sides. The great advantage of the craft was that it could drive right up close to the beach. After many false starts, the Corps finally had a workable amphibious vehicle, and the 1st Marine Division practiced landing on the beach adjacent to Camp Lejeune. We had no way of knowing that the boats were supposed to be a secret, and who would we tell, anyway? The practice landings were something of a spectacle at times. In an oral history commissioned by Camp Lejeune, Billy

Arthur, a local historian and editor/publisher of *Leatherneck* magazine, remembered taking a picture of one of the early models of Higgins boats the marines deployed:

> The Marines piled over the sides, hit the sand and simulate under attack, move forward and this is a good story. The Navy used to run those Higgins Boats. They would beach them and take them back out. The Marines had not taken over Onslow Beach. The only part of the area that they actually controlled was this area up here in Tent Camp. So everybody was headed there. They came through the swamp, they marched all the way from the beach to Tent Camp and some of them stayed in the woods 2–3 days. It alarmed the people who had not been displaced, see not all of the people had been moved out and so there is still a concession stand on the beach, sold beer. Somebody found out about it and so every time one of those Higgins boats would beach in that area, we would see them come get some beers and run right by those Marines on their bellies.[14]

Arthur took a picture of the landings, and it was printed in a Raleigh newspaper, the first public picture of the Higgins boat. He got calls telling him to "cease and desist," and the navy sent an intelligence officer, Lt. Col. Frank Goettge, to investigate.

Goettge was already an old marine hand, a football star at Quantico. *The Washington Post* for December 2, 1923, covered the annual Army-Marine Corps game, which the marines won for the third year in a row—and fullback Frank Goettge, "the Great Goettge," was the star and most valuable player. Goettge was the "irresistible force, which alone cannot be denied." He turned down professional football for a career in the Marine Corps. Our paths would cross again on Guadalcanal.

Goettge told Arthur that the navy and Marine Corps had planned a media event two weeks later, and the marines would do a full-scale landing for photographers and newsmagazines such as *Life*. Arthur had stolen their thunder. (A general asked Colonel Goettge "who the hell took the damn picture," and he told him, "A little man with a great big camera.")

Reflecting on the Onslow Beach exercises, Vandegrift would say, "The maneuvers of the First Division Marines, and First Division, Army, were a great success. There were twelve [battalion] combat teams landed and maintained over a week through surf and by small boats. As it was all within our own area there was nothing taboo and nothing artificial . . . You will see what I mean when I tell you that they landed four hundred tons of small-arms ammunition and moved it inland for the final stage 7.5 miles from the beach. Little did I think when you and I were bushwhacking in Haiti in 1915 that I would ever live to see the sight of thirty-two transports and cargo ships for the sole use of landing force exercises."[15]

In February of 1941 the 1st Marine Brigade became the 1st Marine Division, with three regiments, the 1st, 5th, and 7th Marines. Our unit became K (or "King") Company, 3rd Battalion, 5th Regiment.

According to Vandegrift, at this time "the First Marine Division existed more on paper than in fact. Its infantry regiments and supporting units such as artillery, engineers and communications were understrength some 12,000 men. New

River was largely wasteland. Since their arrival a couple of months earlier the units had been building a billeting area—a most uncomfortable place called Tent Camp One. Few firing ranges existed, almost no roads, but few wooden buildings. In short, we were building a camp from scratch and simultaneously trying to organize and train what was to become a reinforced division of over 19,000 people."[16]

I took my responsibilities seriously, and my officers could see this. Even though I came into the Corps as a very independent young man, I had no problem with military discipline and understood the reason for it. Whatever frustrations I would come to experience being part of the chain of command, I understood the flow of the Corps' leadership structure, and in short order I was promoted to private first class, a short while later recommended for corporal, and before long passed the exam for sergeant. Now I had the three stripes. I was making good on my promise to Dad.

It was a long trip to Otsego, a train ride and bus ride and hitchhike, but I came home to see my family and my girl, Recie (pronounced *REE-see*), as often as I could, leading to a rumor that I had gone AWOL, but I didn't care. I asked Recie to marry me and she said yes.

Learning to be a marine came naturally to me, for I took pride in my uniform, the best clothes I had ever owned, and I liked that people cared about my appearance. I listened closely to various instructors and put into practice what I had discovered in myself in high school: If I listened in class, I did not have to take books home. I watched the experts and learned. This was always noticed by senior NCOs. I learned something else about myself: I wanted and needed structure.

Being in the boondocks of the dismal Carolina swamps in summertime is one thing. Spending a winter living in tents there, as we did, is another. Tents are not so good at keeping out the cold. The winters in that part of the country were pure torture. It didn't snow or frost much, but the cold rains were penetrating, and we had saplings growing up through the wooden platforms of our tents. We had been settled out of humanity's reach. The oil stoves they gave us spewed out soot at night and kept our clothing and gear constantly dirty and smelling of oil. It was an ordeal, and many times we would just as soon stay out in the field as return to the tents, for out there we could build big fires to keep warm. Often we would go to our beds fully clothed and would pile all our extra clothes on top of us, even our overcoats. Our tent city made our already tough group even tougher.

Now in charge of training at New River, Vandegrift focused not just on standard command post exercises but on "small unit training, beginning with the squad and working up."[17] As well, he pushed construction crews to complete the live-fire ranges that the fledgling camp still lacked. Because of peacetime regulations and our lack of facilities, working with live fire was something few of the troops had experienced—except for those of us who had come from Guantánamo. As a result, most men were given only a few rounds of ammunition and were allowed only to point fire.

One morning we were told to fall out with full field packs. The explanation was terse and to the point. "Now, men, we are going on an endurance march. This is the way it works." We were to march from four in the morning until midnight. We would take a ten-minute break on the hour, every hour. We would rest from midnight until four. The march would last a full seven days. There was to be no special mercy shown to those who dropped out, but there would be no penalty lodged against them. It was staged purely to see who could stand up under such conditions. Of the forty-two men in my platoon who began the march, only seven of us finished. There were no prizes, nor was there contempt for those unable to complete the march. If you had made it to New River, you already were tough, so it was no great thing to be just a few degrees tougher.

I turned twenty-two on November 26, 1941, the same day, I would later learn, the great Japanese fleet left its home waters on the way to Pearl Harbor. Now it was the first Sunday in December and I was waiting at the train station for my ride back to the base after a visit home. The headline at the top of the *Charleston Gazette* blared, FDR ASKS EMPEROR TO AVOID CLASH, but the president was referring to the imminent Japanese invasion of British and Dutch colonies in Southeast Asia. The rest of the paper was full of war news—the United States seizing all Finnish ships, German guns blasting Libya, Russia fighting to hold Moscow. (Still, a good Christmas shopping season was predicted.) An editorial spoke of Japan as a "sad story of greed and selfish ambition" after an exhausting four years of war. "Arrogantly, blindly she pursues her course toward her doom. The United States, British, and Dutch airplanes and sea forces can utterly strangle her by blockading and bombing . . . Since the 14th century Japanese have traditionally observed the custom of self-destruction—hara-kiri—as atonement for wrongs done by her nobles and officials. Is Nippon as a nation now bent upon the course?"[18]

Sunday afternoon, December 7. I hitchhiked to Princeton

to catch my ride back to Camp Lejeune. The driver turned on
the car radio, and every station was carrying the same news:
Pearl Harbor. The radio in the Grand Hotel in Princeton an-
nounced, "all marines must return to camp immediately." The
six marines in our group loaded into a borrowed 1937 Chevro-
let four-door sedan and hit the road. We broke the speed limit
in every town we went through. We stopped briefly at a diner
in North Carolina and the entire front page of the afternoon
newspaper summed up the news in huge letters: *WAR*! We entered Durham doing 70 miles an hour. A policeman on a motor-
cycle pulled up alongside, looked into the car, saw that we were
all marines, and pulled around in front of us. He motioned us to
follow him and escorted us through the city, siren blowing and
lights flashing, and we were soon back at the base.

This is it, we said. All we had been preparing for, all the endless training, and now war had come to the United States and
the marines were ready.

Not so! The situation was a classic "hurry up and wait."
Plans had to be laid, ships built, a much larger armed force
built up. The 1st Division was ready, but the nation was not.

Christmas 1941 found me wondering how long it would
be until I joined the fray of World War II. That December
the bombs fell, ships vanished, men died, and such phrases as
"Prince of Peace" and "goodwill among men" seemed to belong
to the distant past. My last visit home was deeply affecting. The
beauty of the hills, the love of my parents, the very freedom of
life caught me up. There were so many things I could have done
with my life, and I began to hate the thought of war.

I was jarred back to reality by the very nature of my training

3

K/3/5

Enough talent

I WAS NOW A SERGEANT IN K Company, one very small
unit in a great division, the 1st Division, one spoke in a huge
wheel. General Vandegrift was originally told to make the division ready to ship to Samoa. However, plans began to shift
with the creation of the 1st Raider Battalion, under the command of Lt. Col. Merritt Edson. To fill his ranks, Edson combed
through the 5th Marines, cherry-picking those officers and
men he thought suitable for his elite units. Men from the 5th
Regiment also were siphoned off to fill the ranks of the under-
manned 7th. It was the 7th that would ship to Samoa. Instead,
Vandegrift was told that he was now to take his men to Wellington, New Zealand, to serve as the landing force of the newly
established South Pacific Amphibious Force. Once in New Zealand, he would have six months to train and prepare his troops.

Vandegrift was disturbed, not only at the abrupt change in

venue but at the lack of combat readiness of his marines. Despite our bravado, Vandegrift knew we were not ready. The 5th Marines had been stripped of much of its best talent; there were very few Fleet Marines left, and Fleet Marines—the Old Breed—were what Vandegrift needed. Lt. Col. Samuel B. Griffith, a Fleet Marine himself, described the Old Breed as

> first sergeants yanked off "planks" in Navy yards, sergeants from recruiting duty, gunnery sergeants who had fought in France, perennial privates with disciplinary records a yard long. These were the professionals, the "Old Breed" of United States Marines . . .
>
> They were inveterate gamblers and accomplished scroungers, who drank hair tonic in preference to post exchange beer ("horse piss"), cursed with wonderful fluency, and never went to chapel (the "God-box") unless forced to. Many dipped snuff, smoked rank cigars or chewed tobacco (cigarettes were for women and children). They had little use for libraries or organized athletics . . . They could live on jerked goat, the strong black coffee they called "boiler compound," and hash cooked in a tin hat.
>
> Many wore expert badges with bars for proficiency in rifle, pistol, machine gun, hand grenade, auto-rifle, mortar and bayonet. They knew their weapons and they knew their tactics. They knew they were tough and they knew they were good. There were enough of them to leaven the Division and to impart to the thousands of younger men a share of both the unique spirit which animated them and the skills they possessed.[1]

Whether enough talent remained or not, the order came to ship out. We arrived dockside in Norfolk, Virginia, with all our earthly possessions, which consisted of a standard seabag, a military pack, and a rifle. The pack allowed room for a change of socks or two and a change of skivvies, a mess kit, and toilet articles. Our regulation belt held a canteen, ammo clips, a standard first aid kit, a bayonet, and a knife scabbard.

The men of K/3/5 were to board the converted luxury liner the USS *Wakefield* (formerly the luxury liner *Manhattan*).[2] The *Wakefield*'s expensive furnishings were stored for eventual reuse, and she was repainted in camouflage. They had not completely finished gutting the ship by the time she took us to New Zealand, and I was lucky to share a relatively large and well-appointed stateroom with Gunnery Sgt. John Cassel, a stocky guy with a lopsided grin.

Our course took us south, down the eastern seaboard of the United States, through the Panama Canal, and into the Pacific. Our destroyer escort turned back not long after we entered deep waters. Our long-range plane escort left soon after. Alone, we sailed in a zigzag course to the southwest. This was a trip of many firsts for me—for many of the men. I was fascinated by the lock system of the Panama Canal and delighted by the pods of dolphins that swam alongside the ship. Less delightful were the sharks that followed behind, drawn by the garbage we dumped. It was with genuine, childlike awe that I saw my first whale.

On the whole, the trip was uneventful. Our only combat excitement came early on, the first day out of Panama, when a Jap submarine threw a torpedo across our bow. It missed, and on we sailed. I was made sergeant of the guard and thus had to make rounds of the ship every eight hours. The rest of the time was spent eating, sleeping, and wandering around topside. Sergeant Cassel had a cribbage board, and we played for hours at a time. We all endured Neptune's baptism when we crossed the equator.

There was a lot of hostility between the sailors and the marines each time we sailed, and earlier on the *McCawley*, and we thought a mutiny might break out. Whether some incident had triggered it or the sailors were just plain mean, I never knew, but the crew did everything they could to make our lives miserable. They stuffed the ventilators full of rags so we had no air down below and were forced to sleep topside. When they would sweep down the decks we would roll up our bedrolls and after they finished roll them back out again, but a short time later they would begin hosing down the decks without telling us. We would find our gear soaking wet. Finally we held a conference with our own commanding officer, who in turn had a serious talk with the captain of the ship. He told him in so many words that if this did not stop he would turn his back while his marines corrected the situation. The situation improved.

Four days from our New Zealand destination we ran into a huge storm that lasted seventy-two hours. We reduced our speed to 3 knots as we headed directly into it. It tossed the huge ship around like a canoe, and at times we thought we would sink, although we never expressed these fears even to each other. No one was allowed forward of the bridge. Jim McEnery recalls that during the storm he went topside aft and "looking up you'd see a wave three stories high; when the ship pitched forward you would look down at the sea six stories below."[3] Several antiaircraft guns at the bow of the ship were ruined by the raging seawater. Many marines got seasick, and the chow lines got shorter and shorter as the storm progressed. I was never bothered much with seasickness, so I enjoyed these leisurely meals.

We put ashore in Wellington, New Zealand, on June 18, 1942. This small island nation was in grave danger of being overrun, and we were the force designated to buffer the island against the encroaching empire of Japan. Ours was not a large military force, but nevertheless it gave these people hope that their nation would not fall to the invading soldiers. A New Zealand military band met us at the dock. The city, set in a huge natural amphitheater, had a tranquil beauty that appeared to greet us as outstretched arms of welcome and relief.

Wellington was hilly and green and beautiful, especially after the storm, yet the port was a disaster. The cargo ships that had preceded us were days behind in the unloading process. The dock was overrun with towers of cardboard boxes, gear, tenting supplies, ammo crates, cots, C rations, cornflakes, you name it. New Zealand dockworkers had scheduled breaks for morning tea, luncheon, afternoon tea, and teatime tea. If it was raining, they didn't work at all. Then they went on strike.

To compound matters, our ships had been commercially loaded, not combat loaded. The essence of combat loading is to have essentials such as ammunition ready to unload first. This meant that everything would have to be unloaded, sorted, and then reloaded. So, instead of acquainting ourselves with the tasty beers of New Zealand, we went to work on the docks. The police ordered the strikers away from us so we could get to work. Unfortunately, the storm we ran into en route to Wellington had followed us, and soon we were awash in disintegrating cardboard, moldering bags of rice, and sodden, useless boxes of cigarettes. One marine ran a forklift off the docks into the sea; others ran jeeps into trucks and trucks into stacks of gear.

Eventually, we were taken to a base that had been hastily put up to accommodate us. At Camp Paekakariki, also known as McKay's Crossing, our four-man tents had no running water except in the toilets. We walked around in mud and sheep droppings up to our shins. We carried stones from a nearby field and creek bed in an attempt, soon abandoned, to construct a kind of sidewalk. An earthquake hit soon after we arrived, nearly shaking us out of our cots; Wellington was badly damaged. We dug in and continued to prepare for a fight with the Japanese.

During a day of liberty in the city, I surveyed my surroundings. I stared at the beautiful mountains, and in my mind I was back at home in Appalachia. Walking through the city, I strolled by a jewelry shop, and my eyes fell on an old-looking gold pocket watch with a long chain and fob. I remembered the old-timers who would come by for a visit with Dad. At the end of an evening, they all would pull their watches out, flip open the double gold case, and announce they had to go. I bought a gold watch from the window of a jewelry store. It cost twenty pounds sterling, a dear price for a sergeant, but the watch carried with it a special value that, at the time, I did not fully understand; I carried it with me every day thereafter.

There was a great sense of urgency in the air, and soon enough the call came to ship out. On July 2, 1942, at Wellington harbor we boarded the USS *Fuller,* one of the best-run ships we had been aboard. However, we didn't sail for twenty days. During that time we had to load and unload massive amounts of cargo again. Finally, everything was straightened out and the ships were combat loaded. As far as we knew, the rush to unload and reload was to make room for the second echelon, whose arrival was imminent. In truth, the rush was due to something far more serious. Battle plans had changed. Following the attack on Pearl Harbor, the operational strategy had been simply defensive: Protect what we could. However, after America's great victories at Midway and the Battle of the Coral Sea, during which the Japanese lost four hundred aircraft, Admiral Ernest J. King began agitating for an offensive to push northwest from New Zealand. While the Joint Chiefs remained cool to the idea, Adm. Chester W. Nimitz, commander of Pacific forces, and Gen. Douglas MacArthur were very definitely not.[4] The decision was made that the marines would go on the offensive and mount an amphibious assault landing on a small island in the Solomon chain, supported by the firepower of the navy.

We sailed in a hurry, and far out to sea on the third day the announcement came over the loudspeakers: *Now hear this . . .* They told us we were going to invade an island with a strange-sounding name: *Guadalcanal.* None of us had ever heard of it.

Reflecting on learning the news, General Vandegrift recalled, "I didn't even know the location of Guadalcanal. I knew only that my division was spread over hell's half acre, one-third in Samoa, one-third in New Zealand, and one-third still at sea."[5] There was worse news to come for Vandegrift. The six months of training he had been promised had been shortened to three weeks. D-day was now August 1.

I looked it up after the war. A Spanish explorer in the 1500s named Guadalcanal after his hometown. Interestingly, his town had been named by Arabic Muslims during their rule of Spain, and it meant Valley of the Stalls, i.e., places of refreshment. How ironic, I thought, that such a hell on earth derived its name from such a pleasant image. I also learned that the Japanese called the island Gadarukanaru, and the first syllable, "ga," can mean "hunger" in Japanese.[6] Before our time on the island was up, both we and our Japanese counterparts would understand the irony.

Most of the Europeans living on Guadalcanal before the war had been evacuated. A nun and her missionary party refused to leave, or abandon their native schoolchildren, after what she described as ten happy and peaceful years on the island, "We knew too little about war to realize what we were doing."[7] In July, a Japanese general speaking perfect English had arrived at the mission to formally take over the island, commandeering anything of value and ordering all inhabitants of the island to work. Locals who gave thirty days' loyal service to the Japanese were promised a "certificate of residence" and were entitled to food but no pay. The general wrote on the mission school's chalkboard, "Out of sight, out of mind, you must obey the Japanese Forces." They put the natives to work building an airfield. The famous native coastwatchers were already in place, and the Japanese heard their transmissions and accused the mission of hiding a radio.

Guadalcanal was to be strictly a navy action, the marines being a semi-independent arm of the navy, and in particular this would be a battle in which the 1st Marine Division would take the lead. Hardened as we were, however, we still were not battle tried. The high command in Washington needed to know whether their amphibious landing theories would work in practice and how our troops would hold up in the jungle. So instead of heading straight into battle, we steamed toward the Fijis, to a small island called Koro, for a rehearsal of the amphibious landing to come on Guadalcanal.[8] It was an amazing sight—seventy-plus ships, the biggest armada in American history up to that point. The event was crucial for the American command to understand the limits of our capabilities, especially since prior landings had shown how shaky Navy support operations really were.

We had practiced amphibious landings in New River, but there were still many issues to be resolved under real-life conditions: loading and unloading cargo, the relatively new Higgins boats, communications, logistics, and so on. The plan was for the entire division, nineteen thousand marines, to go ashore on the north coast of the island. We would land on A-day, July 28, reembark on A+1, July 29, then do it all over again on July 30 and 31. At least that was the idea. Prior to that, cruisers and destroyers would simulate shore bombardment in support of the landings on A-day, then conduct actual bombardment on B-day. Fighters and dive bombers would simulate aerial strafing and bombing of the landing beaches on A-day but use live ordnance on B-day. Radio silence was to be maintained except in the case of "grave emergency" or actual enemy attack.

The timing needed to be precise because we were synchronizing our assault with the navy's bombardment. We were to seize our area, dig in, and spend the night.

My platoon was to land on Beach Red at 1:20 P.M., but the Beach Red landings were running late. It was after 2:00 P.M. by the time we reached the line of departure. When the signal came, my men and I clambered down the ship's cargo nets into the waiting Higgins boats. We carried 70-pound field packs, rifles, and ammunition. Once we were in the flat-bottomed transport, the pilot pulled away from the *Fuller* and sped straight into—a debacle? A circus? Whichever, it was clear when we sighted land that something was dramatically wrong.[9] When Koro had been scouted as a site for maneuvers, it had been at high tide. Now, at lower tide, we saw that the island was ringed by great impenetrable coral reefs. Unable to make it to the beach, Higgins boats, supply transports, and assorted landing craft bobbed about in the sea. Some circled aimlessly, while others actually got hung up on the coral. Many boats lost their propellers. Navy coxswains began ordering the men out of the boats well shy of the shore; following orders to disembark, many marines sank into water several feet over their heads. One navy commander led his troops onto the wrong beach entirely, some 1,800 yards off target. Many Higgins boats simply returned to the ships. The navy beachmasters at Koro were led by Lt. Jack Clark, who was "shocked" by the rough coral beaches and used his ship's Aldis lamp to signal his concerns to the officers on the flagship boats, so many landing ships were diverted from the worst of the coral. Clark saved the navy a lot of propellers and repair time and made enough of an impression that he was named beachmaster for the Guadalcanal landing.

K Company actually did land on Red Beach, and we spent the day wandering about the island, looking around. We tried to figure out how to open coconuts. At one point, when we were hacking at the husk of a coconut with our machetes, two natives came along dressed in just their loincloths. (This was a surprise, because we had heard that the natives had been evacuated from the island.) They had a sharp stick, and I presumed it was a weapon of sorts. They gazed at us strangely for a few moments, put their sharp stick in the ground, and proceeded with ease to completely strip the coconut of the husk. As Richard Tregaskis would confirm in his book *Guadalcanal Diary*,[10] the marines would go on to become excellent coconut openers.

When dusk fell, we pitched our tents and settled in to watch the sailors, who worked throughout the night struggling to free their boats from the coral and repair the damage to the crafts' propellers. The cancellation of the first day's landing exercises, midexecution, forced the commanders to improvise the next day's maneuvers. On the second day the orders were changed so landing boats only approached the beach at about 2,000 yards.[11] Those troops who hadn't managed to land would disembark from the ship into their transports, but the transports wouldn't actually attempt a landing because the navy couldn't risk any more damage to its crafts. However, one marine captain didn't get the word and landed his craft, going ashore along with his men.

Now the situation really went south. Somehow the scheduled hour of the live-fire aerial bombing and strafing runs had been moved forward. Our company was supposed to be a mile offshore, on the transports, headed back to the ship when the bombing commenced. Instead, not only were many of us still on the island from the day before, but new waves of men were landing. At the last moment, one of the destroyers was able to call out to a transport that the beach was about to be shelled. Our lieutenant, Rex McIlvaine, shouted for us to head for the woods and hit the deck. All across the beach could be heard cries of "Incoming!" as men scrambled for cover. Two destroyers

That night, I asked myself the questions all soldiers ask themselves sooner or later. *Will I run? Will I be afraid?*

August 7. D-day. It was exactly eight months since the "Day of Infamy" at Pearl Harbor that America launched its first offensive action against the empire of Japan. These islands, the Solomons, were the first rung on the ladder extending all the way up to Japan. Control of the chain would give Japan stepping-stones to dominate the Pacific and eventually strike at America. Reveille came very early that morning. After a fitful sleep, I checked my watch: 4:00 A.M. Now it was not a matter of D-days but H-hours. I would check the watch repeatedly through sunrise.

The assault on Guadalcanal was part of code name Operation Watchtower, although it soon came to be called Operation Shoestring, as it seemed the entire affair had been drawn up and provisioned with the help of a dart board, chewing gum, and some loose change. Interservice rivalries among big personalities such as General MacArthur and Admiral King produced a compromise plan, and just six days before we landed on Guadalcanal the navy would issue a major revision of its Landing Operations Doctrine, the guide for how the navy and Marine Corps would manage an opposed amphibious landing, covering "the tactics and technique of the landing operation and the necessary supporting measures therefor." It added sixty new pages to an already complex document. Koro had taught both forces many lessons, such as getting marines into boats faster, but confusion still reigned as to which force would be responsible for getting everything off the boat and squared away. Whether Lieutenant Clark was able to absorb all the changes to the Landing Doctrine is unknown.

First, we needed to take back Tulagi from the Japanese and prevent them from taking Port Moresby, New Guinea, from which they would threaten to cut supply lines between the United States and Australia and New Zealand. However, when the Japanese decided first to build an airfield on an old plantation on Guadalcanal, preventing its completion became the first order of business. Vandegrift had originally been told we would probably not be needed until early 1943. But here we were. But where were we?

Information about conditions on Guadalcanal was almost nonexistent. While we were still in New Zealand, Lt. Col. Frank Goettge, now the chief intelligence officer for the 5th Marines, traveled to Australia and New Guinea seeking as much intel on the island as possible. What he was able to gather was sketchy at best. For one thing, he found that the tropical heat, disease, and impenetrable jungle of the islands would present immense challenges; quoting Jack London, "If I were a king, the worst punishment I could inflict on my enemies would be to banish them to the Solomons."[1]

Goettge spent eleven days in Australia, "tracking down miners, traders, government workers, seamen, and missionaries—many of whom had passed through but had never actually set foot in the objective area. He returned to the division headquarters in Wellington on July 13 to begin making some sense of his discouragingly small grab-bag of data" and put together a brief and error-filled report and a rough map of Guadalcanal's northern coast.[2] What Goettge was not able to specify was just how impenetrable the terrain was, and even if he had, I do

not know if the Corps could have foreseen just how enormous
the challenge would be. Appropriate for Operation Shoestring,
other maps were available but were "poor, constructions based
upon outdated hydrographic charts and information provided
by former island residents. While maps based on aerial photographs had been prepared they were misplaced by the navy in
Auckland, New Zealand, and never got to the marines at Wellington."[3] Lacking serious intelligence about the island, Vandegrift also sent several "liaison planes" from the naval escort to
do reconnaissance work. Unfortunately, even their reports were
sketchy. One pilot reported seeing many enemy troops, but it
emerged under closer inquiry that these "troops" were actually
cows.[4]

We knew none of this at the time, only that we would be landing on the northwest side of the island, on Lunga Plain. From
there we were to establish our command posts, set up a Main
Line of Resistance, and proceed to take the almost-completed
airfield. K Company, along with the entire 3rd Battalion, 5th
Regiment, was to take and hold Beach Red. Vandegrift would
set up his 1st Marine Division Headquarters about 100 yards
inland. As we waited for our orders, our platoon leader, Scoop
Adams, gathered us together. As he recalled many years later:

> The night before the landing those of us who were boat com-
> manders were called into a wardroom aboard the U.S.S. *Fuller*.
> The battalion commander informed us that intelligence indi-
> cated that the next morning when we landed we were going to
> run into machine gun fire, heavy caliber anti-bullet guns, rifle

fire, automatic weapons, barbed wire, and land mines on the beaches. He said, "Very frankly, the estimate is that nobody who lands in the first wave will come out of it alive. Now, it's up to you whether you want to tell your platoons this or you want to keep this to yourselves." I thought about it awhile and I decided I should keep nothing from the guys in that platoon. I had plenty of faith in them. I went down to the platoon compartment. They had borrowed a grindstone from the ship and were sharpening their bayonets. I passed the word to them exactly as I'd heard it in the wardroom. I told them if there's anybody who figures tomorrow morning he just can't make it going in there, if he'll come see me tonight I know we can figure out something so he won't have to go in. I got no comment from the platoon guys at all, except Dutch Schantzenbach who said "Let's go get them Japs!"[5]

Our Higgins boats left their rendezvous area, where the ships made slow circles in the sea, and now stood in a straight row at the line of departure. Two regiments stood abreast on the boats a few yards apart as they began their journey toward the beach. At first the land appeared as only a small line of brown against the green of the dense jungle. That line became more jagged as we drew closer. As we accelerated, the beach loomed much wider than we thought at first, and incongruously beautiful; one war correspondent described "blue-green mountains, towering into a brilliant tropical sky or crowned with cloud masses, [that] dominate the island" and the "dark green of jungle growth [that] blends into the softer greens and browns of coconut groves and grassy plains and ridges."[6] This was no vacation, though. As we closed the distance to the island we heard the burst of American shells, punctuated by the deeper sound of exploding bombs, meant to clear the way for our landing force. Not knowing what we were facing was in some ways as bad as if we had been fired on.

As the boats drew closer to land some men made the sign of the cross, some bowed in silent prayer, and others just stared ahead at the unknown. No one knew what the next few minutes would bring. I felt alone in the world. Never in my life had I experienced a feeling of utter loneliness such as I had now. I was at last headed into something from which I might not return. I was truly on my own, but I had a job to do and was determined to see it done. We settled into the boats and watched the navy prepare the beach. A cruiser and gunboat made a pass along the beach. We were in the older-style Higgins boats, requiring us to leap over the side; the new LCVPs with the wide front ramp would not see action in the Pacific until later in the year. This meant we could be jumping into deep water, fully armed for combat; it was imperative we get as far up onto the beach as possible. We were in the 3rd Platoon, Mo's squad in the stern. Again, in Scoop's words:

T.I. rode on the port side, near the Navy coxswain running the boat. [Author's note: My middle name is Irving, and by now I had gained the nickname "T.I."] This was a different Navy man than we had trained with for the past several weeks. I was on the starboard side where I would be first man out of the boat on that side. When we were halfway to the beach I crawled across to the coxswain. Our prior coxswain had told us he would land us "all the way up into the coconut trees" if need be. I tapped this new man on the shoulder and reminded him that when we scraped the beach he was to hold the throttle open and thus hold the boat in place until all the marines were out. He informed me that he was in charge of the boat and would take us in only far enough that he could safely get the boat back out! At that moment, T.I. signaled me not to worry. I knew he had something in mind and I felt better. The boat scraped bottom but we were still in water too deep to negotiate with our heavy packs and weapons. But the boat then pushed further up the beach. As I went over the side I looked across at the Navy man. Someone had knocked him out, and the boat was pushing further up on the beach. T.I. had done what he signaled he would do. The marines thus made a safe landing.[7]

As suddenly as it had come, the fear left. I was filled with the desire to lead my squad over the side of the boat, as soon as the boat ground as far as it would go onto the beach. The first sand we hit as we tumbled out was under several inches of water, and our footing was unsure. As our feet struggled onto firmer sand, our cursing was nearly drowned out by the roar of the boats as the navy men hurried to leave the beach and return to the relative safety of the sea, beyond the land artillery and mortar we supposed the enemy to have installed. Gaining traction, we hurried up the beach, toward the jungle's edge. There, we waited for oncoming fire that never came. There were no bullets, no sound except the men behind us as we ran toward the jungle. We had caught the enemy off guard. Inexplicably, the landing on Guadalcanal had been made without taking a single casualty; the first offensive action against the Japanese Imperial Forces had begun. We were informed that the president had received the message that we had landed and had the situation in hand.

The rest of that day, August 7, 1942, was calm as we unloaded ammo and part of the food supply. The loose and shifting sand made walking with a load difficult, but by day's end much had been accomplished. Still, Red Beach backed up with more supplies than could be squared away, and many ships would never be fully unloaded. Following the landing of infantry on the beach, regimental headquarters came ashore, to be followed by artillery. However, due to overloading and confusion about who would handle the unloading, the march of logistics began to unravel. The 105 mm howitzers arrived very late, as the number of ramp boats able to accommodate them was inadequate. Moreover, the 1-ton trucks that had arrived were not heavy enough to transport the guns. What they needed were deuce-and-a half trucks and the ramp boats to transport them. Forced to improvise, the engineer companies, whose job it was to oversee the off-loading, landing, and movement of matériel, used the new amphibian tractors to move equipment off boats, onto the beaches, and inland to the forces—but the tracked vehicles were lethal to communication wires. Every sort of supply began to pile up on the beach. At one point, the congestion was so great that the engineers radioed the ships to halt the supplies. They could not keep up. Vandegrift couldn't spare combat marines to unload the ships, and the navy didn't assign enough personnel to do so either, and what was unloaded stacked up on the beach with no sense of order or priority. Though no one knew it at the time, the situation would have long-ranging repercussions. One estimate suggests that less than half had even been unloaded from the ships—and that none of the heavy equipment had made it.

The navy had reason to worry about its ships. At midday a Japanese air attack commenced against the fleet. It was quite a sight to see. Hundreds of marines lined the beach as if they were watching a baseball game.

On that first night, we heard gunfire, though likely from marines accidentally shooting at each other in the dark. We were impossibly green and untried. We had trained as a division for only a few weeks, and we had not yet confronted the enemy, but we knew they were there.

Those of us on the ground had no way of knowing it, but the small village of Horahi, about twenty-five huts, lay in the jungle just off the beach west of us, between the Matanikau River and Point Cruz.[8] Until the war, the people of the village lived very simply off the plentiful fish, fruit, and vegetables the jungle and sea provided. A Catholic mission had been established on Guadalcanal fifty years earlier, so there was a small church in the village, and a British government schooner made regular stops at Horahi and other villages and Aola Bay, the British district office. Little was known about Guadalcanal, but a plane from Adm. Kelly Turner's task force had taken aerial photos showing the point and village in May 1942.

The village's first Japanese visitor was Terushige Ishimoto, an English-speaking shipping manager in Rabaul recruited as a lieutenant when the war began. He was assigned to organize labor crews from the natives and to provide intelligence on the island, and a truck would come daily to take the workers to the airfield the Japanese were constructing. Ishimoto warned one young villager to stay away from the soldiers at the airfield "who could be dangerous." The little village would play a major role in one of the most controversial events of the war.

On August 8 we moved out toward the Lunga River, and I began to get a sense of the place. Although I was a child of nature, far more comfortable in the wilderness than elsewhere, I would never encounter anything like the island of Guadalcanal. Author Richard Frank's description cannot be improved upon:

> The lords of Guadalcanal's jungle were the great hardwood trees that soared up to 150 feet and had girths as much as 40 feet across. Their straight trunks sprouted only high branches that formed a 'sunproof roof." Their massive flared roots snaked across the surface like thick trip wires while other leafy vines festooned the trunks of the jungle floor . . . Sheltered in the dark bramble were wild dogs, pigs, lizards, and gigantic bush rats the size of rabbits. Fish filled the streams and crocodiles slithered in and out of watercourses and mangrove swamps near the shore . . . The sour odor of decay permeated the steamy stagnant air, for beneath the lushness omnipresent rot made the yellow clay earth porous.[9]

The backbone of the island is Mount Austen, some 1,514 feet high (curiously labeled "the grassy knoll" on our maps), whose ravines create endless, crocodile-infested runoffs that join up and then separate again, cutting steep banks beneath the canopy of hardwoods. Man-high, razor-sharp kunai grass grows on the open slopes where the mountain finally pushes into the sea.

The rest of Guadalcanal is dense black jungle interrupted only by jutting stone ridges.

We advanced without opposition, moving laterally along the coast through several coconut plantations. Later that day, marines took the Japanese landing field, renaming it Henderson Field. Also captured was a Japanese base camp that seemed to have been abandoned only minutes before. The Japanese had occupied the island for a year, and the matériel they left behind was staggering: antiaircraft batteries, ammunition dumps, a power plant, radio receiver stations, a refrigeration plant, an air compressor plant, over a hundred Chevy 2-ton trucks, road rollers, and fifty to sixty thousand gallons of gasoline all stored in underground pipes. It was a sight of such permanence, of such capacity, that it finally drove home the understanding that we were going up against a seasoned, entrenched, fully supplied enemy. The truth was there before us: Nothing would defeat this enemy but the full force and strength of the United States Navy and Marine Corps.

The full force and strength of the United States Navy, however, were not to be offered. On D-day +3 the sea was vast and empty. There were no American ships to boost morale, no planes in the sky to ward off the planes that arrived every day at noon to bomb and strafe at will. The entire U.S. Navy had left.

Late on the night of August 8, General Vandegrift had been summoned by Rear Adm. Kelly Turner to the USS *McCawley*. Turner was the commander of the Amphibious Task Force and reported to Vice Adm. Frank Jack "Black Jack" Fletcher, who was in charge of all seaborne forces headed for Guadalcanal. Fletcher reported to Vice Adm. Robert Ghormley. I knew none of these men and would never meet them. I was a grunt on the ground. In terms of chain of command they floated in the stratosphere. Yet the decisions they made intimately impacted those of us crouched in our foxholes. Such was the decision taken by Fletcher and communicated to Vandegrift at 11:00 P.M. on our second night on the island, *Fighter plane strength reduced from 99 to 78. In view of large number of enemy torpedo planes and bombers in this area, I recommend the immediate withdrawal of my carriers.*[10]

After only two days at Guadalcanal, fearing for his carriers, and despite Vandegrift's pleas to remain at least a day or two, Fletcher chose to retreat out of reach of Japanese bombers. Fletcher had a right to be nervous; he had already lost the USS *Lexington* at the Battle of the Coral Sea and the *Yorktown* at the Battle of Midway, and without air cover his ships would be utterly vulnerable. It wasn't my job to second-guess decisions about how much of a calculated risk Fletcher should have taken; history may be kinder to Fletcher than marines have been over the years.[11] In any event, thirty minutes after having informed Vandegrift of his intentions, Fletcher instructed his ships to pull out. The marines now stood alone.

"Abandoned" may not be the right word; the decision to leave our division there, "at the wrong end of a nonexistent or easily dominated supply line, was positively taken by sober, courageous leaders who thoroughly understood the risks and the overriding potential benefits."[12] It still felt like abandonment to us; the men on the ground knew nothing of the reasons behind the navy's decision to pull out. As *The Old Breed* put it, after the fleet left with the matériel, food, and supplies we would need, "the feeling of expendability is difficult to define. It is loneliness, it is a feeling of being abandoned, and it is something more, too: It is as if events over which you have no control have put a ridiculously low price tag on your life."[13] Needless to say, we were preparing ourselves for another Wake Island, another Bataan, as we were apparently another helpless, stranded group, left to its own meager resources.

When we woke up on the morning of August 9 the horizon was empty as far as the eye could see; I would learn later that ships remained in the area through the afternoon, but they weren't visible to us, and we felt very much alone. We had no carrier air support, no naval bombardment support, nothing. Due to the congestion on the beach on D-day we also had little in the way of supply; much of what we did have still stood in great piles mounded on the beach, 3 miles away.

The cache of matériel found at the abandoned Japanese camp now seemed like a windfall. Immediately, instructions were given to inventory what supplies we did have, both those left by the navy and those left by the Japs. On final count, the quartermasters determined that the 10,819 marines on Guadalcanal had four units of fire per man and seventeen days of food (at two meals a day).[14] There was a dire shortage of pick-axes and shovels and a worrisome dearth of mines with which to fortify the beaches. Nevertheless, we were marines. We would make do.

Unbeknownst to us, Japan was having its own interservice disagreements. After we landed on Guadalcanal, the Japanese navy insisted that three naval battalions from Rabaul be sent immediately to Guadalcanal to take it back, but was overruled by the army, which instead diverted crack infantry then heading home to Japan after fighting in Java.[15] A vice admiral interrogated after the war called this a mistake: "When troops were on their way home after completion of fighting, their morale was inclined to be reduced, and I felt the same way about the so called crack troops on their way home from Java. They might have been good while the fighting was going on, but when the fight was over, there is bound to be a let down in spirit."[16] The diary of one of Ichiki's men confirms that when they found out their ship was not going home "they were dispirited in a moment. However, remember boys, only the life with a sublime duty to carry out will be worth living."[17]

The war soon caught up with us. By day we could set our watches by the arrival of the bombers. They came in waves and were consistent in their quest to dislodge us from our positions. Japanese destroyers and cruisers would steam along the coast and fire inland at us. Although they had few men on the island at the time, the Japanese began shelling the beach night after night. Combat was difficult, but being sitting ducks for heavy artillery was something else.

One evening some of us sought refuge behind what we thought to be crates of food. When "Charlie" came over and dropped a flare I raised the edge of the tarp and saw that our hiding place was a row of ammunition boxes about 100 feet long and 10 feet high! If a shell had found this mark it would have moved the beach in a few hundred feet.

On August 9 we began to see flashes of light far out to sea, followed by crashing sounds we knew could not be the thunder of a natural storm. The Japanese navy had managed to sneak up on part of our fleet, and through the night a terrible duel was fought off the coast of Savo Island. We lost four valiant ships, the U.S. cruisers *Astoria*, *Quincy*, and *Vincennes*, and the Australian cruiser *Canberra,* along with their entire crews. Those ships and their brave men sank to rest on the sandy ocean floor of Iron Bottom Sound, charter members of the "Lost Fleet of Guadalcanal."

On the island, Vandegrift made finishing the airfield, which we took on our second day on the island, his top priority; the Japanese would soon make it their top priority to take it back. Though we had been left without any earth-moving equipment, the Japs had gifted us with those 2-ton trucks and road rollers. By August 12, the runway at the newly named Henderson Field stretched almost 2,600 feet, big enough to land Admiral McCain's personal Catalina. By the end of the first week we had established a beachhead. Our perimeter of defense was roughly 7 miles long and 2 miles deep. It was rather thin in places, but we simply did not have the personnel to man it the way it should have been manned.

Our intelligence had ascertained that only a small detachment of soldiers and a rather large group of laborers defended the island. They had scattered all over the jungle as the firing began. We even found their breakfast tables with food still on them untouched and their laundry out on lines. Of course, we all knew this could not last. Sure enough, the Japanese began to build up a fighting force on the island at night by bringing fast-moving surface ships and submarines down "the Slot" between the New Georgia island group and Santa Isabel and Choiseul islands. Each vessel carried a small number of troops and each night they left them on the island.

In the meantime, K/3/5 began running patrols to the Matanikau River, the largest river near our position. The Matanikau became the de facto battle line for much of the first months on

Guadalcanal, with Japanese entrenched on the west banks and Americans on the east, both sides pushing across at some point along the water and then getting pushed back. The river was narrow enough that you could hear the enemy talking on the other side, but the vegetation was so thick you often couldn't see the man next to you. At the sandspit at the mouth of the Matanikau, the river widened and the banks became less steep, the only place tanks and other vehicles could hope to get across, and a point we would need to hold at all costs. We repeatedly took fire and knew the general location of enemy positions.

In advance of our August 7 landing, U.S. forces had bombed the nearly completed airfield, and the relative paradise of these villagers of Horahi would be no more. The villagers abandoned their village and would never return. The village wasn't empty when we landed, though: A Japanese Guard Unit moved in on August 8 to set up a defense, digging four large trenches facing the sea, each big enough for eight men. A marine patrol along the mouth of the Matanikau took Japanese rifle fire and pulled back, calling it a "hornet's nest."

Receiving intelligence from a captured prisoner of war that a detachment of Japanese bunkered down along the Matanikau might be induced to surrender, on August 12 Colonel Goettge led a large patrol to investigate. His patrol carried no Browning automatics, no radio, no grenades, but did contain Goettge and other important members of his intelligence staff. They had spotted what may have been a white flag of surrender—or the Japanese flag, with its Rising Sun hidden in its white folds for lack of wind that day. The patrol of twenty-three marines also included a coxswain and the Japanese POW. Platoon Sgt. C. C. "Monk" Arndt was sent along on the mission because he was one of the most experienced scouts on the island. Instead of continuing farther toward Point Cruz the patrol landed just west of the Matanikau sandspit—close to the "hornet's nest" and just down the beach from the dug-in Japanese at Horahi. The patrol's landing craft got stuck in the sand for half an hour and made plenty of noise; the Japanese couldn't help but notice and watched from the trenches. Colonel Goettge sent the landing craft back to Lunga Point, and the marines came ashore toward the village and the dug-in Japanese. Goettge saw an entrenched Japanese soldier and ordered him to stand up. Instead, the colonel was killed immediately with a shot to the head. The Japanese wiped out virtually the entire patrol. Only three men—Sgt. Frank Few, Cpl. Joseph Spaulding, and Arndt—survived, and they told of a gruesome massacre. Sergeant Few reported seeing, as he swam away, "the Japs back on the beach using bayonets on our wounded, and could clearly see the sunlight glinting on the two-handed samuri [sic] swords."[18]

Long after the war Japanese veterans would describe to historian John Innes how some of the remains of the patrol were buried in the trenches, even providing a map of the trenches and village. Some members of the patrol may have escaped east as far as the Matanikau, to be buried where they lay, or their dismembered remains may have been allowed to drift down to the sandspit at the mouth of the river. It has also been speculated that remains were intentionally brought to the sandspit to serve as a warning—a "show"—to the marines then beginning to patrol the area. The Japanese who respectfully recalled the events of that dark, confusing August 12 half a century later, in order to permit the retrieval of American remains, did not volunteer further details of any Japanese atrocities.[19] The description of shallow graves, if they can be called that, fits: According to interviews with Japanese after the war, after killing the Goettge patrol the Japanese pulled back into the jungle, and "they used the hasty fighting holes as shallow graves for the marines and threw sand over their bodies."[20]

The official Marine Corps history stated that their remains were never found, however, within a few days a squad from my K Company was dispatched to search for the patrol. Scoop, Jim, Mo, Slim Somerville, myself, and several others set out along the east side of the sandspit. Our perimeter of defense did not include the river at this time, and so our approach up the coast through the jungle was made with the utmost caution. We were directed to engage the enemy only if necessary; we had permission to fire only if we ran into trouble. Up through the long stands of coconut trees and dense brush, across a dry wash, we crept single file. We spoke very little. At first this was precautionary; soon our silence was that of mourning, and of rage. For just across the sandspit we found what we were looking for. The lush banks of the small river cradled a scent that those of us who were there can recall in an instant. What lay beneath the foliage was no longer human.

We first found what we believed to be a man from the patrol, or what remained of him. Sticking out of the sand was a boot, containing the foot of its owner. I scraped in the sand and uncovered another legging with the leg still in it. McEnery found a severed head and a little farther on the blouse of a first sergeant. No arms, just the torso. We paused on the bank of the river and without another word went slowly across the spit. We

death—more than one marine lost a hand, or his life, reaching for a dead Japanese officer's sword, only to trigger a booby trap. A great prize with a terrible price. Many of us are convinced that the captured Japanese soldier who told of the Japanese detachment wanting to surrender and offered to lead Goettge and the men to them—for that is the tale he told—knew exactly what he was doing: leading Goettge and his men into a trap.

Early books about the war downplayed the significance of the patrol. For example, John Miller Jr., in *Guadalcanal: The First Offensive*, wrote, "Subsequent patrols never found any trace of Colonel Goettge's party," citing the 1st Marine Division Final Report III. George McMillan's *The Old Breed* says, "As far as the Division's records are concerned, the patrol disappeared into oblivion," and the bodies were never discovered.[23] Perhaps this is because the patrol included some of our most critical intelligence personnel. Only decades later was it revealed that accompanying Goettge was Lt. Ralph Corry, a recently arrived intelligence officer who spoke fluent Japanese. Of course, it would have been disastrous had he been captured and forced to talk.

More recent scholarship suggests that the patrol *was* found—and then lost again. Eric Hammel writes in *Guadalcanal: Starvation Island* that a week after the Goettge patrol was lost, men from I Company found similar dismembered remains: a leg in marine leggings and boondocker, an arm—with no hand—sticking out of the ground. They believed it was Goettge or one of his men. They had earlier found what they believed to be another of Goettge's men, Cpl. William Bainbridge, in the sand by the mouth of the Matanikau. That squad found twenty-one bodies in the area, but was called back to base before they could exhume them, and never found them again.[24] Ore Marion of L Company says he saw the shallow graves and "believe[s] that every other active member of L Company also saw those bodies"; according to Marion, Monk Arndt confirmed it: "See the arm sticking up, and the riding boot? That's the colonel," meaning Goettge. Marion continues, "The bodies were badly decomposed, and it would have been impossible to recognize their individual features, but Arndt had known Goettge well. He was certain that he was seeing Goettge's remains, and I have no reason to believe he was mistaken."[25]

Had these dismembered bodies been brought to the sandspit as a warning to us? To frighten us? Whether these were Goettge's men or not didn't really matter. That day on the Matanikau we beheld all the horrors of war, all the degrees of degradation to which the human race could descend. We were hardened by much training, and our reflexes were sudden, our minds alert, but now our killing potential was amplified. A second ingredient, hatred, had been added. What kind of warfare was this? Our manuals had failed us. The Articles of War seemed to ring hollow. We threw away the book that day on the sandspit on Guadalcanal. From now on, we would do it their way. There were no words of agreement, no fanfare, no loud cursing or crying, only grimness and resolve.

It's hard to overestimate the speed and depth at which a story such as this travels among the enlisted. Eugene Sledge wrote of meeting a veteran marine described as "one of the three guys who escaped when the Goettge patrol got wiped out on Guadalcanal. He was lucky as hell." Sledge asked why the Japs ambushed the patrol. "The veteran looked at me with unbelief and said slowly and emphatically, 'Because they're the meanest sonsabitches that ever lived.'"[26] The sneak attack on Pearl Harbor, booby-trapped corpses, deliberately killing our corpsmen—all contributed to our hatred of the Japanese, but no single event fed that hatred more than the story of the Goettge patrol.

On August 19 the marines set fire to the village of Horahi to keep it out of Japanese hands, and that was the end of it. On September 2, 1942, the commandant of the Marine Corps, Lt. Gen. Thomas Holcomb, wrote to Frank Goettge's wife, breaking the news that although he was officially still missing, "I'm certain he did not survive the engagement" with the Japanese, considering the reports from Frank Few and the other two survivors. He also wrote that a recovery patrol sent out early the next morning returned to the scene and "not a trace" of the patrol was found. We now know that the patrol didn't locate the village, and as the war escalated the marines had more pressing matters at hand.[27] Before long, tanks overran the area where the patrol was lost, then the Seabees built a base on it, and in the years after the war the area was developed, and any physical evidence was presumably lost to history. After the war the capital city of Honiara grew up on the site of the village, and a "shanty town" now stands on the Matanikau sandspit.

Since his body was not recovered, Goettge was not formally declared dead until August 13, 1943. A simple square granite marker in the memorial garden next to Henderson Field—now Honiara International Airport—commemorates the patrol and the "22 brave marines who lost their lives 12–13 August 1942 on Guadalcanal under the command of Lt. Col. Frank Goettge, Intelligence Office, First Marine Division US Army [sic]."

The lost patrol became a subject of frequent discussion at our reunions. There have been many attempts to locate the remains of Frank Goettge and his team, none successful.[28] An anthropological expedition in 2008 used ground-penetrating radar and other high-tech instruments, but since 1942 the coast has been heavily developed and excavated, and typhoons have washed away much of the beach. No sign of Goettge or his men, but the researchers heard stories of "this person finding bones when they were doing construction and bones at their dad's house or their cousin's house or on the other island or whatever . . . So there exists the possibility that just piecemeal, one by one, they were discovered or dug up, sold, given to the Japanese. When remains are given to the Japanese, they are assumed to be Japanese. They cremate them right there on site."[29] Perhaps the smoke of our men's bones mingled with theirs, and I wish them all peace, but the island will never be free of ghosts.

After our patrol we returned, reported in, took up our positions on the line, and dug in to wait. For the rest of our time on Guadalcanal we met Japanese brutality with an equally brutal response. The Japanese became less than human to us, and many of us descended to their level, not just taking revenge but also taking body parts, even skulls, as souvenirs. This practice, although officially condemned by the military brass, was widespread and accepted in American society in a way that is difficult to understand today. *Life* magazine published a cover photo of a young woman and a Japanese skull; she is writing a thank-you note to the navy boyfriend who sent it to her.[30] (The public relations branch of the army objected to such pictures, arguing that they could inflame even greater atrocities against American troops.) Every soldier knew, or should have known, that taking teeth, bones, or any body part of an enemy soldier is a violation of the most basic rules of war, but the spiraling cycle of revenge reduced both sides to base animal instincts. We were killing machines fueled by hatred. At Guadalcanal, "the Japanese fought with an intensity that appeared disproportionate to the marines' opinions of their likelihood for success. Fighting to the last man, as most warriors understand, rarely serves military effectiveness, and it barbarizes those who have to kill to the last man. The Japanese Bushido (code of chivalry) quickly pushed the marines farther from their self-image as warriors and closer to that of murderers."[31]

It would be late in the war before I would look directly into the eyes of a young Japanese soldier, ready to die at my hand, and see anything resembling a human.

Throughout August the enemy landed more and more troops until we were outnumbered and outgunned. We were fighting constantly. I read later that a Japanese officer, one of Lt. Gen. Harukichi Hyakutake's men, was told that when he arrived on Guadalcanal "you will fire only one shot from your artillery and the American Marines will surrender."[32] It's difficult to fathom that a leader could be so dismissive of the marines, but at the time the Japanese did seem to be in control; the outcome of Guadalcanal was still very much in doubt, and it only dawned slowly on both sides what a turning point this small island would be.

5

BATTLE

A place to sleep and a good meal

So here we were. Morale couldn't have been lower. Forty-eight hours after launching the largest amphibious assault landing in the history of the United States Marine Corps, the navy had pulled out, leaving us alone, and then we had stumbled onto the brutalized remains of our fellow marines, giving K Company firsthand knowledge of the bloodthirsty Japanese. Our supply situation was dire, with almost no food, little in the way of communication gear, marginal ammunition, and no heavy equipment. By the end of our second week on the island, patrols had pieced together enough intelligence to suggest that Japanese troops were massing on the western banks of the Tenaru River and that decisive action was critical. Our intelligence maps indicated several major rivers on the island, but two of them, the Tenaru and the Ilu, were switched on our scouts' maps. Moreover, the battle of the Tenaru was actually fought on the banks of Alligator Creek, and it was not a creek at all but a brackish lagoon located a 1,000 yards from the Tenaru. Alligator Creek got its name from the fearsome creatures that clogged its waters, which weren't alligators but crocodiles. Such is war.

By mid-August Col. Kiyoano Ichiki, late of Guam, had landed his first echelon of nine hundred soldiers.[1] Armed with plenty of guns and ammunition, the Japs hit us throughout the night of August 21 with snipers, grenades, mortars, and intense artillery fire. This was no probing action but a full-on attack. Exploding phosphorus flares of silver punctured the deep black of night, lingering in the heavy humidity. Tracer fire chased back and forth over the river. Concussions echoed across the island, booming long after the blasts. Twice the Japs made a run at our front line and twice we repelled them, laying down a heavy mortar barrage in concert with the artillery. Gunner John Rivers of the 1st Marines' H Company fed hundreds of rounds into his machine gun. It was said that he fired two hundred rounds even after being killed. Cpl. Lee Diamond took over Rivers's gun until he, too, was shot. With Diamond out, Pvt. Albert Schmid took his place until he was thrown off the gun and blinded by shell fragments, and he fought on, blind, with a pistol.

The land itself seemed to breathe fire, but the Japanese remained entrenched. Watching from a bluff overlooking the river, Vandegrift ordered a tank platoon to cross the river upstream and approach the Japanese position from their rear. Richard Tregaskis described the tanks' relentless progression toward the enemy's position.

On our [west] bank of the Tenaru the tanks halted for a few moments, then plunged on across the sandspit, their treads rattling industriously. We watched these awful machines as they plunged across the spit and into the edge of the grove. It was fascinating to see them bustling amongst the trees, pivoting, turning, spitting sheets of yellow flame. It was like a comedy of toys, something unbelievable, to see them knocking over palm trees which fell slowly, flushing the running figures of men from underneath their treads, following and firing at the fugitives. It was unbelievable to see men falling and being killed so close, to see the explosions of Jap grenades and mortars, black fountains and showers of dirt near the tanks, and see the flashes of explosions under their very treads.[2]

Lacking antitank guns, the Japanese forces charged the tanks with rifles, grenades, and mines. To no avail; it was a slaughter. One Japanese soldier surrendered. Twelve wounded were captured, and two unwounded soldiers became prisoners of war. Many survivors were crushed by tanks or bayoneted. Virtually all the rest of Ichiki's nine hundred men were dead, including Ichiki, who, by some accounts ordered his regimental colors burned before he committed seppuku—Japanese ritual suicide by disembowelment.[3] The losses to marines were forty-four killed and seventy-one wounded. The battle was so fierce in part because Japanese troops would not retreat. "It was contrary to the spirit and teaching of the Bushido. The Emperor's soldiers won the victory or they died on the battlefield."[4] Die they did. Again and again Japanese soldiers would come in great waves, and we would kill them in wide groups until hundreds lay dead on the sand. Their bodies decomposed where they lay until a dozer would come and cover them.

Reinforcements began to arrive, the 2nd Battalion of the 5th Regiment on August 21 and the 1st Raider Battalion and 1st Parachute Battalion on August 30, all fresh from Tulagi. Seabees arrived on September 1 to begin work on the airfield. Feeding all these men was impossible, since the transport ships had been able to leave us only a few days' worth of food, even with what we took from the Japanese, food was scarce. By the end of August we had been reduced to wormy rice twice a day. The rice was unpolished, so it contained much food value, however bad it tasted, but without it we would have starved. The first day we saw worms in the rice and refused to eat it. The second day we picked out the worms and ate the rest. Strangely enough, on the third day, we saw no worms in it. We ate, we lived. We fought off green flies while trying to eat a spoonful of rice and Eagle brand canned milk we'd captured from the Japanese. If it didn't move, we ate it. Sometimes we ate it if it did move. Dick Tweedie remembers the Corps "took the brown food away from us [probably oats] because it had brown worms in it but kept giving us the white food even though it had white worms in it."[5] You could hang your mess gear up and little bitty ants would clean it off completely, leaving dysentery in place of crumbs.

When we found out there was a work party going onto a supply ship, we would pick one of our men to join whatever outfit was resupplying, to blend in and go onto the ship with whatever kind of sack they were carrying, scrounge whatever he could for us, and march out into the jungle again. One of our guys was very good at this. One time he was able to get us some coffee, which we boiled again and again. Once, during the beginning of naval gunfire, someone kicked over our coffee can. When I returned after the shelling I picked up the leaves the coffee grounds had fallen on and stuffed them, leaves and all, back into the can. This marked eight times those grounds had been boiled. Mo says I "cussed everybody in the Marine Corps" over those spilled coffee grounds.

We knew the Japanese, too, were hungry, but we didn't know just how dire their situation was. We would complain of wormy rice and dirty water and the slowness of resupply, but I would read later that General Hyakutake described his troops as "living on grass roots" and that an "average of 100 men starve[d] to death daily."[6] Captain Akio Tani would recall that before the war he loved to go outside and look at the full moon; now, however, he dreaded it, because the Tokyo Express, the Japanese resupply line that ran through the Slot at night, would not attempt to deliver supplies during the full moon, so he knew he would go hungry.[7]

We came across caches of supplies the Japanese had tried to conceal, containing, among much else, Japanese cigarettes, which were better than the Australian or New Zealand versions. We also found Japanese candy, with comics in them, in Japanese for Japanese soldiers. Whether these were propaganda I don't know, as I never learned to recognize any characters of their language.

Malaria stalked everyone, now and for the rest of the South Pacific war, and it is still one of the world's worst epidemic killers. The word "malaria" derives from an old Italian phrase meaning "bad air," and the disease has afflicted the military throughout every major campaign within the little mosquito's climate zone. Neither Napoleon nor the Union Army in Mississippi nor the Marine Corps was any match for it, and by October of 1942 it would claim as many casualties as the Japanese did. Mosquitoes were everywhere, regardless of how much bug repellent we used or how faithfully we later covered ourselves at night with mosquito netting. Only the female mosquito bites, turning human blood into food for her eggs. Up-close photos show what a monster the little insect really is, its snout combining tiny blades, pumps, and tubes. Malaria actually comes from the saliva she sprays onto the skin:

> Carried in the mosquito's salivary glands—and entering the body with the lubricating squirt—are minute, wormlike creatures. These are the one-celled malaria parasites, known as plasmodia. Fifty thousand of them could swim in a pool the size of the period at the end of this sentence. Typically, a couple of dozen slip into the bloodstream. But it takes just one. A single plasmodium is enough to kill a person. The parasites remain in the bloodstream for only a few minutes. They ride the flume of the circulatory system to the liver. There they stop. Each plasmodium burrows into a different liver cell. Almost certainly, the person who has been bitten hardly stirs from sleep. And for the next week or two, there's no overt sign that something in the body has just gone horribly wrong.[8]

For many of our men that "something" came quickly on Guadalcanal; for others, like me, the parasite would remain in hiding, for now.

In addition to dysentery and malaria, fatigue began to take its toll. We stayed awake for days at a time and would sleep lightly when we slept at all. We grew mentally tired of being on guard at all times, which was worse in some ways than actually being in battle. Mo later told an interviewer, "You would wake somebody up careful, or you were liable to end up with a rifle or a pistol in your face . . . Night and day you're living under the threat of death, day after day after day, nothing to eat, no sleep, nothing, sometimes no hope."[9]

Again and again Japanese bombers came, their ordnance gouging 10-feet-deep craters. The sand along the beach had sections of small bushes that allowed us to move unseen, but the hot sand and 110-degree heat made it difficult to move without standing up for a breath of air now and then. Amid the shelling and firefights, the most startling deaths on Guadalcanal were strangely bloodless. Slim Somerville recalls Dutch trying to get a box of grenades open when an incoming shell hit a nearby tree. Slim and Dutch hit the dirt and weren't hurt, but half a dozen others were killed. One young marine lay there lifeless without a scratch—the concussion had been enough to kill him.

The utter strangeness of the jungle was worse for some than others. One city kid recalled that "when we went ashore at Guadalcanal, it was like going back to school. All we had by way of maps were barely legible aerial photographs taken from a vertical angle. The fields showed up as white, and the jungle showed up as black. But you had no feeling of topography— the third dimension. Being from an industrial town, I had no background in dense, jungle terrain, but suddenly I had to move in the forest quietly, read the stars and other signs to find my location."[10]

I was better prepared by my West Virginia background to survive in these conditions and find my way across unfamiliar ground; the jungle was nothing like my own hills, and the stars were out of place, but growing up I learned to listen to the land and the animals that inhabit it. The jungle had a different story but would tell you many things if you let it. Likewise, having no running water and less food than a body should and getting little sleep over a period of weeks were not new experiences to me. As a teen I would leave home for long stretches, not knowing when I left in the morning where I would sleep that night or what I would eat. Guadalcanal was just an extreme case of my wanderlust.

When the uploading had begun on our first day on the beach, all of the "goodies" had gone to division headquarters. An occasional boat would make it in with a few supplies, but often they were diverted elsewhere. We would send out scavengers to round up what they could. A buddy and I once tried making doughnuts with some swiped ingredients. The doughnuts sank to the bottom of the cooking oil, hard as anchors. We ate them anyhow. Once we had coffee delivered to us in 5-gallon oil cans. It tasted and looked like oil.

By now headquarters had received a small delivery of cereal, cake, and other tasties, although in the field we still had wormy rice. A few days after the officers had been resupplied with decent food, we badgered Scoop to go get himself a good meal. He initially refused, but we pushed him until he went to get something. He came back cussing us and said he wouldn't be going back unless his whole platoon had better food. "I already respected him," Mo said, "but I really learned to respect a man who'd say, if my men don't eat, I don't eat. And that's exactly the kind of platoon leader I had on Guadalcanal."[11]

You wouldn't think such a terrible experience as Guadalcanal would be remembered with any humor, but it's amazing how much we found to laugh about there. (For example, one outfit posted a sign, DRIVE CAREFULLY, WE LOVE OUR CHILDREN.) When veterans get together there's usually much more laughter than civilians would expect based on such a serious experience. Scoop said there's always a funny part to a tough situation, and Mo especially had a great sense of humor. Whenever Scoop complained about the bad food and other harsh conditions on Guadalcanal, Mo asked him what he was squawking about. "You're getting a place to sleep and a good meal twice a day, aren't you?"[12]

Division headquarters requested a workforce from the front lines every day, and on the day we were assigned to work for Division it happened that they were baking a big cake for the brass. The inimitable Weldon DeLong had observed how those behind the lines reacted when the cry of *"Air raid!"* sounded, so he saw this as a great opportunity. He let go with the air raid alarm, and immediately everyone vanished—everyone, that is, except our work detail. First DeLong appropriated two steaks for himself and Scoop; then we proceeded very calmly to have ourselves a piece of cake. Unfortunately the colonel came out of his bunker and saw through our plot. He approached our platoon leader, and I wondered how Scoop was going to handle a piece of cake in one hand, a cigarette in the other, and a salute at the same time. I have always admired his quick thinking: He hastily put both hands behind his back, dropped the cigarette, transferred the cake from his right to his left hand, and saluted smartly with his right hand.

They say an army is always preparing to fight the last war, and in our case it was literally true in terms of equipment. Our old World War I–era Springfields had five-round clips; the Japanese had learned this and could recognize the distinctive click of an empty clip. Some men on Guadalcanal adapted their Springfields to fire twenty-round clips, a trick I didn't know about at the time but wish I had.[13] The 8th Marines, however, had been given M-1s. Occasionally, when they were bathing they'd rest their rifles against the coconut trees, and our men would sneak up and take them, leaving our old Springfields in their place. The M-1 is a semiautomatic with eight-round clips; many Japanese were surprised to be shot by a marine they thought was out of ammo. A marine would fire the M-1 five times and wait until the enemy, assuming he was reloading, advanced.

The Japanese certainly looked different from us, but many Japanese spoke perfect English, having been educated in America or England. "Hey, Joe!" they would yell. We'd reply, "My name ain't Joe!" and promptly shoot at the caller. That the Japanese could mimic us worked to their advantage early on. We found booklets written in English that had the typical expressions marines used, such as "Cease firing" and "Knock off the shooting," phonetically marked so they could pronounce them, with a Japanese translation beside them. They were also writing down nicknames that we used among ourselves, including "Scoop." I once heard a guy yell, "Hey, Scoop, knock off the shooting!" I knew it wasn't a marine.

Colonel Edson later said this was why they adopted code

names for all the officers. The Japanese "would yell or speak in the night, 'This is Captain Joe Smith talking. A Company withdraw to the next hill' . . . One night the Japs put down smoke and they yelled 'gas.' We were green at that time and two of our companies withdrew leaving A Company exposed on its two flanks." Edson was battalion commander at the time, and Captain Lew Walt then in command of the 2nd battalion, 5th Marines, called him on the voice radio to inform him of the situation. Walt said, "Who is speaking?" and Edson replied, "Red." Walt responded, "What name do you identify with 'Silent'?" "Lou," Edson replied. "That is correct," Walt affirmed. "Walt explained the situation to me," said Edson. "At the end of his conversation a voice broke in and said in perfect English, 'Our situation here is excellent. Thank you, sir.'"

In the after-action report Edson added drily, and unnecessarily, "This was the enemy speaking."[14]

Jim McEnery, a lifelong Brooklynite, described Georgia-born Mo as having an "accent you could slice through." Looking for him one day, Jim called out his name several times. He heard Japanese soldiers run behind a bush and holler, "Come on over!" Jim said, "They had no southern accent, believe me!"[15] Their trick didn't work that time, and I daresay few Japanese could mimic Jim's deep Brooklyn accent either.

I never interacted with them, but the 1st Marine Division also went ashore with some of the first Navajo code talkers.[16] Their language was impenetrable to the Japanese, and they were invaluable in coding radio communications throughout this and later battles. Some green marines who had never heard Navajo (or Japanese) and had no knowledge of the deployment of their language reportedly panicked when they first heard it on the radio, thinking it was the Japanese transmitting with *our* radios on *our* frequencies.[17]

We also found several dead Japanese wearing Marine Corps uniforms, and at times we thought we were getting rifle fire from a friendly outfit until we discovered the Japanese were using Marine Corps rifles and American .45 pistols, apparently captured on Wake Island.

The air raids continued, and word came that our fleet was on the way. That night, a terrible battle raged at sea. At about three o'clock in the morning shells began to fall on our lines. We knew Henderson Field was taking a beating, for the greatest concentration of the shelling was there. I made myself a one-man air raid shelter. I knew it would not withstand a direct hit, but it would give me some protection from flying shell fragments and spent casings. While the warships shelled us from the sea, the Japanese on the ground began lobbing mortars into our positions. At the same time the ground troops came at our lines from several directions. I had taken refuge in the shelter, which was about 20 feet from a foxhole, and could hear the mortar shells coming closer and closer, and again my heart began to pound. Then the shells began to explode a little farther away, and I knew they had missed me again. I lay back in my shelter to wait for the coming of day. Not so! Word came along the line for the platoon to move out and take up a new position along the ridge. We did so, and as we took up this new position there were no holes to get into, no logs to get behind. We held off the enemy until daybreak from whatever depression we could squeeze into, if we could find any.

With the coming of dawn the shelling stopped. I went back to my foxhole, and 4 feet away was a neat 5-inch hole in the ground. I looked down into the hole and saw the end of an un-exploded 5-inch shell. A near miss.

Later, watching our planes fighting a Japanese Zero truly reminded me of a dogfight between two very mean dogs. Pit bulls' instincts recede to one thought: survival. First one and then the other is on top, and into the soft underbelly come the flashing fangs. Ripping flesh, mingled with yelps of pain. Only the fittest walk away from this conflict with victory achieved, territory claimed, dominance assured. Sometimes there are no winners; often, both perish from mortal wounds inflicted si-multaneously. Any quiet was short-lived, for the next wave of hunters sought to see through a maze of smoke and dust. They also dropped their quota of missiles, and to their screaming was added a new sound: a smaller plane, a different engine noise. Eyes slitted against the sun, we looked upward. We saw a Grum-man Wildcat on a vertical climb, lining his sights exactly be-tween the two rising suns on the wingtips of the Zero. The Zero hurtled earthward, spewing his bullets, and we again dove for cover—as spent shell casings rained about us and bullets kicked up leaves and dirt. The Wildcat was in turn being lined up by another Zero coming from the same level. The stalker was being stalked. It was assumed that any fighter plane in the sky had sights lined up on him, regardless of which side he was on.

Suddenly explosions ripped the sky. Two rising suns and a Wildcat disintegrated in full view of the earthbound audience. Farther out to sea, one ship's ammunition magazine took a di-rect hit. After the explosion the ship lasted only two minutes until it disappeared beneath the waves. The air was heavy with smoke when two more fighters appeared, headed directly at each other. It was evident they could not see each other through the haze. The winds continued to diminish the pall, but it was too late for them. Destiny now had them in a grip from which there could be no release. Even on discovering their plight, their reflexes were not fast enough to take the mechanical steps needed to steer their planes away from each other. The head-on collision created another huge fireball, and smoke hung in midsky for a long time, as if reluctant to release its reward. From out of the ball of smoke the larger parts of the planes appeared first, followed by the lighter bits of debris spiraling like buds from a maple tree. Off to the left, a wing somehow remained intact and spiraled to earth in front of us. On that day hell swiped its hand across the face of the sky.

A couple of days later some marine pilots came looking for the Zero. One guy asked where it was, and Scoop pointed to the jungle. "What kind of shape is it in?" they asked him. "I haven't any idea," he replied. "Well, haven't you been out there?" "No." "Where's the road that goes on out there?" "There isn't any road." "No road? By the way, where are the front lines?" "You're sitting on them." "You mean these are the front lines here? Let's get the hell out of here!"[18] And away they went.

We used to think about the guys flying around up there and didn't want to be up there with them—but they didn't want to be down where we were either. I later retrieved a bit of armored glass from the windshield of a downed Zero that crashed 100 yards in front of our lines and whiled away a few hours carving a cross and dog tags from it, scraping my name and rank into the latter. I still have them.

6

THE MATANIKAU

No men to spare

THE SAND OF GUADALCANAL NOW held the smell of death. Maggots crawled everywhere. Dysentery, malaria, fungus, dengue fever—these were just some of the jungle maladies that began to take their toll. We had bad coffee for breakfast and rice for dinner. That was it.

During the first week of September, Gen. Kiyotake Kawaguchi outlined a plan to retake the airfield. He would split his force into three divisions, to attack from three sides. Edson's Raiders discovered intelligence of just how many Japanese troops were on the island, and Edson and Vandegrift strategized to protect the most vulnerable approaches to the airfield.

The Japanese attacked on September 12, and over the next few days the vastly outnumbered American defense lines sagged but did not break, thanks to Edson's Raiders. With their failure to overwhelm the Americans in the Battle of Bloody Ridge on September 12–14, the Japanese began to realize that

Guadalcanal was probably lost and could become the turning point for their entire strategy in the South Pacific. To compound their problems, just as with our division more of their men had been rushed in than could be supplied, and starvation would begin to afflict the Japanese. One Japanese soldier wrote in his diary of the failed attack on Henderson that "the attack that was carried out full of confidence seems to be a failure. Enemy planes are already taking off safely in the morning. How mortifying! We buried our guns in the sands of the position and went ahead to [the] gathering point. We had the last ration of rice cut down to 1.8 dl/day [about 6 ounces] for breakfast, and we had nothing for lunch . . . The Japanese army had never experienced such a battle in its history."[1]

Where we were defending there was little fresh water, and lack of water is the bane of every fighting man. Looking back on his Guadalcanal experience, Gunnery Sergeant Beardsley of Company G would say, "I been in the marines 16 years and I've been in three expeditions to China and five engagements since I have been in the Solomons. I will say that this 1942 model recruit we are getting can drink more water than six oldtimers. We have to stress water discipline all the time. They don't seem to realize what real water discipline is."[2]

We didn't have time to argue, though; there wasn't enough water, whatever the reason. We had been issued halazone water purification tablets, a form of chlorine, but we soon ran out of them; anyway, they made the water taste terrible, and there was always a question about their effectiveness against dysentery. The 10-foot craters left by Japanese shells quickly filled with rain and with "wiggle-tails," but we didn't let that stop us from dipping into the crater when we were thirsty enough. We also filled our canteens with what appeared to be clear, pure water from the Matanikau. Even in wartime the silent jungle is for a moment beautiful. Then a storm blew in and the river swelled almost out of its banks, leaving bloated bodies of dead Japanese soldiers, dislodged from upstream, rocking gently with the current before being caught by another wave and washed out to sea. Pure water indeed.

Eventually we had water delivered for drinking, but none for bathing. Sometimes when we were fording a stream everyone made sure his weapon was above his head and proceeded to dunk his whole body into the water. It wasn't much of a bath but did cool us off. Bathing wasn't safe in the jungle battlefields, but anytime we were in back of the lines on a short rest we always found a way. Once we got a 55-gallon drum, made a rack about 6 feet high, and put a spigot on it that we stole from the cook. From a nearby stream we filled a 5-gallon drum with water, dumped it into the big drum, and showered. It was understood that before or after showering the bather was to put in 5 more gallons for the next man. Some goofed off and didn't refill it, but almost everyone complied.

It has been said that the weather of Guadalcanal has two settings: Wet and Less Wet. Wet was now upon us. During the afternoon hours, the water sheeted down in a great silvery deluge. It made the ubiquitous mud deeper, the mossy cover of rocks and tree roots more treacherous. Our uniforms grew mold, as did what food remained. When the changing breeze brought the monsoon, foxholes filled up, and it became an ordeal just to stand up in such conditions, and in the middle of scraping mud off your boots with a bayonet comes a *Banzai!* charge. The mud began to color everything the same. The island itself seemed to be fighting back against us trespassers, gradually reducing the contest from the collision of two great nations until it was just two infantrymen battling each other to stay alive, battling each other and nature, which always wins in the end.

It had been six weeks since our first major engagement, the Battle of the Tenaru. In that time, we untested marines had learned the fundamentals of jungle warfare. *Stay low.* The Japs frequently fired without a target, hoping to flush out a response. A man bent low was safe from everything but ricochets. *Look high.* Jap snipers tied themselves and their guns to tree branches. That way even if one was shot or wounded, he would not fall and give away his position. *Factor in the weather*—the enervating rain and humidity were always with us—*and the decay.* Eleven marines were killed by falling trees, trees simply listing over because they had been rotted from the inside out by fungus and insects. *Factor in the canopy;* certain mortars need hard compression to explode, and the billowy nature of the forest's canopy impeded our shells. Even our grenades might explode harmlessly against the all-enveloping greenery.

No jitterbugging—this was what we called it when a nervous marine started shooting at shadows. *Be patient. Impatience is deadly.* Lt. Col. Frank Richards of the 164th Infantry would later emphasize that "if I were training my Battalion again [for jungle warfare] I would have training in *patience*. I would have patrols wait for the enemy to expose himself. They move around too. They have to relieve themselves and have to get food. I would have the men in this patience training be made to stay still for hours at a time."[3]

MILLER, Thurman I.
Enl 3 Sept. 1940
Photo taken 8 Sept. 1940

The author's recruit photo from Parris Island. *(COLLECTION OF THE AUTHOR)*

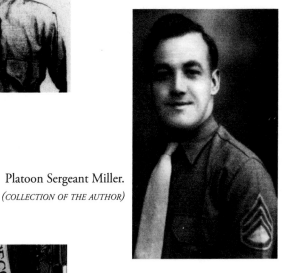

Platoon Sergeant Miller.
(COLLECTION OF THE AUTHOR)

A. L. "Scoop" Adams, a great platoon leader and eventually a lieutenant colonel. *(COLLECTION OF THE AUTHOR)*

K Company's Sgt. Lou Gargano *(left)* and squad leader Jim McEnery. *(COLLECTION OF THE AUTHOR)*

Dick Tweedie, a great scout. A friendly fire bullet from I Company wounded Dick and killed scout Jim Snodgrass. *(COLLECTION OF THE AUTHOR)*

As a private first class at Parris Island. *(COLLECTION OF THE AUTHOR)*

The inimitable Weldon DeLong, *(left),* with his sister Phyllis DeLong Mack and friend Skipper Mitchell. *(COURTESY OF CONNIE VEINOT)*

Propaganda the Japanese dropped on New Britain. "Mad Mac" MacMahon saved me a copy. *(COLLECTION OF THE AUTHOR)*

On Pavuvu an unknown artist would post cartoons having fun with the gunnies. *(Left to right,)* Mo Darsey, David Bailey, the author, and John Malone. *(COLLECTION OF THE AUTHOR)*

My ration book from Camp Lejeuene. *(COLLECTION OF THE AUTHOR)*

The watch I bought in Wellington, shipped home from Guadalcanal, and eventually passed to my oldest son. *(COLLECTION OF THE AUTHOR)*

Recie and I at Camp Lejeune.
(COLLECTION OF THE AUTHOR)

"The Mighty Goettge" bursts through the line at Fort Benning, 1924.
(LIBRARY OF CONGRESS)

Supplies being landed at Iwo Jima, giving some idea of the vast supply effort required for such a battle. Our Guadalcanal landing demonstrated how much could go wrong. *(U.S. COAST GUARD)*

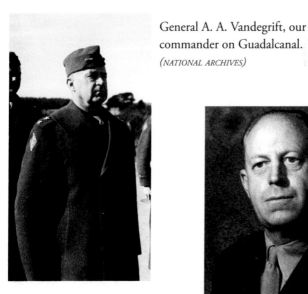

General A. A. Vandegrift, our commander on Guadalcanal. *(NATIONAL ARCHIVES)*

Brigadier General Merritt Edson, who kept my record clean. *(NATIONAL ARCHIVES)*

A shot taken during the New Britain battle, capturing some of the jungle setting but none of the mud, snakes, mosquitoes, or bullets. *(NATIONAL ARCHIVES)*

The real Old-Breed Marines, in a recruiting photo pose, 1918. *(NATIONAL ARCHIVES)*

A Coast Guard LST crammed with supplies and Marines, heading for Cape Gloucester. *(NATIONAL ARCHIVES)*

LST 204, which took my Combat Team to Cape Gloucester and then stood by for wounded. *(U.S. ARMY SIGNAL CORPS)*

A more recent photo of the graveyard at Guadalcanal. *(U.S. ARMY SIGNAL CORPS)*

General Lew Walt. *(U.S. MARINE CORPS)*

USMC artist Donald Dickson captured the roughneck nature of our 1st Division. *(COURTESY OF FORTITUDINE: BULLETIN OF THE MARINE CORPS HISTORICAL PROGRAM, VOL. XXII, NO. 1.)*

Andrew "Close Crop" Haldane, here a lieutenant but eventually a captain, and a good leader. (He became "Ack Ack" for Peleliu.) *(U.S. MARINE CORPS)*

That would not be easy in such a terrain, as the jungle preys on mind and body and weapons. There were strange noises at night, even for a country boy like me. "The jungle is not still . . . The land crabs and lizards make a hell of a noise rustling on leaves . . . and there is [a] bird that sounds like a dog barking."[4] *Keep your wits about you and don't shoot at barking birds.* It sounds like common sense, but it's hard to keep everything in mind at a time like this.

Such knowledge was gleaned the hard way, through fatal mistakes, stories passed from unit to unit, and endless observations made on patrol. On patrol, routine was the word, patience was the style, caution was the rule of thumb. On Guadalcanal, amid the forces of nature and the violence of our human foe, each patrol was at once routine and always different. There were recon patrols, line patrols, food patrols, and just plain patrols. Patrols were the eyes beyond the lines, the fact finders that largely determined the movements of the entire unit and very often made the difference between victory and defeat. Patrols have a way of shifting perspective. A squad or platoon may leave the lines on a recon patrol and have it turn abruptly into fierce combat. An unexploded mine may turn a patrol into a rescue mission, to return the injured to medical care.

The scout was point man for the patrol, and each advance man had his own method of staying alive. I respected our scouts immensely; they were a breed apart. Monk Arndt would tell an interviewer later, "When I am scouting and come to an opening in the jungle, and have to cross it, I generally run across quickly and quietly. Going slow here may cost a scout his life."[5] Good advice like this was passed from the veterans like Monk down to the brave but green scouts assigned to each platoon.

(I wouldn't meet Monk personally until we were both in Australia, but we knew him by reputation. Arndt got his nickname in Puerto Rico in 1939 because he was small and lean and could climb and scramble up a tree like a monkey.) What makes a good scout? Dick Tweedie and Jim McEnery could tell you better than I, but the keys are stealth and practice. Monk himself came by his reputation by the hard, silent work of repetition, "walking quietly over rocks, twigs, grass, leaves, through vines, etc. I practice this around this bivouac area. I received instructions in scouting and patrolling at Quantico but I still practice this around here in the bivouac area. I believe because I practice, this is the reason I am still alive." A marine walking around a quiet camp might be going mental or might just be practicing stealth. "Some of the other NCO's laughed at me because I am always seeing how quietly I can walk around and because I go out and practice on my own. But they have stopped laughing because I have been on more patrols than any man in the Regiment, and I am still alive."[6] I have no doubt his stealth and quickness kept him alive not only on the Island but throughout his service in Korea, too.

More often than not patrols are made up of volunteers, men who go out of curiosity or even boredom. Many go because they are dedicated to their fellow marines, willing to go before the rest and glean the answers to make the way safe. To mark the trees, as it were. Patrols are hell, for the enemy is always there, if only in your mind, behind any bush, in any tree.

Since our August landing, all 1st Division Marine units had been involved in heavy combat. Those of us in K Company, 3rd

Battalion, 5th Regiment had fought alongside the Raiders in three separate engagements and endless smaller actions on the Matanikau River. The 1st Marine Regiment had turned back the enemy at the Tenaru River. The 2nd Battalion had cleaned up at Tanambogo. Such continuous action was not sustainable even for battle-hardened troops, which we were not. Admiral King's original plan had called for the immediate replacement of marine forces by army personnel once the airfield had been taken, so that the marines could be moved to amphibious operations on island chains to the north. Though we had taken the airfield on the second day, it was six weeks later and still no army.

The grinding conditions of Guadalcanal sharpened and perfected our jungle combat skills. This was the hands-on training the division didn't have time for before being thrown into battle; it had turned all of us into the Old Breed. Coupled with our mastering of amphibious landing tactics, our new edge and understanding of the enemy's tactics and strategy made understandable General Vandegrift's impatience to take the battle to the enemy, all the way to Tokyo if necessary. This was not to be. Gen. George Marshall's commitment to Europe would not allow army troops to be siphoned off to the South Pacific.

On September 18 the 7th Marines arrived, under the command of the already legendary Lewis B. "Chesty" Puller, bringing food, tanks, ammunition, fuel, and aviation support. Like Vandegrift, Puller—who started out as a private—was known for mingling with his frontline men and bucking up their spirits. Those spirits would begin to slacken as the island absorbed the 7th and its men grew hungrier and more fatigued by the brutal heat, malaria, and utter strangeness of the jungle.

At about this time Vandegrift received an odd message. The nun and her mission party and her native schoolchildren who had refused to leave Guadalcanal just before our invasion had now walked for weeks across the island, always just a few hours ahead of the Japanese. When they walked on the beach the protective natives would walk in their footsteps, covering the sandal shoeprints that would have given away the presence of Westerners. The nun and her party hid in the mountains for weeks before finally making it to Tangarare, where coastwatchers tried to get help for them. With all the other problems Vandegrift had, he asked, "Is this what war is all about, rescuing missionaries and Nuns? I have no men to spare nor a small boat to send to an unknown area of the Island. I cannot send my men on such a mission. Why didn't those missionaries leave when ordered to do so?"[7]

Yet he did. He sent a message via the coastwatchers that a transport would arrive on October 4. The nun joined a manifest of twenty-six passengers on the 40-foot launch, including a U.S. pilot and a coastwatcher, and they sailed through Japanese-controlled waters. American planes dipped their wings over the small craft as it rounded Cape Esperance, but no one had told the navy. A ship rounded its guns on the little craft, but the commander hesitated to fire. "Let me check with headquarters," he said. The reply came quickly, "For God's sake, don't fire!" The USS *Fomalhaut* carried the group safely to New Caledonia.

Fighting along the Matanikau continued throughout October. Our 3rd Battalion was in support of the 2nd Battalion along the Matanikau and had to rely on semaphore signals to get the word that we had been called back to set up a line behind the 1st Battalion, 5th Regiment. Eventually we came to the banks of a small stream. On our side the bank was steep, and in some places it was 10 or 12 feet down to the water. On the other side, the enemy's side, the jungle sloped gently downward to the stream and provided much more cover for the enemy to hide in. The Japanese knew jungle warfare; they were veterans of the ruthless conquest of much of Asia. We were veterans now also, but we had just begun to be schooled in atrocity. However, we had learned much from their tactics and engaged in a screaming bayonet charge that drove the Japanese back to the banks of the river.

War is a game of objectives. Take 01; 01 taken. Stand by for orders; 02 is designated as the next objective. Take 02 and rest. The temperature is around 110 degrees, and 02 is hard to acquire. We lose some men. Yet, though costly, 02 is achieved. Stand by for orders. Take 03, then you're relieved. Or not. "Men, I need you to take 04." "Hell, man, we already took more than our allotment." Our weariness, the draining reserves of strength and morale, didn't matter. On Guadalcanal, we began to learn that war didn't come in allotments. You took what you could, held what you had, and took more if the job demanded it. These lessons would be tested to their limit on Cape Gloucester.

We held the ground we took, and the fighting waxed and waned as we waited for the great land assault we all knew was coming. Digging yet another foxhole, I heard a *chunk* as my entrenching tool hit something in my pocket. I had broken the crystal of my gold watch. Saddened, I put the watch and shattered crystal in my pocket and continued digging in.

On October 7 the men of the 3/5 were deployed along the

Matanikau, where we had begun probing actions to the west. The airfield was at our backs. We had learned by this time that holding this line was essential to protecting the airdrome. If the enemy crossed the river, he could establish an artillery cordon that would put the airfield within reach. If we could keep the enemy at bay, his only redress would be to use heavy-caliber, long-range weapons. Deadly but less accurate. We crossed the river on October 9 and forced them to retreat from their position on the east side, disrupting their plan to attack Henderson Field. Their casualties were heavy that day.

On October 11 came the next great sea engagement, the Battle of Cape Esperance. Our Navy intercepted Japanese heavy cruisers and destroyers set to bombard Henderson, sank one cruiser and destroyer, and forced the rest to retreat. The Japanese supply convoy still got through, but after discharging its cargo it turned to help the crippled Japanese ships, and our fliers sank two more of their destroyers. It wasn't a decisive battle, in that neither side completely controlled the sea around Guadalcanal. Still, after the disaster at Savo this first victory over the Japanese naval forces was a great boost for morale, which by now was very low.

The second week of October brought a period of extended, violent shelling that would become known as "the Bombardment." Imagine the devastation wrought by a thousand shells, each as heavy as a small car, raining down to explode on this little island. We had been shelled before, but this was different. These shells were big, and we knew they were coming from a battleship. (The Japanese navy was firing 14-inch shells; McEnery said they looked more like 14-foot shells.) Nothing is more terrifying than to be crouched in a foxhole in dark of night, wondering if the next shell has your name on it. Later, when Guadalcanal was far behind us, the men of K Company would agree that the shelling was one of the worst experiences of the island. As Mo put it, "When we were fighting with small arms, we didn't have time to be scared. But when the shelling started it seemed we were at the mercy of fate."[8] Many factors contributed to the breakdown of men from combat fatigue—lack of sleep, lack of food, seeing buddies killed—but shelling by enemy warships was by far the greatest single factor, especially when it continued night after night.[9]

After the Battle of Cape Esperance, in the strait between Savo Island and Guadalcanal, the battleships *Kongo* and *Haruna* (the ships that had been pounding the hell out of us) arrived at our shore. From our perch on the bank of the river, and with grim understanding, we watched the two ships unload several hundred men, four 150 mm howitzers, field equipment, and ammunition.

Admiral Nimitz visited the island to buck up our morale and hand out medals and to see for himself the conditions on the ground. Most of us stayed on the lines; medals were the furthest thing from our minds. Throughout the battle, Vandegrift toured the division perimeter every morning, talking to enlisted men and officers alike, to keep a close eye on his command but also to keep up our morale during the constant shelling and the rising supply crisis. Compare this to what we now know about General MacArthur, who was made a national hero early in the war because we needed heroes, but who made a series of terrible military decisions. "Dugout Doug" was known on Bataan for staying in his well-equipped and comfortable quarters with his wife and family rather than hobnobbing with his lowly soldiers. Not Vandegrift.

Now, rumors were being whispered across units that the fleet was returning. From our positions up and down the lines, we squinted at the waves, straining to see the ships. Soon we could make out the silhouette of a bridge and con tower. There *was* a fleet, streaming directly toward us. They had come back with what we assumed to be a carrier battle group. Cheers broke out among the men at their approach. Once they were upon us, our joy fled, the emblem of the Rising Sun manifest on the underside of the wings. There was indeed a fleet, but as one man put it, *"Hell, they ain't ours!"*

No ships with Old Glory waving in the sun, no big guns replying. So it was to be a repeat of Wake Island after all. Through a telescope we watched the enemy begin to deploy. It looked like a complete task force of the Japanese Imperial Navy, and its stirring was leisurely, as if it had all the time in the world. We counted off the ships one by one. Destroyers, troop transports, and cargo ships unloaded tanks, infantry, and other troops. By the planes, we assumed an aircraft carrier was in the area. Adding this to what they had already brought down the Slot, they had indeed become a formidable force.

Dig in? No, the order was not forthcoming. If we ever needed air support, it was now—but I later learned MacArthur had no planes to send. With no planes on the field and no guns that could reach the ships, we had to stand by and watch them unload. Suddenly there came a sound we hadn't heard before: a huge, awkward U.S. Navy PBY, "PB" meaning a patrol bomber, more a flying boat than a combat aircraft. Somehow, the navy had fitted her with a bomb. As she flew over the task force, the cry went up all over the ridges, *"She's diving, she's diving!"* Sure enough, the PBY was plummeting, aiming as best she could at one of the Japanese ships. Their antiaircraft guns began to burst flak all around her. We cheered her on. She dodged their bullets, finished her dive, dropped her bomb, and left in her wake a smoking transport. Then out of the blue came a squadron of B-17 bombers. They dropped their loads and two more ships were ablaze, and they were gone, leaving behind the smoking ships . . . and marines filled with new resolve.

As the evening sun sank behind the horizon and dark began to fall, we set about the task of seeing to our positions, making sure of ammo and cover. Alone with my thoughts, I searched for a reason for being here in this unheard-of chain of islands. I had received a small New Testament from a minister back in my hometown and resorted to reading it at times. I didn't consider myself a Christian, but in periods of stress we draw a little closer to the spiritual. As I look back I remember no atheists on Guadalcanal, although I vowed I wouldn't let fear drive any religious belief I might come to profess. I began to read about love, family, and devotion and came across a scripture that spoke to me as no other had: *Greater love hath no man than this, that a man lay down his life for his friends.* If this were true, it would all be worthwhile.

The Japanese hit Henderson Field hard; they destroyed some of our planes and blew up some aviation fuel but didn't disable the airfield. Meanwhile, they still controlled the night seas but were successful in replenishing their troops only little by little because they didn't have enough barges, and perhaps more importantly because the destroyers typically used in the Tokyo Express transports weren't designed to carry a large volume of supplies.[10] Finally realizing they were facing not a division but a regiment, a Japanese convoy landed at Tassafaronga on October 15 and began unloading a large contingent of troops. Our planes bombed the convoy throughout the next day, destroying several cargo ships, but the convoy was able to deposit 4,500 fresh troops and most of their food and equipment. These were the last reinforcements they would be able to land, bringing their total on the island to about 20,000. We couldn't know it at the time, but conditions on their side of the lines were no better than ours, and possibly worse. One of the Japanese officers landing in that final troop convoy recalls making his way to a Japanese gun emplacement near the Matanikau. He asked what the terrible smell was. "The dead," he was told. "American dead so close to our lines?" "No," came the reply, "our dead."[11]

The situation on our side was still critical. We were low on everything—food, medicine, you name it. Gas was in short supply. Our planes were stranded by the shelling. Resupply had been difficult as the Japs had engaged the navy across the Slot. Each night, we squeezed into whatever depression we could find. Hidden in foxholes and shallow creases in the land, we held on until morning. Every morning, with the coming of dawn, the shelling stopped. The sun came up through the mist and was beautiful, bizarrely normal. The stillness wouldn't last, though—it never did. Spiraling bombs dropped by Japanese Bettys would soon split the air with an ever-increasing wail until suddenly displaced by the deeper sound of explosions rocking the earth, splitting trees, hurling bits of metal, glass, and the remnants of men and equipment into the valley. Then, silence again.

Japanese artillerymen would move frequently to prevent our targeting them. Shoot, move, camouflage. Their matériel supply situation was as bad as ours, and in November and December their artillerymen were so low on both powder and shells they were forced to scavenge for spare gun parts and make packing material from old shoes or anything else they could find.

After ten days of intense sustained naval bombardment . . . nothing. When would the assault come? Night after night we were shelled, and day after day new Japanese troops wearily trudged up the beaches and disappeared into the jungle. Nothing more.

Nevertheless, Vandegrift took action. There were two main crossings of the Matanikau, one at the mouth of the river, where it emptied into the sea, and a log bridge the Japanese built on the river farther inland. Anticipating a Japanese flanking move from inland, Vandegrift moved the 7th Marines south and west of the airfield. The land crossing at the mouth of the river provided the only crossing for tanks, heavy weapons, and large numbers of enemy troops, and that's why K Company was deployed to take and hold it. We ensured that it was within firing range and sight of both our rifles and antitank guns.

On October 21 our engineers threw a footbridge across the Matanikau in preparation for a new assault, but the next day the line was at a standstill; we were being held down by a well-placed enemy machine gun. Second Lt. Charles J. Kimmel of I company shouted, *"Who will help me get that gun?"* Weldon DeLong immediately jumped up, yelling, "Let's go, men!" The whole line jumped up to join him and came out yelling and screaming, *"Banzai!"* The Japanese forces turned and ran. Mo recalled, "We all just started runnin', hollerin', and shootin.' It was just a crazy thing to do."[12] We had learned early the famous *Banzai!* charge of the enemy. We were so convincing that battalion headquarters reinforced their position in preparation for a Japanese attack, thinking they had overrun our position. The Japanese were fooled by their own style of fighting, and our rush took us within a few yards of the mouth of the Matanikau River.

Try as we might to keep squads connected, the jungle seemed to envelop all of us. Mo and Weldon were ordered to go out and see if they could contact the left flank of L Company, and they came across a wounded PFC, Emil Student. Mo recalls:

It was almost dark and me and DeLong went out in the direction where we'd been ambushed that afternoon, where we knew Student was. We got pretty close and DeLong called Stu, and Student told him, "Don't come out here. Don't come out here. Don't come any closer." About the time he said that they just sprayed machine gun fire over DeLong and myself, and we just lay flat on the ground. A few minutes later we called for L Company again. They laid another barrage right down on our heads, so DeLong and myself fell back to our lines at just about dark. Of course, DeLong always thought if we could have gotten to Stu we might have saved his life. He was shot through the stomach. Stu kept saying *Don't come out here. Don't come out here.*[13]

Even in his dying, this tough marine was protecting his buddies. He couldn't move, we couldn't reach him, and he died that night.

Darkness caught up to us just before we reached the river. Word came down the line, "Dig in where you are." In the darkness you never knew if you were in a foxhole with friend or foe. We slept, when we did sleep, two to a foxhole because early in the campaign the Japanese were so close and so quiet they could creep into a foxhole and kill one man without the other detecting them. Robert Leckie aptly said of the deep jungle darkness, "Everything and all the world became my enemy."[14] We had been advancing more or less on our stomachs and knees. I happened to wind up on a pile of dry bamboo, and every time I moved I sounded like one of the large lizards that came crawling out of the jungle at night; I couldn't dig a foxhole or risk giving away our position. I lay quietly for a long time, scarcely breathing. During the night a small Japanese patrol crossed over the sandspit. Suddenly we were in a hot close-quarters fight, and amid the noise I rolled over several feet and found myself a deeper hole of sorts, which I proceeded very quickly to deepen further, providing me cover until the Japanese abandoned the skirmish. At dawn the firing dropped off to an occasional burst. I raised up to survey my surroundings. I could hear the river to the front. A few yards to the side I saw a young marine lying on his back, his pack under his shoulder and his head resting on a rotten log as if asleep. A closer look told me he had died in that position. His wound had been sudden and sufficient to drain all the blood from his body, and he was very white. Nature had already begun the process of returning his body to the dust from which it had come. Little bugs crawled in and out of his nose holes, and a wiggle worm crawled out of one ear. Maggots had begun to eat away his flesh. His gear already had started to mold into a blue greenish color. As I stepped across his body, the ultimate question came to my lips. *How long?* This boy had given all he had.

As is inevitable in wartime, we had some losses from friendly fire. A single bullet from someone in I Company killed scout Jim Snodgrass and wounded Dick Tweedie. At the time we relied on runners to carry messages from one unit to another, as there were few radios, and as a consequence of this poor communication, we were sometimes shelled by our own artillery units or ships. Other marines were victims of their own carelessness. One guy in I Company picked up an old grenade and was going to throw it into the ocean to kill some fish, but as soon as he pulled the pin the grenade exploded in his hand.

On October 23, it was getting close. The jungle on the other side was so thick you could see only a few feet into it, but we could hear the enemy digging in. As the day wore on, we could see the gathering of troops and equipment. So we dug a little deeper, cleaned our weapons again, checked on our buddies, made small talk. Where I was, about 50 yards upstream from the spit, the river did not exceed 40 feet in width. Huge rainforest trees loomed overhead. Here and there a lone coconut tree spread its palms to the sun. The jungle vegetation covered the ground on the riverbanks with such beauty that I lost myself in it for a moment.

It was just at dusk that hell discharged her fury. Across from us, the Japanese 2nd Battalion, 4th Infantry (2/4) and the 1st Battalion, 4th Infantry (1/4) began firing, the sound of their artillery punctuated by the thud of mortar fire. The noise of our .30 and .50 caliber machine guns mingled with our own mortar and rifle fire. Under the covering blanket of the ask-and-answer of the machine guns, Col. Nomasu Nakaguma began to move his 1st Independent Tank Company into position. This was it. Tracer bullets lit up the sky with a ghostly green flare. All around us, the dark earth exploded in small geysers. Grenades flew over the river in both directions, passing in the air. Artillery and mortar fire rained down. Some Japanese grenades reached our lines; some of our grenades reached theirs. In the darkness, men sank, dying, into the waters of the Matanikau.

Then, for a moment, the firing ceased. I looked at the man next to me, and we both strained to hear what we knew was coming. We had watched their unloading more than a week ago, the 17-ton Chi-Ha tanks. An ominous rumble began behind their lines. This was what we had been waiting for. As the tanks made their way toward the beach, lurching slowly over downed trees and their own dead and dying, waves of artillery fire continued to break over us. The rumbling held steady, not ready to advance until light. We dug in and continued to trade fire and artillery. Our lines were very close, close enough for us to have a conversation with the enemy, had we been inclined to. Across all these years what stayed with me most about this long night is a single voice, the piteous crying of a dying boy, alone. His words carried across the water, *"Ashamoto, Ashamoto."*

To whom was he pleading? Father? Brother? God? How is it

that I could hear him? I do not know, but his voice has stayed with me for seventy years.

Just at dawn, before full light, the tanks began their crossing in single file. Apparently not to be denied, believing they could hit us at their leisure, the first rolled onto the spit, then the second. They tracked forward, making way for those that followed. In only minutes they were halfway across. Then two-thirds. We held our fire. As their last tank reached the crossing our half-track, upon which we had mounted a 75 mm cannon, let go a mighty salvo. Two direct hits rendered the lead tank useless. With the lead tank stopped and no way for the others to turn around, the rest became sitting ducks. One hatch started to open. A marine ran alongside and threw a grenade into it. The hatch closed for a second and then burst open. The body of the driver hung there, suspended, his helmet seared onto his blackened head, his eyes wide open.

Throughout that day and into the night, we took out the entire tank company and both Japanese battalions. At sunrise, the night's devastation was revealed. The trees were all gone. The beautiful greenery was no more. For hundreds of feet the vegetation had been erased as if it had never been. The remains of the enemy lay scattered about. Nothing intact, just parts of limbs and equipment, flesh and bone.

Our battalion lost 6 marines that night, with 25 wounded. Action reports list the number of Japanese dead at 1,050—the size of a large battalion. Over the next three days, as the 1st Marines and the 7th Marines added their totals to ours, that number would rise to 3,500. So much loss, so many lives ended here before me, one boy's simple cry, and now a whole field of what was left of human beings. Some compassion crept into my

mind and sat down beside the hatred embedded there; the resolve that followed the mutilated Goettge patrol diminished
slightly as I considered the carnage that lay before me.

Gen. Masa. Maruyama's boast that he "would exterminate the
enemy around the airfield in one blow" was shown to be the
gross underestimation of the United States Marine Corps it
was. A German naval attaché stationed in Japan, interrogated
after the war, recalled being "astounded" at the Japanese over-
confidence in their South Pacific positions he visited early in
the war. "The Japanese there were thoroughly enjoying the lush
life. They had parties continually and were drinking all the liquor they had captured. I asked them why they did not prepare
fortifications and do something to make these places stronger,
but they said that the Americans would never come, that they
could not fight in the jungle and that they were not the kind of
people who could stand warfare in the south."[15]

  Our part in the battle was done, but the Japanese were not
to take the failure to regain the airfield lightly:

> Maruyama was not yet finished. He reorganized his spent
> troops for a final effort. Soon after dark on the twenty-fifth,
> the Japanese assault began. The slaughter continued until even
> Maruyama realized the futility of it all. The Sendai Division
> was shattered; half of its officers were dead, and the hungry,
> tired, dispirited survivors were forced to retrace their steps . . .
> The failure of the Japanese offensive was due not only to the
> courage of the marines and army personnel, but also to the ri-
> gidity and overconfidence of the Japanese commanders. The

senior officers, who had gained battle experience either in China or earlier in the war against vastly outnumbered green Allied troops, no doubt felt contempt for the Americans and believed that the raw courage of their infantry combined with aerial and naval superiority would assure easy victory. It didn't work out that way. Hyakutake's ambitious plan failed to take into account Kawaguchi's earlier failure, Maruyama launched frontal attacks with tired troops before all his men were in position, and Colonel Oka did not send out reconnaissance patrols to study the terrain. In the final analysis, the Japanese commanders had destroyed one of their finest infantry divisions for absolutely no gain.[16]

Yet how could Maruyama have done otherwise? If Japanese success depended on control of this small airfield, how could he have ceased fighting for it, poor logistics and all, given the code of war under which he operated? Looking back on it, the failure of coordination among the Japanese is a startling departure from their traditional regimentation. As quoted in the after-action report, Col. G. C. Thomas, chief of staff to General Vandegrift, observed that

all of his efforts have been in the form of attacks on a narrow front at rather widely separated points. These were mass attacks and although orders and operations maps captured have shown that they were to be simultaneous attacks this was never the case. Our feeling is that his failure to estimate the terrain difficulties caused the lack of coordination. The result has been favorable to us as it has permitted the shifting of our all too small reserves from one area to another. We believe that the

told we could send a letter if we could find something, anything, to write on. Needless to say, there were no writing tablets
or envelopes available, and almost everything made of paper or
leather rotted quickly in the humid island air. Jim somehow got
hold of a Japanese envelope and wrote home on it. I found a
small piece of brown paper bag. Of course, I couldn't divulge
the location of my 1st Marine Division, but I penciled a note to
my father and mother and told them I was all right. No more
could be said. I folded it up and gave it to the company clerk.
That small piece of paper made its way out of the Solomons and
across the Pacific to the Fleet Post Office in San Francisco, then
across the breadth of the United States to the post office in Otsego. In those days the post office was kept in a private home
and had just a few mailboxes, casual hours, and a small bag of
mail each day. Every morning my father would go faithfully
down to the post office in hope of hearing from me. Every day
he was disappointed. I had always been close to my father, and
he had no idea where I was, and I had been gone many months.
This particular morning the postmistress, Mrs. Vancamp, sadly
told my father once again that there was no mail for him, but
just before closing time she noticed a small scrap of brown paper lying on the floor. She had walked on it all day. She picked
it up to discard it. The first thing she noticed was my name on
the bottom of it. As she read the few words she realized this was
important to my parents. She immediately closed the post office and walked the mile up to our house and gave it to them.
My sister Gladys wrote to me years later, "I remember it was
way after dark. I thought they'd come with bad news about you
and I started to cry. But it was good news. They had found a
little folded piece of paper, a letter from you, no envelope or

stamp. Our poor old mom then and there got down on her knees and thanked the Lord for that little folded up note."

The air raids continued by day, and Washing Machine Charlie came each night. The enemy had hit us with a three-pronged attack, up the beach both ways and in the middle of our perimeter, and had been repulsed.

Every day there were patrols. One patrol was directed to seek out and identify the remains of one member of an earlier patrol. They found his grave and upon digging out the remains found that the jungle had already begun to claim the body. They recognized a tattoo on the forearm of the man, but since there were no dog tags on him they simply had to list him as missing in action. The strange thing was, the grave had a crude grave marker—a piece of board with the man's name: Sweeney. Apparently the Japanese had buried him, marked his grave, and kept his dog tags. Why? Our Graves Registration Service wouldn't have left him there. Was it an apology? A warning? Or was it the natives? We would never know.

Scoop recalls leading one patrol into a large ravine that had to be crossed. He could go around it, taking a greater chance of running into the enemy, or he could ignore it and return to the lines. His orders, however, had been explicit, so he decided the best recourse was to go over or through it, depending on the natural opposition of the jungle itself. He spread his men sparingly with instructions to find the best passage. Scoop saw a large tree that had fallen almost all the way across the deep ravine. He told Mo he'd see if the tree was stable enough to use as a bridge. He stepped gingerly on the trunk and it seemed to be solid. He went a little farther across. A third of the way across he ran out of vines and limbs to hold on to and had to depend on balance alone. All was well until he stepped on a section of the trunk that had been rotted away. The bark separated from the trunk and he lost his footing and fell headfirst down through the vegetation, lodging himself in a tangle. His first thought was of the various forms of jungle carnivores that would soon be fighting over his body. He struggled briefly and found that that only made him sink deeper. He yelled for the sergeant. All he could do now was wait. Meanwhile, Mo, not seeing his platoon leader, thought something was amiss and hastened back to the fallen tree. Scoop was nowhere to be seen. Mo heard a muffled sound from below. All he could see from the base of the tree was a pair of boot heels. He reached down and extracted the muddy lieutenant from the darkness below.

On with the patrol. Eventually the men worked their way across the ravine and regrouped on the other side to decide the best course to take. Weldon DeLong stopped and began sniffing the air. He whispered to the platoon leader he smelled Japs.

"Hell, they ain't none around here," another man said.

"Oh yeah, I can smell the bastards a mile off," DeLong replied.

"Spread out and have a look," ordered the leader.

"Here he is, hiding under the brush!"

DeLong got hold of the Japanese soldier by his boots and dragged him, blinking in disbelief, out into the bright sunlight. Upon seeing the size of the patrol, the Jap resigned himself to being taken in. "Take him back to headquarters." Casually Scoop shifted his Reising gun to his other hand. Quick as a flash the prisoner was on him. He grabbed the barrel of the

Reising gun with one hand and the lieutenant's arm with the other. Round and round they went. Scoop recalled later that all kinds of thoughts were going through his mind. *What if this guy's a black belt? What if he throws me out into the jungle? If he does, it sure will embarrass the hell out of me in front of my men.* He knew he had to do something quick, but if he wasn't careful he could cause the Jap to shoot into the rest of the patrol and maybe kill or wound one of them. Can't have that happen. The Jap turned Scoop's arm loose and popped him once on the cheek. From over the lieutenant's shoulder came Weldon's fist, scarcely missing the lieutenant's head before it slammed into the Jap's jaw. The fist brought the problem to an end, but it presented another, for one of the other men put his service knife up against the Jap's belly and asked permission to sink it home. That, too, was not the answer. By now our officers had been warned that we needed the intelligence prisoners could provide. Scoop delegated two men to take the prisoner back to rear headquarters. He was not escorted back gently, however; as they disappeared out of sight he was receiving numerous kicks to his behind.

Some patrols are made without the men ever knowing what they are actually looking for. One of Scoop's patrols left early in the morning and walked around the lines of defense just observing, occasionally venturing outside our lines to have a look at a new section of jungle. At length they came to the top of a ridge and found themselves in the deep grass. Shortly they were enveloped by the darkness that came on suddenly after sundown in the jungle. They decided that their only recourse was to move off the trail, post sentries, and bed down as best they could. Sometime during the night the rustle of tall grass

awakened one member of the patrol, and he could see in silhouette a group walking the trail. He counted enough to deter-
mine that the enemy was at least platoon sized. Not knowing
the exact mission of his patrol he decided to not yell out, since
they were not dug in for combat. He heard no one else mention
it the next day and assumed he was the only one who had seen
them. The patrol returned without engaging the enemy.

We retained our position on the banks of the Matanikau for
the remaining days of our stay on the Canal. The stench of the
dead grew worse by the day. Food and water became even more
scarce. The rice was coming to an end. Green flies covered our
mess gear so you could barely see the food. One time a cow
wandered into a booby trap the engineers set up. John Cassel,
my old bunkmate on the *Wakefield,* was a butcher in civilian
life and cut a quarter from the carcass. We boiled it all day and
tried it that night, but it was still too tough, so we kept cooking
it all night, holding ponchos over the fire so it couldn't be seen
out to sea, fighting the smoke all the while. We tried it again in
the morning and still couldn't cut it. We kept boiling it until
that evening, thirty-six hours after we started, and still couldn't
cut it, so we gave it a decent burial.

Mo and Scoop were involved in one detail that had the unpleasant task of disposing of the bodies of many Japanese soldiers killed in heavy fighting with the 2nd Platoon. There were
far too many to bury individually, so Mo had a friend in the
Engineers blast a large pit, and the Japanese bodies were
dropped into it. A barrel of captured Japanese oil was rolled
into the pit, and a tracer bullet set fire to the oil. This was effec-

tive, but it burned for days, and even then, as Scoop recalls, the bodies wouldn't stay buried—an arm or a head would be sticking up.[18]

We lost DeLong on November 3 at Point Cruz. His Navy Cross citation summarizes his heroism and death succinctly and almost poetically. "After leading his squad forward in numerous assaults upon enemy positions, Corporal DeLong with two other marines, when the advance of his company was threatened by a Japanese 37-mm gun firing at almost point-blank range, unhesitatingly rushed forward, seized the gun after disposing of its crew and put it out of action. Finally, in a violent bayonet assault, he advanced to the front of his unit and engaged the enemy in hand-to-hand combat until he was mortally wounded." Slim Somerville was right behind DeLong when he was killed. Slim recalls that marines were very short of ammunition at the time, and had the enemy known it they could have overwhelmed our forces. We were sorry to lose DeLong, the big fullback who was always ready for a good laugh. Fittingly, a destroyer escort was named after him, the USS *DeLong,* DE-684.

Scoop came down with a severe form of malaria and was evacuated back to the States early; it would be forty years before I would see him again. We all knew we couldn't hold our units together, that the man next to you could be gone in an instant, but I would miss Scoop's leadership for the rest of my time in the Corps.

On November 4 the 2nd Marine Division's 8th Regiment arrived. The few days needed to replace troops and rebuild squads and platoons and companies provided a short period for us to relax. During lulls in the fighting, once our work was done we passed the time however we could. Some men gambled. Jim remembers men playing blackjack and hitting on 17 or 18. What good was money to us there? Many of us wouldn't live to spend it. On the other hand, some marines won a lot and sent thousands of dollars home. One man drank some homemade "raisinjack" liquor and got so drunk he climbed onto one of our .50 caliber machine guns and commenced firing. He turned it 360 degrees and everyone hit the ground before he was finally dragged off it.

During our last few days on the island we got a replacement company commander fresh from the States who wanted to make a name for himself very quickly. He at once tried to turn us back into the spit-and-polish image of the Corps. He ordered our platoon leader to take us on another combat patrol. Our gunny was wise and led us around within the confines of our own lines, the CO never suspecting. The CO also arranged for us to attend lectures and assigned me to give one on night patrols. I thought he was out of earshot when I began my lecture. "Now men, I'm supposed to give a lecture on night patrols. Personally, if I were given the order to go on night patrol, I would tell whoever gave that order to go to hell." The men began to look at me funny. Turning, I looked into the face of the CO. He ordered me to his tent and asked, "Were you serious?" "Yes, sir," I replied. "Dismissed," he said. "Give your lecture tomorrow on barbed wire entanglement instead."

they know much about what we were going through. On Guadalcanal somehow the rumor spread that I had been killed, and the news made its way to the father of another West Virginia guy on the island, a family friend of ours. He knew he had to break the news to my parents, but he couldn't bring himself to do it, and the situation was straightened out just before he made that awful, long walk to our house. My sister Gladys went to a movie that showed a newsreel before the feature, and she was sure she had seen a Japanese soldier stab me to death right on the screen; she had to be removed from the theater because she was crying so loudly.

We did know the war effort was in full swing, from paper and metal drives to rationing to women working in factories—and even becoming marines. America needed every effort to replace what we'd lost at Pearl Harbor and to fight on two fronts, and fortunately our country had both abundant raw materials and a can-do attitude. Conversely, the Japanese leaders did not trust their people. Interrogated after the war, a Japanese admiral would lament, "Although it was known from the start that there would be basically a shortage in resources as the war progressed, the rapid depletion of what we had to start with was not made known to the people as a whole. To be sure, individuals realized that there was a shortage in activities with which they were directly concerned, that is true; but they were not given a chance to find out the overall shortage that was increasing from day to day, because that shortage was kept under cover as a national secret, and the people had no chance to find out how bad the situation was becoming."[2] The Japanese never had the chance to experience the same sense of coming together, of shared sacrifice, that America did during World War II.

A greater problem for the Japanese was that their warrior code would not let them be honest even within the military hierarchy that depended on an honest and sober assessment. "As long as Japan, despite the setback at Guadalcanal, still seemed to be winning the war, the Japanese high command did not find it necessary to conceal the number of casualties or to distort the results of the fighting. Before long, however, the official communiqués became unreliable, exaggerating or even inventing enemy losses and minimizing their own. Rumors filled in what the communiqués failed to reveal."[3]

We were officially relieved at 1400 on December 9. Four months and two days from our arrival on the island, we marched down to the beach to board ship. Our packs were light now. The sand crunched as it had when I had jumped out of the landing craft. I joined the many men who stopped to bid farewell to their friends at the cemetery holding most of the marines who perished on the island. Their graves were covered over with palm fronds, and many had tombstones of wood scraps, with handwritten farewells. It was near the beach, and the graves were laid out in perfect rows so that any way you happened to look they were straight. All the palm fronds on top of the graves had been laid so all pointed the same way. Every man in the division left a part of himself on Guadalcanal. Every man who served there feels, and has a right to feel, a sense of possession about the island, and an interest in the ground that holds his friends.

As I looked down at this display I thought some higher power must have kept me from lying here beside my comrades. Their faces flashed before my eyes. Beltrami. Student. De-Long, and so many others. I had come with many of these men through the pain of boot camp and advanced training. I would leave them there to go again against the enemy on another island and take my chances of joining them. My mind drifted back to shortly after our arrival on the island, when dozens of men went down to the beach in response to the chaplain's call and were baptized. I had decided I would not do so while I was in danger. It was sad to see these same men later commit such deeds as we were called on to perform. I was ashamed of them even though I didn't claim to be Christian myself.

We prepared to embark. A great number of marines were too weak to lift themselves into the ships that would carry us away from the island; our traditional nemeses, the navy men, helped us up. Lt. Cmdr. E. Rogers Smith, MC, USNR, a doctor from Mare Island, California, examined the men evacuated from Guadalcanal and described a "picture of physical and mental strain that combines the best of Edgar Allen Poe and Buck Rogers":

Never before in history has such a group of healthy, toughened, well-trained men been subjected to such conditions as the combat troops of the U.S. Marine Corps faced during the days following August 7, 1942. . . . These men do not like to exaggerate their trials—in fact they do not like to even talk about them . . . Rain, heat, insects, dysentery, malaria, all contributed. But the end result was not bloodstream infection nor gastrointestinal disease but a disturbance of the whole organism—a disorder of thinking and living, or even wanting to live. And this incredible strain lasted not one or two days or nights but

persisted and increased for months. This was not the quickly
terminated but terrific rape of Pearl Harbor, not the similarly
acute days of Dunkirk. This was the worst of both of them,
prolonged seemingly without end. . . . They were alone on this
island and their expected relief did not come. They had no
way of knowing why it did not arrive. Soon they were sure
none of them would get off the island—they were expendible,
doomed. . . . Fatigue produced by all these factors increased
and wore them down. Painful aching fatigue that they felt
could never be relieved. And this in men trained to such an
extent that they had known no fatigue during their periods of
training.[4]

It's difficult to describe the desolate look of many of the men
once aboard the transport. Doctors would give the name "Guadalcanal neurosis" to a "new and unique psychiatric malady"
that haunted these men and made them nervous, jumpy, wild
eyed, always exhaustingly ready to confront an enemy no longer present.[5] The condition would follow the most invalided
men back stateside, rendering them unfit for combat. Still,
these were marines. A newspaper article on Dr. Smith's find-
ings reported, "One of the first duties of the medical officers
was to assure the men that no one could ever consider them
cowards. Their trembling, nervous, upset state made them fear
being thought yellow. It was pathetic, Commander Smith said,
to see how grateful they were when being assured no one would
think them yellow."[6] Oddly, the doctors naming this disease
suggested that blonds were most susceptible; the "average white
man is not 'geared to the tropics' and blonds are especially likely

to crack, Lt. Cmdr. James L. McCartney declared."[7] Perhaps my dark coloration had protected me.

Innumerable books and movies have used the island's name as shorthand for deadly warfare. Our taking and holding Guadalcanal not only stopped the Japanese advance in the South Pacific, it enabled the Americans to make advances of their own. At the time, we soldiers on the ground had no context for any of this. Only the perspective of a few years established it as a decisive moment in the war, for both sides. Guadalcanal became the forward base for MacArthur's Southwest Pacific action, and Point Cruz was turned into a giant dock and warehouse. American planes of every type flew to and from Henderson Field.

The small island gave the 1st Division the first of three Presidential Unit Citations in the war, at a cost of 650 killed in action, almost 1,300 wounded in action, and more than 8,000 cases of malaria. Thirty-one would remain missing in action.[8] By comparison, we killed over 14,000 of the 36,000 Japanese troops who fought on the island, and they lost another 9,000 to disease or starvation. Moreover, they had lost thousands of their best infantry and airmen, neither of which could be replaced quickly enough throughout the rest of the war.

Guadalcanal also became a byword in the ranks of the Marine Corps. Less than a year after our fight on the island, the Corps would purchase fifty thousand additional acres at the marine base in Quantico, Virginia, and immediately name it the Guadalcanal Area. The 1st Marine Division adopted the symbol of the Southern Cross as our emblem. For years afterward, everywhere we went people would ask, "You served on the Canal, didn't you?"

Many army and marine men continued to be stationed on Guadalcanal for varying lengths of time until the end of the war, so there are many soldiers who can say they "served on Guadalcanal." There are really two Guadalcanals, though: the one we fought to take from the Japanese, and the one we left for others to hold as an American base. Our experiences were very different from those of the troops who came later. They would describe an island of beautiful beaches, hot food, clean clothes, even creature comforts like record players. I do not begrudge that these men, including my brother Buck and my uncle Russell, both of whom also served in the South Pacific, faced little or no battle.

What if we had *lost* that small island? Historians still speculate. If the Japanese had retaken Henderson Field,

it is difficult to imagine any critical mass among US decision-makers to commit more men and assets to counterthrusts in the Pacific until the European war was well in hand. If no American troops were committed to the Pacific for two or three years, one might ask whether the US public, following the battles to defeat Germany, would have retained enough residual hatred to support the great human sacrifices necessary to dislodge Japan from dug-in positions in these southern islands, and then start moving up toward Japan. More likely, a stabilized Russia would have entered the Pacific war, and from Siberian bases American planes would have bombed the Home Islands. The Pacific war as we know it simply would not have happened.[9]

Whether this is an overstatement we'll never know, and we had no idea of all this at the time of the fighting. Great strategies of world power were not in our job description.

What tactics and strategies had we learned from Guadalcanal that might help us prepare for the next battle? The Corps interviewed both enlisted men and officers soon after the battle, interviews commissioned by Gen. George C. Marshall and published in the Fleet Marine Force after-action report, *Fighting on Guadalcanal*, in 1943. The army chief of staff said the island "proved to be the critical learning experience on how to meet and defeat a tenacious and proficient enemy in very difficult terrain under most adverse conditions."[10] An understatement. Marshall himself wrote, "The American Marines and Doughboys show us that the Jap is no superman. He is a tricky, vicious and fanatical fighter. But they are beating him day after day . . . We *must* cash in on the experience which these and other brave men have paid for in blood."[11]

In the report, General Vandegrift himself weighed in on how to train for the type of warfare we faced in the South Pacific. He advised that we "go back to the tactics of the French and Indian days. This is not meant facetiously. Study their tactics and fit in our modern weapons and you have a solution. I refer to the tactics and leadership of the days of *Roger's [sic] Rangers*."[12] It seems odd at first that Vandegrift, a tough veteran who'd spent his early Corps service in the tropical heat of Haiti, Cuba, and Nicaragua, would reference the tactics of a New Hampshire militiaman from two centuries earlier, a major who fought in the deep snow of New England rather than the hellish heat of the Solomons. However, as I look back on the lessons we learned the hard way on Guadalcanal, I see the wisdom in Vandegrift's advice. "Rogers's Rangers" were a colonial militia that fought on the side of the British in the French and Indian War, operating mainly in the vicinity of Lake George, New York, and what is now Vermont. A fictionalized version of Rogers's story was told in the best-selling novel *Northwest Passage* in 1937, so it isn't unusual Vandegrift would have it in mind.[13] What is unusual is that he would think of mentioning it in the context of a South Pacific jungle war.

The Rangers were known for their winter raids on French towns and garrisons, trudging across the frozen rivers. Rogers adapted Native American scouting and survival techniques, and his well-trained force of about six hundred men fought in some of the worst winter mountain conditions imaginable. In addition to being well trained, Rogers's men were at a technological advantage, as they wore snowshoes, while the French had none (thus, the "Battles on Snowshoes" in 1757 and 1758). Similarly, we adapted ourselves to the ways of the jungle, from discarding insignia and Marine Corps ceremony when that made sense to using Japanese-style banzai charges.

Rogers was also an innovator of guerrilla warfare, writing out twenty-eight detailed "rules of ranging" and training his men under live fire. His force was trained to live off the land, wherever they were, for extended periods. (The U.S. Army's Ranger force identifies itself as inheriting Rogers's principles.) Unusual for a guerrilla force, his Rangers were expected to attend a daily roll call and weapons inspection (with "a firelock, sixty rounds of powder and ball, and a hatchet") "and to be ready on any emergency to march at a minute's warning," well armed and in good fighting trim. He gives detailed directions about marching in different types of terrain ("keeping at such a distance from each other as to prevent one shot from killing two men"), setting a rendezvous point in case of retreat and dispersal, dealing with prisoners, and the importance of secrecy and silence among sentries. When stopping to drink water, "dispose your party so as not to be surprised," and where possible avoid the usual paths and roads. Rogers also emphasized fire discipline. "In general, when pushed upon by the enemy, reserve your fire till they approach very near, which will then put them into the greatest surprise and consternation." It's amazing to me how much of this advice was incorporated in my Marine Corps training: Study the articles of War; daily roll call; weapons inspection; spread out when marching, "keeping at such a distance from each other as to prevent one shot from killing two men"; keep prisoners separate until they've been interrogated; save your ammo and don't get trigger-happy.

Had I then known of Vandegrift's admiration for Rogers's Rangers I would have become a scholar of them, which would have better prepared me for teaching young officer candidates later in my career. He could just as easily have been talking about modern strategy when he says, "If you find the enemy encamped near the banks of a river, or lake, which you imagine they will attempt to cross for their security upon being attacked, leave a detachment of your party on the opposite shore to receive them, while, with the remainder, you surprise them, having them between you and the lake or river." I thought of our line along the Matanikau.

Looking back at the lessons we'd learned, the biggest surprise may have been the lack of individual and NCO-level initiative among the Japanese. Japanese artilleryman Capt. Akio "Pistol Pete" Tani later said of Guadalcanal that American ranking officers were superior and American infantry "performed their duties on the basis of what was necessary, or logical. In contrast, our soldiers only carried out direct orders. I regard that mental flexibility and greater degree of personal initiative an important strength of the American soldier."[14] The famous regimentation of the Japanese was a drawback when fighting conditions required improvisation and self-reliance, two traits the 1st Division showed daily.

The German attaché quoted above traced the Japanese command problems even further up, blaming corruption in Japan for the lack of a coherent strategy among ranking officers. "Sometimes very good men were kept at their work only a very few weeks or months because someone else would get the job through corruption. You cannot be efficient with key positions constantly changing."[15]

The same respect for authority so deeply entrenched in Japanese culture that prevented them from acting on their own also prevented them from taking the commonsense step of reducing the recognition of their leaders by our troops. Our officers discarded their insignia, so as not to be recognized by rank, and if an officer was killed, you took the insignia off his body. When two marines were sent back to the jungle to confirm Goettge was dead, for example, they first removed his watch and insignia so the Japanese wouldn't identify him as an officer. By contrast, you could tell a Japanese officer by his saber and leather leg wrappings, and often by his relationship to his men; it was clear who was subservient to whom.

Finally, World War II occurred just at the front edge of a

technological revolution, and technology played an underappreciated role in Guadalcanal. Asked what lessons he would take from Guadalcanal, a Colonel Sims advised to "concentrate on communications. We depend to a large extent on wire communications. It is tough work but it can be done. I have had to loan the Communications Regimental Section men to help carry wire through tough places but *I want communications*. Your information has to be timely and properly evaluated."[16] While for the most part we stretched hundreds of yards of wire in a complex web, wire that could be cut by heavy transport treads or the Japanese at any time, the Japanese had early model handheld radios. In the report Colonel Puller bemoaned that advantage. "The 'walky-talky' the Japs have operates. Why can't we have a similar one? To HELL with the telephone wire with advancing troops. We can't carry enough wire. We received an order. 'The advance will stop until the wire gets in.' THIS IS BACKWARDS!"[17] Our commanders did have TBX radios, but they were in short supply in the early days of the war and were "portable" only in a broad sense, as they required three men to carry their transmitter, batteries, and hand-cranked generator. They were also inadequately waterproofed, a definite problem in the jungle, where a downpour could commence without notice.

Now we were resting, exhausted, aboard ship, with a decent meal in us, and had been led to believe we were going home. Then, just a day out of port the loudspeaker blared, "Now hear this. This ship is bound for Brisbane, Australia." We sailed away from the Island of Death aboard the USS *President Jack-*

son for the five-day trip to Brisbane. We looked back at the islands and saw them again as we had first glimpsed them. Savo
still stood defiant, and the green hell of the jungle still looked
as beautiful as ever from a distance. The sand gleamed.

When we pulled into Brisbane much of the population of
the city was there to greet us. They had heard of Guadalcanal
and read of the combat in their papers, yet they must have wondered about this motley bunch of men. We were not the well-
groomed Yanks they had expected. We had landed on the
Canal with only one change of clothing and hadn't been issued
new uniforms yet. The raggedy-assed marines were once more
on parade. The city met us with great acclaim, however, for
they knew we had halted, for the time being, the march of the
Japanese army toward their continent. Their country's entire
population was less than that of New York City at that time and
would have been overwhelmed, with their troops off fighting in
North Africa.

In true marine fashion we were not assigned clean barracks
to live in but were shipped a full 40 miles out of the city and
ordered to live in tents. There could be no lights after dark, for
the Japanese had been known to fly sorties that far south, and
we could take no chance on being bombed.

We had time now to look at ourselves and each other. Malaria had taken its deadly toll on the 1st Division; our flesh
hung on us like limp cloth. The circles under our eyes deep-
ened, and the look of age came upon all of us. We had beaten
one enemy. Could we beat this one? Malaria still ate away at
many of us, consuming our stamina, reducing our days to shiv-
ering and high fever and general misery.

When I joined the Marine Corps, I weighed 160 pounds;

by the end of my time on Guadalcanal, I weighed only 115. I felt the only reason I had not come down with malaria was because I had taken the preventive atabrine very diligently, all the time and at the proper time, and it had been effective. The disease would haunt many of the men who served on Guadalcanal for the rest of their lives. There is no known cure, nor is there an effective and permanent prophylactic. Quinine is given to patients once the disease makes itself known, but there was no quinine to be had—once the Japanese had taken the Philippines and Java, they controlled much of the world's supply. The side effects of atabrine were awful, and many men simply gave up on the tablets. As a result, when we landed in Brisbane, the malarial rate was a staggering 75 percent. Of the four thousand men with whom I arrived, three thousand already were infected with the disease.

The medical community's knowledge of the disease at the time was limited. Though originally deemed a "nonmalarial plain," our Camp Cable in Brisbane turned out to be in a region infested with the anopheline mosquito, the same mosquito that already had given so many men the disease in the first place. As Vandegrift bemoaned, "The troops would infect the mosquitoes which in turn would re-infect the troops, a vicious circle."[18] The only solution was to move the troops elsewhere, and Camp Balcombe in Melbourne was chosen.

In the meantime, paperwork began to catch up with us. Marines then were graded on a scale of 1 to 5 on military efficiency, neatness and military bearing, intelligence, obedience, and sobriety. Those categories seemed strange when considered in context; I had fought on Guadalcanal, killed a lot of the enemy, hadn't gotten killed myself, and kept the men under my command as squared away as I could. There had been little opportunity to be neat or less than sober. On the last day of 1942 Lieutenant Chisick reviewed my performance for my official record and gave me the highest marks.

At Camp Balcombe all the companies were required to take turns posting guards, and when it became K Company's turn, we didn't yet have enough men to mount guard for the whole camp, so we combined with L Company and posted their men. I was sergeant of the guard, and just as aboard ship, the sergeant of the guard has to make rounds every eight hours. I took the corporal of the guard and two supernumeraries—spare men, not otherwise assigned at the time—with me. I came up to one post and found the L Company man asleep at his watch, rifle leaned up against the wall 10 feet away. I woke him up and sent him back to the brig with the corporal of the guard, leaving a supernumerary in his station. At the next position, another L Company guy was sound asleep and appeared drunk. I sent him to the brig, too. About two weeks later I was ordered to appear for their trial. Lo and behold, the L Company commander, Captain Kramer, tried to reprimand *me* for posting men who were drunk! I had never seen these L Company men and wasn't the one who posted them, but I knew that the L Company commander didn't like K Company. K Company's commander, Captain Murray, went to bat for me. He referred the matter up to the regimental commander, Col. Merritt Edson, who told him to bring my record book. After going over it thoroughly Edson said, "This man's record is perfectly clean. Don't put a mark on it." A close call, and that was the end of that.

Capt. Andrew Haldane had been with the 1st Division on Guadalcanal but only joined K Company afterward, and he took charge of reviewing my performance for the rest of my overseas duty. Haldane was a natural leader, captain of his college football and baseball teams, student body president, humane and charismatic and courageous. He was only a couple of years older than most of us, but he seemed more grounded. For the rest of my time overseas I received top scores across the board, which meant something to me coming from an officer we all respected so much.

Again we boarded ship, this time traveling just outside the Great Barrier Reef for the trip around the coast to Melbourne. I watched a young marine die of fever on the voyage. It was not a pleasant sight. Somehow it was different in combat; one expected to see death there.

From the ship we boarded trains, and the moment our trains pulled into Melbourne, our time in Australia became a time of recovery. The seasons in Australia are opposite those of ours in America. In the land down under, the Southern Cross dominates the sky, and everything rotates the opposite from our North Star. The beautiful and varied colors of Australia's mountains contrasted vividly with the lush, dark jungles of the South Pacific.

For the next nine months we slowly healed. I fell in love with the Australian accent and became familiar with their odd slang and complex monetary system of shillings and pence and pounds sterling. There was finally time for writing letters home, washing ourselves, and relaxing some. We generally got along well with the Aussies, and during my stay there I met a very lovely girl who lived in the city. She was a hat designer, and we dated all the time I was in Australia. We spent many happy hours together, and our relationship never went beyond just having a good time. I had told this girl I had someone back home whom I intended to marry. Her parents had me out to their home for dinner on several occasions, and to my regret I once went into their home drunk. I look back on this incident with a shame that has never left me.

Our living quarters were some 40 miles out of Melbourne, again by train. This time they were Quonset huts, and we had outside toilets with running water, a place to wash our clothes, and even lights. We still were a beat-looking bunch of marines, and they began to issue us dress clothes along with "Ike" jackets.

As the new year of 1943 came, our company was rebuilt. Our retraining in Australia began in earnest in mid-January. We were still physically weak, and the first month was light duty as we focused on disciplinary drills, resupply, and building up our strength. Then we added in more small-unit tactics and heavier physical conditioning. This intensive training was especially needed for the new guys. We, and the rest of the companies, were really at only about half strength when we arrived in Australia and had to be brought up to combat level, so new recruits began to trickle in from all over the United States. Now, the situation seemed reversed from that in the jungle: My men gradually regained the art of drilling, dressing, and conducting themselves as marines, but by contrast, many of the new marines failed in every respect, refusing to conform to the image of parade-ground marines. They talked in ranks, stayed out of step, and generally did everything wrong. In the field they excelled, for in open country they could act naturally. They enjoyed the fresh air and sunshine. Back at the base they resumed their lax ways. At precisely 0800 each morning, the same thing was repeated. The CO's runner would deliver a message to my hut, "Sergeant Miller, the CO wants you." I faithfully reported. "Sergeant Miller reporting as ordered, sir!" He would then proceed to chew me out over their attitudes.

Meanwhile, being a pretty good judge of men, I would always try to explain to the CO that these men would never make parade-ground marines. They just didn't care. They were late for roll call, always out of step, wouldn't call me "Sergeant" in ranks, and didn't respect anyone for any reason. Out in the field, I told him, they were as good as any of the others. I had watched them, and I knew that when we returned to combat I could count on most of them to give a good account of themselves.

There were also tense moments of discipline, however. I had one replacement in the company who had become something of a problem. He would ignore orders and smart off in ranks. His platoon sergeant could not cope with him. One day as I dismissed the company, he yelled something. I knew he had directed his remark at me, so I called the company to attention and told the man to stay at attention when I dismissed them again. When the rest were gone, I stood in front of him and looked him in the eye. I began to read him off, and when I finished I told him to follow me into a large clump of jungle growth just a short distance away. I started down toward it but didn't hear him following, so I turned around to see what the matter was. He was sitting on a log, crying. I sat down beside him, and he began to pour out his misery. I listened as he emptied himself. He was only eighteen and had never been away from home. He was just so miserable he couldn't be a good marine. I talked with him for a while, and when he had calmed down I told him that he could come into my tent anytime to talk if he felt the need. I found a friend in this boy.

We hadn't been long in Australia before we began to again take pride in our looks and so were allowed to mingle with the people of the city of Melbourne. The city was ideal, for there were no other troops there, and we enjoyed the restaurants, bars, theaters, and parks. The food was very good; Australia was cattle country and we ate lots of steak, eggs, gravy, and milk. No more wormy rice and green coconuts. I began to gain back the 45 pounds I had lost. The bars were also plentiful, and we spent considerable time in them. We drank their beer, listened to their music, and generally enjoyed ourselves. Sometimes we would drink too much. One young man was refused a drink due to his age. True enough, he was too young to frequent bars, but we reminded the barkeeper that the "kid" had manned his post on the Canal, just as other men had done. "Now serve him, or we'll tear your damn bar apart." As I write this, I am not proud of some of the things I did and the places I went, but I wish to tell it like it was. I drank along with the rest and did all the things they did.

At Camp Balcombe, after we had recuperated, Colonel Edson's order came down for all hands to hit the firing line, and they asked us NCOs if we would go for the entire seven weeks, the time it took for all the regiment to do the range. We were each promised one furlough day for each week we instructed there, and command came through on their promise. We took our seven-day furlough in Melbourne.

Our retraining became more intense, and we went on longer marches. Soon a 20-mile march was routine. After a few months our commanders decided to test our recovery. On a Thursday at about noon they suddenly put out the word that weekend liberty call was at 1600 hours, or as soon as we got back to the base. We were 20 miles from the base with full field packs. We began jogging. Each of the companies in the battalion started at about the same time, and we all arrived at the base at about the same time. The whole 20 miles had been covered without the usual ten-minute break on the hour.

By April we began landing exercises along with the 7th Marines in Port Phillip Bay. We replaced our Springfield rifles with new M-1s and trained on them into the summer months on Williamstown Range. By the end of July we were using live ammo in large-scale Landing Team and Combat Team exercises. Then came intensive ten-day field exercises with all hands, Combat Teams and all support, with overhead artillery, mortar, and rifle and machine-gun fire to give us a sense of real combat.

By now I had been promoted to platoon sergeant, second in command of the platoon with which I would go into combat. My hometown paper carried the story of my promotion "somewhere in the South Pacific." Soon after coming to Melbourne I had been offered a promotion without the necessity of being examined for it. I respectfully refused, telling the CO that if the chance came up again with the exam I would accept. Why hold out for the exam? Because otherwise the men would say the promotion had been given to me, that I hadn't earned it. This way I could receive the promotion with no hesitation on their part. About a month later the chance came. I took the exam and passed.

Word came in late September that we were to ship out.

Each liberty became a maybe good-bye, and each time I told the girl I dated I might not return. Finally, we were given the order to depart. I packed my seabag carefully, and again I took only my field packs with a change of clothing in my combat pack. I left with a memory of the kind people of Australia and the girl who had filled so many lonely weekends. I will always be grateful to them for being good to us and for expressing their thanks so well. My link to the people of Australia is still strong. My Australian acquaintance Rob Crawford writes, "I can't tell you how many people I've talked to who know nothing about Guadalcanal, Savo Island, or The Slot. In my endeavor to learn more about Australia's role in World War II, I became obsessed with what happened in '42 in the Solomon Islands. If the Yanks had not fought and held the islands, of course, I wouldn't be here now. How many American men gave their lives so that the people of Australia would be safe? That's worth remembering, worth talking about, and they did not die in vain."[19]

Rob also very kindly sent me something I never thought I would see again: sand from the beach at Guadalcanal. It is only a small glass jar about 4 inches tall and 1.5 inches in diameter, but looking at it brought back many things I have tried for sixty-six years to forget. In fact, I can forget very few things about that time, for the images are embedded in my memory so deeply that the mere mention of these islands, where my life changed forever, brings them back immediately.

Life on the troop transport was nothing new to the Fleet Marines. We found we were headed for Milne Bay, New Guinea.

We stayed there three months for training. During that time an occasional nurse rode by in a jeep with a member of the brass; otherwise, we saw no member of the opposite sex.

I now was recommended for gunnery sergeant, or "gunny." It took us three days to take the exam, and you would think it was an exam for colonel the way they did it. Thirteen out of the regiment who were up for promotion reported, and seven dropped out the first day. We had to fieldstrip every weapon the Marine Corps used, from a .45 automatic pistol to a 37 mm antitank gun. I passed the test but was not formally promoted until later.

A small group of islands off the coast of New Guinea is named the Goodenough Island Group. What a name! They took us there for a day's relaxation and fun. There had been no bombs, shells, or any other firepower directed to these islands. They were a paradise. There were tropical birds with such beautiful coloring it was impossible not to stop and admire them. The foliage was incredible, and strange but delicious fruit was abundant.

We chanced to meet one of the local natives coming down a trail clad only in a loincloth and carrying a large stalk of bananas. One member of our company started dickering with him for the bananas. The marine gestured with his arms, pointed to the stalk, showed the native a pack of cigarettes, and pointed again. All the while the native stared with seeming ignorance. Finally, it appeared to dawn on him what the marine wanted. He responded, in perfect English, "Oh, you want to trade your cigarettes for my bananas. Sorry, marine, I don't smoke." We all had a long laugh at this, even the marine who was the butt of the joke.

We were sorry to leave the comfortable air of Australia for a hot and muggy island, but we put our time in New Guinea to good use. We conducted advanced training in the staging areas for the next two months in a climate similar to those where we'd be sent. We began to train with various transports, such as LSTs and amphibian tractors and trucks. By now it was December 1943. It still seemed funny being in the tropics in the winter. Then word came—another appointment with the forces of Japan, to contest their domination of another island. Our staging time had come to an end, as 1944 quickly approached.

New Britain:
Suicide Creek and Walt's Ridge

Tully's ring

Lying 100 miles to the northwest of the northernmost Solomons and 400 miles from Guadalanal, New Britain is the largest island of the Bismarck Archipelago. In 1942 the Japanese invaded the island and remade the capital, Rabaul, into their most formidable advance base by building multiple airfields and taking advantage of a natural deep water anchorage for their fleet. The base put Japanese bombers and troops perilously close to Australia. From here the Japanese launched their counterattack in the battle for Guadalcanal. From here they ruled the South Pacific by air and by sea. It was of the utmost importance—or seemed so at the time—that the Allies capture the airfield called "Unfinished." If we could choke off Japanese supply lanes and recapture the island, we would also take a giant step in our slow march toward their homeland.

The 1st Marine Division's invasion of New Britain was to coincide with the day so many set aside to worship the Prince of Peace. Christmas was D-day for the invasion, but it dawned with no heralds, no carols. The long barrels on the big ships would roar their missiles shoreward amid the ominous sound of the high bombers. The high-pitched scream of fighters would strafe the beach, phosphorus smoke bombs providing cover. It was a Christmas devoid of worship, save the individual prayers of those who were wont to pray.

I had no way of knowing it at the time, but I would be drawn into the vortex of an incredibly detailed plan to retake control of the entire South Pacific. The 1st Marine Division was at the heart of this step in the plan, and we were rested and ready, battle proven by Guadalcanal. We were a mix of old steel like Pop and Mo and fine new men who would go on to represent the 1st so well on Peleliu and Okinawa. I was truly one of the Old Breed now—an old man just past my twenty-fourth birthday.

Scoop was gone, evac'd from Guadalcanal, and I didn't know his status for the rest of the war. I still had Mo with me, and Jim, out scouting silently and then ready for a good laugh and chat when things settled down.

Operation Cartwheel was a marvel of military planning. The first page of the declassified special action report is handwritten in good, clear military form by some nameless clerk corporal: "Phase I: Planning and Training."[1] Then, illogically, part 1 is "Training." This describes the 1st's time in Australia, spread out to Camps Murphy, Robinson, Pell, Balcombe, Mount Martha, and Ballarat, and the training we went through. The code names in the Planning section were designed to confuse the enemy: Amoeba Force, Backhander, Alamo. There would be two initial landings, one at Arawe (code name Director) to the enemy's rear, where those forces would set up a radar base and PT boat base and block any attempt by the Japanese to send reinforcements along the southern coast of New Britain. The second landing, at the Cape, was code-named Backhander.

One of the greatest challenges in planning for Cape Gloucester, and for researchers looking back at the battle, was not unique to that island: A lot of the time even the officers didn't know where the hell we were.

Since the natives of New Britain speak many dialects, spelling of local place names is necessarily phonetic. The Australians during their regime listened carefully as the natives pronounced the words, then adapted these sounds to the English alphabet and thus set them down on maps and pertaining documents. The Japanese, in turn, transliterated some of the Australian names into Japanese characters, coined some new ones, and rendered native versions of place names phonetically into their own language. U.S. translators, encountering these several versions in captured enemy documents, transliterated them back into English, again phonetically, as they thought the Japanese had thought the natives pronounced them. Checked carefully against the earlier Australian versions, the results often made sense, but in many instances this triple translation produced some decidedly odd results . . . During later phases of the campaign, when marine patrols roamed the hinterland at large, intelligence officers contributed further to the confusion by attempting their own phonetic renditions in a well-meant effort to bring earlier maps up to date. On entering a village, they would inquire its name of their native guides, then spell out the reply as they thought it sounded to American ears, often with results that bore little relation to Australian versions owing to certain differences of pronunciation in the dialects of the two nations (example: U.S. phonetic rendition of what our allies called their own country would be spelled "Orstrylia"). The guides themselves were less than helpful at times. Jungle-bound all their lives, few had traveled far beyond their own localities; often they did not know for certain which village was which, and with the characteristic desire of these people to please their new friends they agreed readily that it was what the marines believed it to be, even when they did know better. As a result, the same village may appear at several different locations on different maps, sometimes under different names, and may be spotted still elsewhere in reports using target square coordinates. Trail routes vary similarly.[2]

The planning documents for Cape Gloucester reflected this confusion and ordered that only map names be used, not local village names: If a village or other locality is found to be located in a place different from that shown on maps, or a new village or other locality is found bearing the same name as one shown on maps, then the new village or other locality will be referred to as village (given name) No. 2, No. 3, etc."[3] Add to this the standard additional layer of complexity of code names and the overarching element of time—initial battle plans were laid, then revised, and the plan as actually carried out differed from either. Such is war.

Preparation for an offensive of this magnitude is truly spectacular. For every fighting man on the front lines there will be a dozen in support, with food, ammo, vehicles, and so on, all packed aboard ship and ready to deploy. Everyone was ordered to take 0.1 gram of atabrine daily "under the direct supervision of an officer."[4] Absolute secrecy was the order; no diaries, maps, documents, even pictures of sweethearts were to be brought forward into the operations theater. The marines knew first-hand from captured Japanese documents how much could be made from even a little information. (Some marines hid diaries in their Bibles or other personal effects, creating vivid memoirs after the war, but exposing all of us to harm should they be discovered. The Japanese apparently had no rule against diaries and they were a source of great intelligence during the war and of great historical interest afterward.) Marines were ordered not to take souvenirs from the battlefield "or the person of the enemy," although they could tag an item with their name and outfit and it "may" be returned to them once it had served its military purpose.[5] The Reising submachine guns that had first been tried on Guadalcanal performed no better on New Britain; in the humid jungle conditions the stock would swell up, and each time the weapon was fired the mechanism would jam on the swollen wood, requiring us to trim down the stock. Not a very good weapon for the jungle, and we once again came to rely on our M-1s.

At dawn on December 26, 1st Division forces—but not our 3rd Battalion—were landed on Yellow Beach 1 and Yellow Beach 2 on the western side of the island, several miles south of Cape Gloucester. The password for D-day was "Guadalcanal." The Japanese airdrome there was the first objective. Because the island was over 370 miles long and 40 miles wide, and enemy positions unconfirmed, my battalion, 3/5, was held in reserve as

Combat Team 35, Amoeba Force, McDougal Group, until January 1 when the situation could be reassessed. We were considered an elite force, capable of handling anything they threw at us, so it's not surprising we were set aside for a few days as an ace in the hole. We had a war correspondent attached to us, and we heard him complain that he would have no story to tell with a reserve unit. An officer told him not to worry, the 3rd Battalion would plug the biggest hole on Cape Gloucester.

The men landing on the day after Christmas faced combat landing and soon thereafter an immense storm, with deadly lightning strikes and even an earthquake. By New Year's Eve, it had been determined that the enemy was massed in an area called Borgen Bay, to the south of the initial perimeter. Our unit, reinforcing the 7th Regiment, was to advance to Borgen Bay and clear the enemy. We went ashore on Yellow Beach 2— no combat landing was needed there now—and moved inland and took up positions alongside what would become known as Suicide Creek.

Our battalion spread out across a 500-yard line. Slowly, painstakingly, we cut our way through the vine-matted underbrush. The Japanese we were advancing against were the 141st Infantry Regiment, a veteran group of their soldiers cited for bravery on Bataan. They had been on New Britain since early December and were dug into their invisible redoubts. Their snipers were hidden high in the canopy 200 feet above our heads. The main body of the Japanese infantry was entrenched on Aogiri Ridge, a jungle rise hidden by dense foliage. We had no idea where it was, but captured Japanese intelligence suggested they considered it a key defense point. Our ultimate goal was to take this ridge and command the heights.

Between our position and the ridge lay a small, winding creek that was not on any of the maps. Sometimes 15 feet across, the creek was only 2 or 3 feet deep. What posed a serious problem was its precipitous banks, at some places 20 feet high. On the far side of the banks the Japanese were dug in deeply, waiting in camouflaged pillboxes and machine-gun emplacements, all positioned so as to give them interlocking fields of fire on both the creek and the banks. It was an untenable situation, but there was nothing to do but cross that creek. When we reached the creek, one by one marines began sliding down the banks, their rifles held high over their heads. One by one they were picked off by snipers. Those still on the banks retrenched. Those clinging to the muddy walls of the creek took cover under fallen trees, unwilling to retreat without their dead. Slim took out the first Japanese rifleman of the battle. Calvin King, a sergeant from Pennsylvania who took his platoon over the creek four times, said, "When we got across the creek, the fire was so hot we couldn't do a thing. You couldn't see a single Jap. All you could see was where the bullets were hitting around us. And men getting hit. But no matter how bad it got, I never saw one of the boys pass up a wounded man."[6] We made a second charge with more success, and marines began scrambling onto the Japanese-held banks, but now their machine guns and snipers opened up. There was no place to hide from the snipers, and our platoon got mixed up among others.

Lieutenant Andrew Dykstra was leader of the 1st Platoon of K Company. How he and I came to be side by side, I never knew. Suddenly he cried out, "T.I., I'm hit! I'm hit!" I glanced over and saw that his entire elbow had been shot away. I reached for my first aid pack and found I had only a compress. No sulfa powder to go into the wound, nothing to tie it up with. I stretched out his arm as best I could, bandaged it with the compress, and cut two small pieces of wood for splints. I used my mosquito net to secure them.

We were pinned down, but across the stream I could see movement. I thought this would be a good time to cross, and I stood up and yelled, "Let's go, men!" I jumped down the bank and into the water. Bullets began to burst around me, shredding the leaves from the trees. I looked to my right and to my left. No one had followed me. The Japanese counterattack had started just as I had jumped into the stream, and the other men had had no time to jump. I scrambled back up the bank and found cover behind a rotten log.

For the next two days our men clawed their way up the banks only to be blasted by fire and forced to roll back down to the creek to whatever cover could be found. We managed to get our own machine gun across, but it wasn't enough. Technical Sgt. Asa Bordages wrote later that "a man could only walk on slowly through the jungle waiting for the next shot; trying not to think that he might be dead before he could take another step . . . The next day, they'd be blasted by invisible machine guns, and leave a few more marines dead in the brush as they fell back across Suicide Creek. Then they'd do it all over again. There is no other way to fight a jungle battle."[7]

Help was coming, though. In the rear, marine engineers were frantically building a "corduroy" road of sand-covered logs strong enough to transport our heavy equipment. At the end of the second day they arrived with a bulldozer, which we used to push down the banks of Suicide Creek. Again and again, snipers picked off the driver. Again and again, another marine was there to take his place. In the end, we made it across and cleared the enemy, but we paid a dear price; by the time we were across, the waters of Suicide Creek ran red.

After a day's pause, we pushed on toward Aogiri Ridge. Aogiri wasn't much of a ridge, only a couple hundred yards long with a gentle rise until steepening just before the crest. It stood above and protected the main Japanese supply route; they must hold it or lose the island. The Japs had dug in, with machine-gun emplacements and camouflaged bunkers and riflemen hiding in foxholes; from their higher vantage they could spray fire across every inch of the approach to the crest.

For two days, our progress could literally be measured in yards. The first day we gained 10 feet. That night, we did not pull back to our former positions but rather dug in and held on to that 10 feet. Next day, we took 10 more. The terrain sided with the Japanese, the rain forest preventing any supporting fire. There was never a moment we weren't under fire. Our commanding officer, Lt. Col. David S. McDougal, was wounded on January 7. He was hit in the right shoulder as he was firing his pistol at a machine gun. He rolled over and said, "I guess I can't use that hand anymore." He lay there, "firing at them with his left hand and hollering for a telephone."[8]

His replacement, Maj. Joseph S. Skoczylas, was shot five hours later. Chisick got hit, too. Chesty Puller, who was then with the 3/7, assumed command until a replacement from the 5th Regiment could be found. Puller was a piece of work, and we were lucky to have him. He had enlisted in the Corps as a private and went through boot camp at Parris Island; after seeing action in Samoa, his brigade joined the 1st Division on

Guadalcanal in mid-September, in time for heavy fighting along the Matanikau and the Battle of Henderson Field, where his 7th Marines held the field against a fearsome Japanese regiment. (This is the night of John Basilone's legendary near-solo standoff against what should have been an overwhelming Japanese force.) Puller would go on to fight on Peleliu and Korea before retiring in 1955 with a chest full of Navy Crosses and other awards. He loved the Marine Corps, he loved the 1st Division, and he loved the enlisted man. He was one of us, and our morale lifted somewhat.

The next morning, Lt. Col. Lewis W. Walt took command. First he had to pull together our scattered, depleted units into a battle line. He ordered us to push out our flanks to close up the gaps with the rest of the battalion. Snipers were everywhere. Continuing toward the ridge, we penetrated far into the jungles and found ourselves ahead of our supply system. K rations ran out, and we sent two or three men of each squad back along the lines to gather up the hardtack we had thrown away. By now it had turned green as the mold started to grow on it, but we cut away the mold and ate the rations. The supply system managed to get some gallon cans of fruit cocktail up to us but we were not allowed to stop and eat. We had no spoons, so the lead man in each squad opened it with his bayonet and took out a handful and passed it on to his buddy. Our hands were not dirty to us; we were hungry. Thirst was a greater problem, as the jungle heat sapped our reserves quickly, and while humans can go without food for many days, not so for water; we must have it, even if supply can't get clean water to us, even if it's dirty and we know it will make us sick, as it did many men on New Britain.

The undergrowth was so thick with vines and crazy tangles of limbs and roots that neither side could see more than 10 yards ahead. We had to crawl between the stumps and roots of the giant mangrove forest, many already filled with mud. Between the rain, the snakes, the heat, fungus, dysentery, and malaria, Pop Haney, a veteran of World War I and Guadalcanal and by now pushing fifty, said the Cape was the worst conditions he'd ever fought under—but he would go on to Peleliu.

Still pushing toward the ridge, our platoon had received an order to encounter and destroy a pocket of the enemy. I gave Sergeant Archie Thompson, one of my squad leaders, the order to attack. He told me it was a suicide mission. I told him it was an order. Without another word he turned, gathered his squad, and left. That was the last I ever saw of him. Our lines were so close I heard him engage the enemy. I heard him cry out when he got hit. I heard him dying, and in the din of battle, the rattle of his breathing was sharp and unnatural. He had been shot in the throat, and the air sucked into the hole made the sound of snoring. He was about fifteen minutes dying. Thompson was twenty-three years old, clean cut, and a good man. His death became a personal thing with me, and for many years the sound of his dying would awaken me from sleep. Even now it's as if it happened yesterday.

We had been assigned a new platoon leader we liked very much, a Hoosier, 2nd Lt. Lowell Toelle, whom we all called "Tully." He had been in the South Pacific less than six months and hadn't been married long. As we prepared to hold our line at any cost, I saw Lieutenant Tully raise a rock and put something under it. "My wedding band, T.I.," he said. "I don't want these yellow bastards to get it." That night, all hell broke loose again. We could see the summit and also watch the enemy's movement. All night the Japanese attacked, time and again. We drew all the firepower at our disposal to repel them. Dawn came, and we counted heads. Tully had been killed in action. His instinct had been true. I intended to go retrieve his wedding ring and get it to his new bride, but we had our hands full.

Tully wasn't the only newlywed in our outfit. One of my best buddies, Sgt. Lou Gargano, had come back from furlough in North Carolina with a twinkle in his eye. "T.I., I got married!" Others who married before shipping out got the inevitable "Dear John" letter before long. It became obvious to me that fighting a war is a business for young, single men who have no binding ties at home to distract their attention from the terrible task they have been asked to do.

It was January 8 and though our progress to the ridge was tortured and at times barely discernible, it was, incredibly, greater than that of the 7th Regiment on our left flank. The 3/5 was now on sharply rising ground, and Captain Haldane was leading the company right into the ridge face. We couldn't hold our position against constant machine-gun fire raining down the slope, however, and that night were forced to fall back. There were "long periods of quiet, of the waiting that saps men's will and strength, saps even faith. The enemy sat back. Whenever the Marines tried to move, he pounded them with fire, a storm of fire that stopped them; held them; left a few more dead crumpled in the brush. There were Marines, good men, who gave up hope that afternoon." Colonel Walt would later remember it as "the lowest ebb of spirit."[9]

We crawled, gaining inches at a time. Our lines were ragged, and every foxhole was a new war, a fight to the death for the marine or the enemy, and often both.

Soon it began to rain. Even in clear weather we could never see more than 20 to 30 feet ahead of us. The stress of fighting got to some men; one private lost it, frothing at the mouth like a rabid dog and swinging his M-1 around. I walked slowly and calmly toward him until I got close enough for him to hand over the rifle.

Our ordnance included a 37 mm antitank gun—a massive, wheeled machine gun that weighed about 900 pounds, fired high explosive and canister rounds, and was used as both an antitank weapon and antipersonnel weapon. Colonel Walt called it his "last card" and believed that if we could get the gun up the ridge we could ease the way for the units who were pinned down next to us—that we could break the impasse. Crews began a rotation with the wheeled gun. At times the ridge was so steep that we were forced to our knees, and we spent much of the time crawling. All the time we were under fire; the Jap and marine lines were never more than 10 yards apart. We hewed a trail out literally by hand until the cannon reached our lines. Then we loaded it with antipersonnel shells, which would spray out in a wide path.

Foot by painful foot, marines pushed the cannon up the hill. Firing, reloading, firing, reloading. When one marine went down, two went forward; one to take his place, the other to retrieve the fallen. Our forward elements had reached the crest of the ridge by nightfall, but those rolling the 900-pound gun were failing. It was then Colonel Walt called us forward, put his own shoulder to the wheel, and began to push that gun up the mountain. Watching our colonel stride forward saved us. As the gun was struggled up the hill, men would join briefly to help lift it over the stumps of trees left by the shelling, then return to their cover. (I helped once as it went by me; over the years the number of men claiming to have personally pushed the gun up the hill has grown to the point that, had they all really been involved, the gun could have been lifted and carried to the top.) Finally, we reached the top of the ridge—but could we hold it?

On January 9 at 4:00 A.M. the Japanese charged, screaming, *"Banzai! Marines, prepare to die!"* They wanted the field piece we had inched up the ridge, and they wanted the ridge. They still held an adjoining hill and sprayed machine-gun fire over Aogiri. Again and again they charged, four, five times. It was close combat, hand-to-hand, bayonet and pistol, man against man. Gargano shouted to fix bayonets; he would be dead before the night was over. We couldn't fire the big gun, lest we give away its concealment. In the dark we had no idea what was happening in the next foxhole, or from which direction the enemy might come; our lines were thin, and they could break through at any point. Colonel Walt called for artillery fire on the ridge, closer and closer to our position, 200 yards, 75 yards, then 50.

In the rain a shell might not ignite with its intended force, and a short round from a 105 mm shell got Dutch. Another short round got Lou. Both would win a Silver Star for their bravery on Cape Gloucester.

The rain continued to pour down. Pop Haney's men were in charge of ammo but couldn't get it to us fast enough. At one point my platoon was short of ammo, so I made a run back to get more.

The Japanese brought in a reserve unit for yet another charge. That charge, too, failed as Walt's artillery fire dampened it. The Japanese charged again and again, abating only gradually until at last they withdrew. It was "almost dawn when the last charge broke, when the conquerors of Bataan backed down before the victors of Guadalcanal."[10] In the first quiet moment in many days, men were dead on their feet and fell asleep wherever they could.

Lew Walt would win his first Navy Cross for his role in taking the ridge, and we renamed it Walt's Ridge. Captain Haldane would win a Silver Star for his leadership on Cape Gloucester, including our repelling five bayonet charges by the Japanese in a single night. As one news story about him put it, with complete accuracy, "His men held, taking their cue from Haldane. He was their captain, but he was one of them."[11]

Our company had been reduced in number to such an extent it was no longer regarded as a battle unit and was therefore relieved from frontline duty. On January 1, the first day of our assault, there had been 242 enlisted men and 10 officers in our company. By January 10, there were 88 enlisted men and 2 officers. I still see so many of these men clearly in my mind's eye today. Dutch and Lou. Ray Newcomb being carried down through the jungle with his kneecap shot off, his last words to me, "So long, T.I.—I'm headed for Tennessee!" Another man dying from a Japanese bullet, his groin the size of a quart fruit jar. As well as sending Sergeant Thompson to his certain death.

Little of the heroism of marines ever gets formally recognized. For example, R. R. "Railroad" Kelly got hit on Cape Gloucester and was pinned down, lying just in front of Mo and Private Teskevich. Teskevich said, "I'll creep over you, you put your arms around me, and we'll get out of the fire that way." Teskevich crept over him, Kelly grabbed on, and Teskevich started creeping back to our line. On the way Kelly got hit by another bullet. Still, Teskevich kept crawling and eventually got Kelly out. Kelly survived, and lived until well after the war. "As far as I know," said Mo, "Teskevich never got a medal or other recognition for this feat."[12]

We were changed out by platoon. The replacement platoon leader, a lieutenant, asked who was the leader in my platoon. On a head count, I was the senior NCO. Counting myself, I had thirteen men left. I informed him he could relieve my platoon with one squad. The lieutenant paled.

After the battles for Suicide Creek and Walt's Ridge, we pulled out to a safer area and made camp. We were given hammocks with built-in mosquito netting in which to sleep, and we strung these between trees and suspended them about 2 feet above the ground. Every morning when I climbed out of my sack I found myself covered with a strange pink substance. I decided I would find out what it was and so began unloading my hammock piece by piece. I raised up my pack, and there was a spider with the leg span of a large saucer. I had been literally webbed in by this creature of the jungle. I turned it loose, and it went on its way. Turn loose a spider and seek out a fellow human to kill? I wondered about this later.

By night a small biplane—"Washing Machine Charlie"— would circle overhead. His motor had a nerve-racking, unsynchronized sound. He would circle until just before dawn and then drop his 100-pound bomb. Charlie did not care where he hit; his aim was to keep us up all night. One evening one of our searchlights caught him, but for some reason we didn't fire on him. The next night they couldn't see him but shot anyway, to no avail. One morning we miscalculated his position and heard the bomb hurtling down before we could unzip our mosquito nets and dive for cover. The bomb exploded, and I heard a piece hit under my hammock and at the same instant felt a burning sensation on my back. I yelled for my friend L. W. Wingate, a.k.a. "Gator." He ran his hand down my shirt. He said, "Hell, T.I., I burnt my hand!" I stripped off my jacket and shirt and found a red-hot rivet about an inch long and half an inch in diameter. It had enough speed after hitting the ground to bounce up, hit the bottom of the hammock, burn through it and through my shirt and jacket, and stick itself to my bare skin. It left a blister but never scarred. Gator complained about my getting a Purple Heart when he did not, but I explained later that I never got one, never even went to a corpsman.

We occasionally went down to the beach to wash and rest, but these beaches were not as beautiful as those of the Solomons. They were riddled with coral and generally dangerous to be in. The water was hot in places, and the entire area was very muddy. I crossed two small streams that ran totally independent of each other, one side cold water and the other hot from the volcano underlying the island. I pulled a rusty razor from my pack and tried shaving. Twenty-one days of beard growth, together with the mud and grime, made it difficult. One swipe and the razor had to be taken apart and cleaned. I spent the greater part of an hour in this effort. The little stream reminded me of my home back in Appalachia. I was raised beside such a stream, and as I sat and shaved I pondered the distance, the

hillsides, so bright and constant you could read a newspaper by it, had there been any newspapers there. In the flash I could see the dark green of late summer in the leaves. My shuttling thoughts expanded time, and I watched the forest shudder in the wind. Years dividing, time blending into one anxious moment. Just a young man in my early twenties, I longed for the clasp of a hand hardened from work but still gentle, saying that all is well. I pulled my poncho a little closer around me to help keep out the rain and wondered if the storm of war would swallow me up, never to see my parents again. I looked up at the huge trees in the rain forest. I could see their dominance over the jungle, but also their frailty amid the raging wind, and knew we were both in the grasp of nature itself. I fell asleep again, and in my dream I heard the soft sound of a door opening, quiet footsteps, a calloused hand gently touching my fevered brow. Peace settled over me, and I slept.

I awoke in my foxhole. The sound of sloshing water in the hole told me that last night's storm had been a fearful one. The feel of the hand on my brow in my dream was real enough that when I woke up I absentmindedly raised my hand to where I thought my father might have touched me.

The days wore on, and the main fighting subsided. Training became a matter of briefing new recruits. Lew Walt was evacuated back to the States in February for treatment of his wounds and malaria, but he would be back for Peleliu, where he would again lead K/3/5 when its officers were killed; he would win a second Navy Cross for his bravery there.

Soon our replenished outfit had a new mission, to land on

the peninsula of Talasea. The enemy had a stronghold there, and we could not reach it by land. We were to seek it out and destroy it.

As I mentioned, I had taken the exam for gunnery sergeant on New Guinea and had passed easily. Just before debarking for Talasea word came that my promotion was confirmed. The promotion gave me another down stripe and moved me up a pay grade, though money wasn't on my mind at the time. A "gunny" is a rank unique to the Corps, just above a staff sergeant and below a master or first sergeant. The gunny is generally in charge of day-to-day logistics for the company, about 180 men, and is chosen for his professionalism and leadership. The gunny has to be familiar with all the weapons (as opposed to technical sergeants, who might specialize in communications or anything else not involving ordnance) and be a good judge of his men and a capable leader. "Within the closed, stratified society of a company or detachment, both first sergeant and gunnery sergeant were obeyed with alacrity and afforded unfailing respect, but there seemed to be a more discernable warmth in the attitude of the men toward the latter than toward the first sergeant . . . He was the archetypal marine who confidently demanded the respect from superior and subordinate alike, and received it ungrudgingly."[13] Gunnies call the roll, run close-order drill, and in general look out for the welfare of the men in the company. People I respected, such as Chesty Puller, described senior NCOs like gunnies as the backbone of the Corps, and I had no reason to doubt it. It was a role I felt well prepared for. I would demand excellence from my men, and would receive it.

When my promotion came through, Company Commander

Haldane invited me to his tent to talk. He asked—not ordered—me to continue leading my platoon rather than immediately taking over as gunny. We already had a good gunny in the company, so I agreed and remained as platoon leader throughout our time in New Britain.

That evening we boarded small landing craft and set off on the all-night journey to the landing site. It rained all night, but it was just as well, for "Washing Machine Charlie" seemed to have followed us here from the Canal and was busy dropping flares. This night, he could not see us. We approached the shore, landed with little opposition, and established a beachhead. We lost a few men to Japanese stragglers. Our primary mission, it turned out, was not the peninsula itself. Rather, the Japanese were on the run, and the high command needed live prisoners to use in the program. We were ordered to bring back prisoners. Whether this was for interrogation and intelligence purposes, or to blunt the public relations problem with our well-deserved reputation for no-holds-barred combat, I do not know, but the 1st Marine Division had earned its reputation for taking no prisoners. Armed or unarmed, it made no difference to the 1st. Knowing this, the supreme commander of the South Pacific forces issued a specific directive, "Any marine caught killing prisoners without just cause shall be automatically court-martialed." With this in mind they attached fourteen unarmed army stretcher-bearers to our group. We were ordered to fill the seven stretchers with prisoners—but we couldn't very well take a man prisoner if he was shooting at us, could we?

The mission was laid out in a leapfrog strategy: One reinforced platoon would march a day's journey up the coast and move out to the beach and establish a perimeter of defense. Another platoon would land by boat and the next day do the same thing, and so on until we controlled the entire area.

It was now mid-March 1944. We encountered many Japanese patrols whose duty it was to delay us, for we also learned that the commanding general of the Japanese forces of New Britain was on the run up the coast on his way to Rabaul. The confusion about village names I mentioned earlier had given the Japanese time to move out: "Quite early in the campaign the marines learned from enemy sources that General Matsuda's headquarters lay at or near a place transliterated from the Japanese as *Egaroppu* (sometimes rendered *Aikaroppu*), a locality wholly unknown to any available sources until someone finally associated it with what the Australians had mapped as *Nakarop,* a factor which contributed no little to the success of the Japanese withdrawal."[14]

Day after day, we chased the enemy up the coast, destroying his supplies but keeping his rice and sake. The Japanese would make a stand and then retreat a quarter mile or so and reestablish their 75 mm gun in a new position to slow us again. The original time allotted to our mission turned out to be overly optimistic, as the Japanese fought back to provide retreat cover. They tried to blow up their supply caches as they retreated, but we found some intact, containing weapons and supplies. We stripped the guns and threw the firing mechanisms into the jungle and broke the stocks. We ate the Japanese food and tried to smoke the dreadful Japanese cigarettes.

Compared to Cape Gloucester, Talasea was a paradise. It had civilization in the form of a German mission, a coconut grove, and very pretty beaches, with hot springs. The beaches were long and shallow, with pockets of warm water propelled up from the volcano below.

I had been introduced to one Lt. William B. Bowerschmidt before starting for Talasea and was informed he was our new platoon leader. I could tell that he was fresh out of stateside and very green. It had always been our practice for two men to share their ponchos and make a small tent. I invited the lieutenant to share mine, but he informed me he was perfectly capable of caring for himself. So be it, I thought. Next morning, after the hard rains, there wasn't a dry thread on him. I wasn't altogether dry, but then I wasn't altogether wet either. That same day I noticed he still had on the little gold bars that indicated his rank. I begged his pardon but told him it would be better if he would remove his bars. Again he gave assurance he was capable of making such decisions himself. I never said much after that, but before long I noticed that he had removed the bars and rid himself of any semblance of authority.

He frequently gave orders that were unwise for this type of warfare. The men, some of whom I had served with since boot camp, would look to me first. I would either nod or shake my head as to whether to follow his orders. Once we came upon a clear mountain stream coming down into a waterfall on the trail. It looked good for drinking, and he yelled for the platoon to gather around and fill canteens. No one moved; they all stood where they were. I held up two fingers and said, "Two at a time." I explained that one grenade would wipe out the whole outfit, and my way only two would have been killed. They say there is safety in numbers, and it's a natural instinct to want to stick close to your buddies. A marine is fighting his own individual war, however, and must be ready to act on his own or in small groups whose membership can change instantly. He must be ready to leave his best friend behind if ordered to do so.

We began to put the Army K-9 Corps to work. As much as has been written about the war in the Pacific, too little attention has been given to our canine companions. My platoon was one patrol that had to be particularly quiet, with no unnecessary gunfire. To carry out the mission a tracker was needed, a dog of great intelligence, with a devoted trainer and a disciplined patrol. The dog and tracker led the way toward a small clearing. The trainer passed the word to be quiet: There were Japs up ahead. The dog had smelled them. The Japanese were in a makeshift shelter a short distance ahead. They had posted no sentries. Sure enough, inside a hut made of palm fronds a group of Japanese soldiers were at ease playing cards. The dog and tracker led the patrol even closer.

Picture, if you will, sixty or so of us men forming a large circle around a small hut. On a silent command we all began to converge on it. Very slowly, very quietly, we crept up to it. We could hear laughter inside. They were completely unaware of our presence. On signal we all rushed it at the same time and tore into it. We scattered bushes, leaves, equipment, and Japs out around us. They had a look of shock and disbelief on their faces, for they had been led to believe they were winning the war. Certainly they still thought they had won the island of New Britain. The entire group was captured without a single shot being fired. The lessons I learned that day were patience, stealth, and respect for the world of canines.

The Japanese we captured prepared to die by going to their knees. They touched their foreheads to the ground and lay there waiting for the doom that was sure to come. They had been taught that capture meant certain death. Ordinarily, this would have been their last living position. I touched one directly in front of me on the head with the toe of my boot. He glanced up, and I motioned for him to stand. I had the power in my trigger finger. I controlled his destiny. I looked at my men and saw nothing but hatred. I looked into my own heart and saw nothing but contempt. I stared at the Japanese soldier in front of me. Scarcely 2 feet separated us. For the first time I had come face-to-face with one of the enemy. Our eyes met. Just two men facing each other, both far removed from their homes, separated from their families. Each alone in a hostile land, each seeking to survive at the cost of the other's life.

I had been filled with the desire to kill. Yet, as I looked into his eyes, I knew that he, too, had been indoctrinated with hatred and the desire to kill, without hesitation or regret. To him, he was the oppressed and I was the oppressor. A sadness crept into my heart, a feeling for this man whose life I held in my hands. Ever so slowly, the pendulum began its backward swing, away from hatred, toward sanity. There surely were men in my platoon who did not share my thoughts, but reason, for me, had begun to return.

I turned the prisoners over to the army men. Prisoners were tagged with WD, PMG Form No. 1, showing the date, hour, and place of capture and the force making the capture, whether army or Marine Corps. The prisoner of war tag made it clear— NO TAG, NO FOOD. I told them to set two men at a time on watch through the night and told them they were responsible for the prisoners' safekeeping. After setting out our defensive lines, I lay down on the beach to sleep. The night was clear. From my position, I would see anyone who passed by. As the night wore on I watched the moon cast a dim glow on the water. The sea was an unholy calm. The waves were very small and made only a slight rustling on the sand. I lay still and listened for the jungle to speak. Its very silence bespoke the presence of intruders. The natural residents were gone; the human animal had caused them to depart. Sometime after I fell asleep, I was awakened by a movement a few feet in front of me. There were two men crawling along, one army guy and one prisoner. The former rose up and threw the prisoner over his shoulder like a sack of potatoes and then back in with the rest. I heard the soldier grunt and say, "Now lay there, damn you!" I turned over and went back to sleep.

We billeted in the rain many nights. One evening we came up on about ten grass huts in a small village. They were built on stilts about 10 feet high to protect the natives from wild animals. A ladder hung down from each hut. The huts were about 12 feet square and 7 or 8 feet high at the sides. In the center of the floor was a box about 2 feet square filled with 6 inches of sand, and we could see evidence of recent fires. In the center of the cone-shaped roof was a 6-inch hole for the smoke to go out. *What a find,* we thought, as we got out of our field packs and laid out our gear. Just to lie down on something dry was pure luxury.

After posting guards we opened our meager daily K rations and stretched our weary bodies out for some much-needed sleep. I don't remember dreaming that night but do remember being abruptly awakened by the CO's "Fall out!"

Hastily gathering our gear (we had learned to arrange it in

such a way that we could gather it up in seconds in total darkness), we scrambled down the ladder and found our place in ranks. As we came down the ladder we could hear the jabber of natives. We added two and two together. The natives had returned and were somewhat irritated that we were camping in their homes. The CO had only two words for us, "Let's go." We had learned very soon after coming to the South Pacific that the natives were helpful but suspicious. As long as none of their stuff was bothered they were all right. One could make off with a wife, but by all means do not bother their chickens or their pigs or their gardens. Or their huts. It was nice for a couple of hours anyhow. We marched through the darkness for a time and set up another perimeter for the rest of the night.

Our last engagement with the Japanese was in mid-March, when Company K reached Kilu Village on the Willaumez Peninsula, and by April our mission was complete and we stood by for relief. The K/3/5 roster had again been depleted, filled with KIA and WIA, and the remaining men of the first version of Company K saw few familiar faces from their original landing in Wellington. When the ordeal of Suicide Creek and Walt's Ridge was over, we had lost three-quarters of our men and eight of ten officers. The 1st Marine Division had been used to its fullest. It was like pouring water into a leaking bucket. Pour it into the top and it runs out the bottom. So again went the rebuilding of our outfit. Replacements came and went without my knowing them as fighters, for they never had a chance to prove themselves.

With our success on New Britain, the Japanese hold over

the Philippines began to slip.[15] The Japanese would pull their planes out of Rabaul, which now were beyond their supply control. American bombing of the airfield destroyed many aircraft; equally important, it also killed a lot of highly trained Japanese aircraft maintenance technicians, just as the Japanese had lost many pilots and support personnel on Guadalcanal. A Japanese commander would confirm that "later operations were hampered because too many skilled personnel [were] stuck at Rabaul unable to get out."[16]

Ironically, we would spend four months and two days on New Britain, the exact amount of time we spent on Guadalcanal.

Again we boarded ship. As we sailed away I looked back at the skyline with the live volcano in the background. The rugged coastline and the rain forest fell away; it was a place I would never see again, but its memories are constant in my soul: the sound of Sergeant Thompson's dying. Tully hiding his wedding band. Suicide Creek, where the balance of power shifted so many times. Hordes of the enemy screaming *"Banzai!"* and coming on and on, proudly dying for their emperor. The sickness, the rain, the spider.

Each time one leaves a battlefield he leaves behind a part of himself embedded in it. Disease and lack of food and water had again taken their toll, and again I was down to close to 110 pounds. My skin had wrinkled up. My fingernails and toenails had dried up, and I had picked them off and thrown them away. My skin hung like folds in drapes. I felt old and worn out.

Talk now began of the rotation system. You needed a total of 92 points in order to be sent home. Points were given based on time in the Corps, overseas duty, and the number of campaigns you fought in. When they gave us the details I started counting. I had been given credit for three separate battles, Guadalcanal, Cape Gloucester, and Talasea. I had 138 points. I had done my job and was entitled to go home—but where was home? Back in the hills of Appalachia? In a tent city in North Carolina? Could it have been somewhere in the "land down under" I had loved so much? Or had the Corps become my home?

We learned we were headed for the Solomon Islands again. We wondered if the Canal was our destination. No, not this time, just the small island of Pavuvu for recuperation and, for some of us, to prepare to come home. It should have been a pleasant respite, but that proved not to be the case. Huge rats ran about, seeking food. The first night it rained and rained, and just at dawn I swung my feet out of my bunk into 14 inches of water standing in my tent. The quagmire in the company "streets" made walking impossible; there were deep mudholes everywhere. You just had to chug along as best you could.

Nature was one thing I could always cope with; I had learned to live with and respect it in my younger years and understood its delicate balances. Human nature was another thing. It had been four months since I had been paid. I had no material to write on and wanted to write home. I went into a Red Cross station set up for our benefit and asked for a pencil, paper, and an envelope. They quoted the price: ten cents each item. I explained my predicament of not having any money. No matter, they could not let me have it. Next I visited their bookshop and was told I had to deposit a book in order to check one out. "To hell with it," I said. It was easy to understand why they had no library. We hadn't gone there to read.

One Sunday the officers received a shipment of assorted drinking materials and chose to give each of the first three pay grades a fifth of wine. Another gunnery sergeant and I decided to pool ours and drink just a little of it each day. It had been about eight months since we had left Australia, and I hadn't had anything with alcohol in it in that length of time. I remember it was my turn to hold roll call the next morning. We opened one of the bottles and sipped along. I'm sure we only had a few drinks, but when I looked at my watch it was ten o'clock in the morning! I jumped up with a start. I looked out at the dawning and hurriedly put on my clothes. I stepped out into the company street and yelled, "Company K outside for roll call!" The response was very slow. I yelled again. "Get the lead out!" They still came out of their tents very slowly. Soon I had the company at attention. I received the report from each platoon sergeant. "First Platoon present and accounted for," and so on down the line until all had reported. I did an abrupt about-face, saluted smartly, and opened my mouth to report to the company commander, but there was no one there to receive it. I then noticed that the men were a funny-looking detachment. Half of them in their underwear, half without shirts, and all just sort of standing there looking at me. I could read their expressions: Poor old T.I. had finally gone bananas.

"What kind of marines are you?" I yelled. "Where the hell's the company? Even the officers are crummy!" Still they stared. About then I felt mud ooze between my toes. I looked down— down at my bare feet. The whole company started laughing.

Not just laughing, roaring, as they pointed and laughed some more.

I had called Monday morning roll at dusk on Sunday.

The wine had found an easy mark. It was not the quantity we had consumed but rather the tropical heat along with the fact we were not used to it. The following day I noticed some cartoons on the bulletin board, and they looked exactly like me. One showed me crawling in the company street. Another showed me leaning up against a coconut tree excusing myself. I often drank, laughed, and joked with the men in town, even breaking the rule of not going on liberty with those of lesser rank, but I never lost their respect—and not many can claim to be the star of a wonderful set of cartoons.

The artist missed one excellent opportunity. On New Britain, even after we were out of battle, there were still all the dangers of the jungle and the Japanese stragglers, so we were required to wear or carry a weapon at all times, even to chow. I had "acquired" a Japanese flag, and one marine struck up a trade with me, the flag for a .45 automatic pistol. A bit later another approached me with a trade in mind, this time for a .38 special revolver with a belt and cutaway holster. I traded with him, and consequently when chow time came I carried the revolver. Because it was so hot in the jungle, we wore only our skivvies around the camp and would twist the bottoms and roll them up until they looked like modern-day bikinis. Imagine me going to chow with a pith helmet and skivvies, the .38 slung low around my hip at a 45-degree angle, ready for the draw!

It may seem odd to think of tough marines drawing cartoons, but comic books were among soldiers' main reading materials (though perhaps less so for marines than other branches of the armed forces, though I have no data to back that up). Comics were easy to read, kept soldiers in touch with America, and in many cases reinforced the patriotic themes of the war. Of course, we were all familiar with Bill Mauldin's Willie and Joe characters, but soldiers were also ready for plenty of escapist fantasy comics, and the USO and other organizations passed out many to the troops.

On Guadalcanal I had known Monk Arndt only by his reputation as a talented scout and Goettge patrol survivor, but we were both at Camp Balcombe in Australia. He and I were chatting one day, and I noticed he was reading a comic book—a comic book about marines fighting in the South Pacific. "Look, T.I.," he said, "they got us in the comics now!"[17] An Australian company published such titles as *Gripping Yank Comics* in the hope of cashing in on soldiers' appetite for escapist stuff. It was strange to see a marine reading a comic about marines in the South Pacific.

Of course, comics—along with books, magazines, and especially movies—were an important part of the war propaganda effort at home. War is as much mental as physical. In addition to pro-war propaganda efforts back home, there were radio transmissions such as Tokyo Rose's attempts to demoralize Allied fighters. The Allies used every medium—cigarette wrappers, chewing gum, comic books—to get across the message that we were the liberators. Also, propaganda leaflets or "paper bullets" were dropped into many combat areas by both sides, including on New Britain. The Japanese version would typically tell men their wives were being unfaithful, the war wasn't worth fighting, they would be buried here, and so on. "Mad Mac" McMahon saved a copy of one such pamphlet for me.

It isn't surprising that there would be comic strips and books about Guadalcanal. Capt. Donald Dickson, an adjutant of the 5th Regiment, was also a very skillful cartoonist. Before the war he created a popular character called Stony Craig, a gunny sergeant like me, working with writer Frank Rentfrow, also a gunny and former editor of *Leatherneck* magazine. Dickson's work was very detailed and true to life, and both his paintings and drawings captured the marine experience well, even as cartoons. Stony went on to many adventures in the South Pacific, including in *Gripping Yank Comics*. Years later *Fortitudine: The Marine Corps Historical Program Bulletin* would feature Dickson's Stony Craig character.

Dickson and Rentfrow's personal Marine Corps experience gave "Stony" an air of authenticity, however, as far-fetched as some of his adventures might be. An example is the rifle-range sequence of 1939. A less well-informed cartoonist might not think to show Marines cleaning their Springfield '03 rifle barrel with boiling water from an immersion burner, at the rear of the firing line.

Another example—from the cover of this issue—shows Jeb Fink in the sitting position wearing a shooting jacket seemingly made from an old khaki tunic with scorebook, pencil, and cigarette pocket added on. The slim '03's leather sling seems adjusted correctly to support Fink's left wrist, and unseen—but felt—is its pull on Fink's left bicep. Scorebook at his feet, rear sight raised, finger taking up trigger slack, cheek resting against a linseed-oiled rifle stock, Fink in Dickson's mind must be headed for the "V Ring" in the next day's panel. The sequence in the rifle range butts could be a lesson in target pulling, marking, and paste-up.[18]

It was amazing that any sort of scribbled lines could have captured an aspect of our experience, but Dickson did, with a great flair and sense of humor.

With my points in, I was ready to ship out for the States. Captain Haldane called me in again and got right to it: "T.I., I will make you top sergeant if you stay for Peleliu." I had great respect for Haldane and was honored he would ask me, and especially honored by his confidence in me. He already knew the next island the division was to take. Lately, though, I had been troubled by the thought that my luck was running out. I couldn't know all this at the time, but General MacArthur, of whom the marines were not big fans, was fresh from several beach landings with movie cameras in order to get a good "take" for his Philippines return, and he needed the Peleliu operation to protect his flank as he attempted to retake the Philippines before striking at the Japanese homeland itself. Peleliu would last over two months and cost almost 1,800 American lives and more than 10,000 Japanese. Our leaders underestimated how well the island was fortified and how deeply the enemy was dug in. The battle for Peleliu became one of the bloodiest of the Pacific war, costing the U.S. Marines and navy thousands of casualties. (The story is well told in *Islands of the Damned* by my friend R. V. Burgin.[19]) With such high American casualties, the Japanese command affirmed the success of their strategy of attrition, which now set the tone for the even bloodier assaults on Iwo Jima and Okinawa the following year. Meanwhile, the Japanese suffered the near-total destruction of their garrison, with over 10,000 killed. Peleliu turned out to have even less strategic value than New Britain, although in war there's no way to predict the future; you take what you're ordered, and hold it.

Now I had a choice. Haldane and I had always gotten along well, so I called him by his code name. "Close Crop, you keep your top sergeant stripes. I'm going home." (He would come to be called "Ack Ack" for Peleliu.) I'm glad I turned it down.

Haldane later called Mo in and asked him to stay on for Peleliu. Unlike me, Mo went on to that battle, surviving but leaving a thumb and finger behind on that island. As I prepared to ship out, I assumed I would never see Mo or Scoop again.

Those of us who were headed home were told to pack up and prepare to embark at 0800 the next day. No big deal for me; my bag had been packed for a long time. That night, long after dark, there came a knock on my tent door. It was Lieutenant Bowerschmidt. In his eyes was the look of an honest man who had found himself. He had been tempered by battle, hardened by life in the jungle, and was wiser in his ways. He held out his hand and thanked me for my help. I told him I was only doing my job and it had been a pleasure knowing him.

Once again we boarded ship. As the small island receded I stood on deck and watched whales come roaring up, blowing, their great tails seemingly waving us farewell. Dolphins leaped up and down; sharks circled the fantail. I tried in vain to dump

captured the grit and grime and honor and terror we all felt. The errors and omissions we find in the book now, with the benefit of hindsight, can be attributed to the conditions under which it was written: None of us on the ground had a strategy-level understanding of the South Pacific counteroffensive. I had the occasion recently to again see the 1943 movie version of Tregaskis's book. It is very much a product of its time, in that historical accuracy is sacrificed for dramatic effect. America needed a victory then, and Guadalcanal was it, our first true victory of the war. Popular culture during wartime can't be expected to tell the truth; in the movie our navy *wins* the Battle of Savo Island, with the colonel saying, "We lost four cruisers but we beat them off good." Of course, losing four cruisers left our navy with few heavy boats to protect troop and supply transports, not to mention the thousand sailors who lost their lives. Nor were the Japanese massacred on the beach as shown in the movie; their Adm. Raizo Tanaka was able to evacuate many starving men under cover of night. (Of course, some inaccuracies are just due to moviemaking sloppiness, such as the Japanese carrying weapons that were used in an entirely different war or that didn't exist at the time.) Overall, however, the film is less "Hollywood" than many other war movies from that time, which were merely Westerns or gangster pictures transplanted to a battlefield. One character spoke for all of us marines when he said, "I don't want no medals, I just want to get this over with and go back home." Now back home we were.

When we came down the ramp we were still in battle fatigues. Our gear was beaten up and bullet ridden, and we were skinny and run-down and had to be fattened up some before being sent home. Finally, we were on furlough and ready to mingle once more with our kin, heading east on our way across the great desert of the Southwest. All across the country I could see the effects of the war. The factories, shipyards, and other industries were working full-time. The balm of wartime production had soothed over the scars of the Depression. Prosperity was on every hand, but I thought of the price tag. The cemetery on the Canal flashed through my mind. Visions of Beltrami, Gargano, Tully. A man sitting against a coconut tree with his guts lying in his lap, a little life left in him, but dying too slowly. I live a moment, I die a lifetime.

I disembarked from the train in Pittsburgh and caught a Greyhound bus to Charleston, West Virginia, changed buses again, and came on to Beckley. The mountains were beautiful and serene. They were far removed from the endless oceans, the sandy beaches, the sandspits, the shelling. I got off the bus in Mullens, the same spot from which I had departed. I had been gone a long time, and when I looked around for a familiar face I saw none. I walked to the side of the road to wait for a ride. The first person I saw was one of my former schoolteachers. When he saw me, he merely glanced aside without really recognizing me. Then he snapped his head back and asked, "Is this you, Thurman?" I told him it was. He told me I looked like warmed-over hell. My morale dropped a few degrees, and he went on his way. Had I changed so much? Would I ever be the same? A friend of mine came along next and asked if I needed a ride. I told him yes, and he said he had to go read electric meters in my direction anyway. He dropped me at my house without having read a single meter. He had made a special trip just to take me home.

I set my new seabag down and greeted my family one by

one. Mom hugged me and cried. Dad gripped my hand tightly. My sisters hugged me, too, and all I could think was how good it was to see them again. I had lain in the darkness and visualized how they would look to me if I ever got home. Mom and Dad had aged considerably, stricken with worry over me. My heart went out to them. A great lump came into my throat, and that was strange to me. I had yet a streak of tenderness in me; love remained in my hardened heart.

I reclaimed the gold watch from my father.

The coal company and the citizens of Otsego and Caloric organized a banquet in honor of seven local men who had just returned from combat. Recie and I used this gathering to announce our coming marriage. Our engagement had been only by mail and mutual understanding, although I had written her many times of my intentions.

She was beautiful, so beautiful. When we married, she had long auburn hair and the most extraordinary brown eyes. We had known each other for many years. Her family, the Marshalls, lived just down the mountain, in Otsego. Her father was a coal miner, and our families had been friendly for years; she and I both went to the same elementary school. We began dating when I was seventeen and she was thirteen. When I went to war, our future was understood but not stated. Though I knew she would be my wife—there was never any other—even as a young man, even before war, I knew I could not tie her to me until I returned. Even so, I did manage to put the fear of God into every male friend I had: She was off-limits. (Years later, she actually told me that she was puzzled by the utterly hands-off manners of my friends—none of them had made a pass at her.

I just nodded and agreed, yes, that *was* strange.) I was home now, and we married very simply, with no fanfare or trimmings. For the next sixty-two years she would be my rock. The love of my life.

My thirty-day leave passed quickly, and by its end I had gained a little weight and was feeling better both physically and mentally. I was not especially anxious to rejoin the Corps and meet whatever lay ahead, but I knew the job of the 1st Marine Division was still a long way from finished.

I got my brother Huey to take me to catch the bus in Princeton. On the way over, I felt a sudden chill come over me. By the time I boarded the bus, I was very sick—I had not taken any atabrine for thirty days, and malaria had finally caught up with me. My world tilted, and I became lost in my delirium. I barely remember pulling into Lejeune. Some of my buddies found me wandering around and took me to the base hospital. When I came to myself I learned I had been delirious for three days. The atabrine I had taken so long had staved the malaria off, but I could not take it indefinitely.

That August 7, and every one since, my dreams returned to Guadalcanal. Strangely, the intruding memories are never in chronological order. They sometimes enter at the point where I climb down the cargo nets to wade ashore on the island. Other times a night storm brings the crash of mortar shells. It is never the same place in my memories. My mind shuttles from the mutilations at the Matanikau River to shredded foliage on the banks of the Ilu to the bloodless form of a marine resting with his head on a log. August, the first objective taken. September's hunger. October's firefights and sea battles. November's memories of home and falling leaves and frosty mornings.

I settled back into the base, but malaria wasn't done with me. I came home for a week's leave, and Recie and I spent the night at her folks'. I woke up Sunday morning with the all too familiar chill spreading over me again. Seven o'clock, nine o'clock, and still the chill persisted. I got very sick to my stomach and began to vomit blood. A dark gray spot appeared before my eyes. It grew and blotted out my vision until I passed out. In my mind, I had been on patrol. I gathered my pack for a landing, called my platoon to attention. During my oblivion, I went to the movies in Melbourne, got drunk with Wingate, cried when Tully hid his wedding band. I woke up Sergeant Thompson and told him he was snoring too loud. I came to several days later and reached for my carbine. "I have to get the hell out of here. I'm AWOL from the Corps and I'll be put in the brig," I shouted.

"No, no, Thurman, you're just sick," came Recie's soothing voice through the fog. She had someone call the base and get my leave extended. Back in the hospital again, delirious, sick, and helpless, I wondered who the real enemy had been. When I was finally able to leave the hospital I regretted having caused so much trouble and worry.

This was the beginning of many years of recurring nightmares, sickness, and misery. Although I wondered why my Creator had brought me to this, he had already provided a woman who kept me from a shortcut to hell and judgment, who took care of me, waited on me, talked to me, and bore my children; I owe her my life, for she gave me purpose and a reason to live.

We had decided to live on base at Lejeune. Formerly Marine Barracks New River, it had become Marine Barracks Camp Lejeune in December 1942, just as I departed from Guadalcanal. Each day, from roll call to taps, I would search for someplace for her to live. I finally found a converted chicken house next to a beer joint for rent. It wasn't much, and it was just temporary, and there was a catch: The whole place was restricted, and marines were forbidden to be there. The lady who owned it saw we were desperate for a place and took Recie under her wing. She told me not to worry about her. I did worry, but worry wouldn't change the facts. The next yard over wasn't a restricted area, and there was a huge oak tree in the middle of the yard with an old car parked under it. The owner more or less turned the car over to us. Recie and I spent many evenings walking or just sitting in that old car talking.

Things had changed at Lejeune and in the marines and in America in general. More women were working in factories and on farms, doing what had theretofore been men's work; the genie would never go back in that bottle. The marines now had blacks, women, and even foreign marines.[1] The Netherlands had had a Royal Dutch Marine Corps for hundreds of years, but now that the Nazis controlled Holland they had nowhere to train, so they trained at Lejeune. They had American-issued uniforms and base privileges and were based at Hadnot Point and trained in amphibious landing just as we did, with them destined for the East Indies. The Dutch were still at Lejeune when I returned there, but I was sorry to learn that the American marines were less than gracious hosts and gave the Dutch a lot of grief. The Dutch moved to Montford Point, the camp for black marines, where they were accepted as equals and became close with them. My future daughter-in-law is a first-generation American of Dutch descent, and looking back I believe that had the Camp Lejeune marines known then of the privations the Dutch experienced under the Nazis, they would have treated our guest marines much better.

I was assigned to the Infantry Training Regiment (ITR) as a trainer, and it was a tough assignment. Essentially, the ITR was to prepare new recruits for the harsh reality of combat. As a result, it was much like being at war, although there were no bullets. We performed mock-up assault battles; we taught the men to use a compass and map and shoot an azimuth. We slept outside in the rain and mud, survived on short rations, dug foxholes, lived in pup tents, and built barbed wire entanglements. I hated it. I had had enough of war.

On Monday morning I was given an infantry platoon. I stepped out into the company street, walked two times up and down in front of them, and began my speech. *"All right, now, you men were not drafted into this outfit!"*

Forty-two voices yelled in unison, *"The hell we wasn't!"*

These weren't the Old Breed. I took a second look at my troops and realized that the toughness of the 1st was lacking—I was not dealing with the kind of men with whom I had served. I thought about the veterans of World War I, or of South America or Haiti, men like Pop Haney, who earned a Silver Star on Cape Gloucester before deciding during the fighting on Peleliu that he'd had enough killing. Haney may not be the best example, as he was different, odd, on his own mission to kill Japs, but the older guys in general were reserved and quiet and took the Corps seriously. They had enlisted, volunteered. I believe the Marine Corps gave structure and meaning to these men's lives, these old-timers in their thirties and forties. There is a sense of security to living "by the book," but these new guys had no desire to live by any book.

I began with rifle inspection. By doing this I could look directly into the eyes of each of them individually. The command was "'Port arms!" I snatched the rifle from one recruit's hand and found dirt on the stock. "How long since you cleaned this piece?"

"A week."

"Clean it tonight and again in the morning," I said as I flung it into his chest. He almost missed it. By the time I had finished with them, they were all good at catching their weapons. Nevertheless, my time there dragged on interminably.

One specific incident made me decide to look for a new job. Word came down from the top that all noncommissioned officers were to take a course in field fortification. It was mandatory, and no one was excused. Now, who do you think the expert instructor was? Not me. I was no expert. No, the "expert" was a corporal whose first journey out of the Bronx had taken him all the way to Camp Lejeune. I and several other veterans of the South Pacific just laughed at him.

It was time to make a change, if I could. Before I went to ITR, I had been offered a job with the Officer Candidate Applicant (OCA) battalion but turned it down.[2] The OCA at Lejeune was a kind of second boot camp for future officers.[3] Young recruits—potential officers—had to get through it to make it to the formal OCA at Quantico. These applicants were fresh out of college and were very smart. I had been reluctant to accept the assignment because I thought my vocabulary was not sufficient to talk much to them. Now, however, I decided to have a second look at OCA.

I went out on a Friday afternoon and visited a few contacts. I was told that Capt. Rex McIlvaine, whom I knew well, was commander of one of the companies, and with this in mind I knocked on his office door. It was after recall, the end of our workday, and he had his feet propped up on the desk. He grinned at me, knowing I'd been at ITR and what an unpleasant experience it was. "I've been expecting you," he said.

I explained how trying I had found the conditions at New River.

"Do you want to be transferred to here?" he asked.

I replied, "In the worst way."

"Well, today's Friday and I can't do anything about it today or this weekend, but when you come in from the field Monday evening, your first sergeant will inform you to pack up and report to Hadnot Point."

Most OCA instructors were like me, "haggard, with haunted eyes, and skin yellowed by the quinine and Atabrine they had taken for malaria," as one writer put it.[4] The Marines were pushing those of us with battle experience to train their new officer recruits—that was the purpose of OCA, to remedy a desperate shortage of second lieutenants and get them prepared for battlefield command—but I didn't think McIlvaine could pull it off. Nevertheless, when I came in from the field on Monday, I was told to report to Hadnot.

The first Special Officer Candidate School (SOCS) class of four hundred graduated in September 1944, just before I began teaching, and went on to honorable service on Iwo Jima and

Okinawa and Guam.[5] Theirs was a special class of the "best and brightest" candidates, the only candidates who, if they passed our OCA school, would not go on to Quantico but would go straight into their commissions as lieutenants. Because of the accelerated training necessary to produce enough NCOs they were no longer even "90-day wonders" but "77-day wonders." However, these men by all accounts acquitted themselves well in battle.

I was to be chief instructor of the next class. My men would have to get through me and the other OCA instructors in order to go on to Quantico and then to their commissions. We were stationed not 400 yards from where I had originally trained at Tent City. The difference was that now I was the trainer.

These candidates got new uniforms, thirty dollars a month, and the chance to become officers in the Corps, but they had to become proficient in all weapons and had to be physically challenged even beyond a brutal boot camp. One man's experience reflects the training at Lejeune very well:

Every other night they went out on an 18-mile hike carrying a full pack. For a good portion of the hike, the terrain was sandy—not the best surface for hiking. It was exhausting work. After about an hour of hiking, the platoon leader called for a 10-minute rest. It was not long before the Marines decided that they would just as soon forgo the ten-minute rest stop and keep going, the sooner to get it over with . . . The Marine Corps was preparing them for the most harrowing and frightening of experiences—mortal combat. They were subjected to everything the Corps could think of to get them as ready as possible. This training reflected experience gained by the Marines fighting the Japanese in earlier Pacific island campaigns such as Guadalcanal and in the central Solomons.[6]

How could I generate the proper mood of hatred, just when I was returning to some semblance of normal life? How could I prepare them to fight? I could make them tough in a physical sense, but how could I tell them to kill, when I was tired of killing, of seeing human blood, brains, and bones mingled with bayonets, packs, and ammunition?

Although I was now at Camp Lejeuene I remembered the basic training all marines received, wherever they first came to the Corps. A sign on Parris Island sums up the gravity of training officers to take over the very lives of other men: "Let's be damned sure that no man's ghost will ever say, 'If your training program had only done its job.'" In short, if these candidates were going to fail, they needed to fail here, not in combat. Our battalion commander had been my battalion executive officer in the islands. He gathered all the instructors in his office and told us bluntly to make these men crack up here in the States, if we could. If they endured us here they could make it overseas. This was one of the great lessons of Guadalcanal: "Not one man in 50 can lead a patrol in this jungle" in the words of one colonel; he had to "get rid of about *25 officers* because they just weren't leaders. I had to *MAKE* the Battalion Commander weed out the poor junior leaders."[7] Friendly-fire deaths are unavoidable in war and are an honorable way for a soldier to die, however regrettable, but one corporal from I Company had bluntly declared that on the Matanikau "we got to firing at each other because of careless leadership by the junior leaders."[8] Failure of leadership leading to that kind of death is not excusable. Each man must be prepared to become a leader on a second's notice, ready to rely only on his own training; he must first win the war with himself. Colonel Edson said that leadership "resolves itself down to being hardboiled. By that I mean getting rid of the poor leader, even if you like him personally, because this is a life and death affair."[9] He was right. (Edson also suggested more training with live ammo, "even if you get a few casualties.")

I saw many boys who should not be in OCA, who just weren't officer material. Many were there just because of their connections, including the son of a sitting governor. I saw the uncertainty in their eyes and knew they were probably thinking that it was a tough world. I offered a silent prayer to the God I had failed to acknowledge that he would let me train them to be good marines, good officers.

Calling on my own experiences, I thought of Bowerschmidt, which gave me incentive to talk to the would-be officers about code names and not flaunting their rank. Bullets, I told them, had no respect for rank or your family pedigree. I adopted a standard speech for each new class as they arrived. I would tell them that they would be judged thusly: "If I had a kid brother in the marines, would you be good enough to be his platoon leader?" If the answer is no, you simply don't go. Some were in the officer candidate school by special favor, as sons of generals, nephews of congressmen. We put it to them simply: We don't care whose son you are, if you're good, you pass, and if you're not, you fail. So it was with one Mr. Boccard, who happened to be from the hometown of the captain of the company. I determined that he was not officer material. The captain called me into his office and informed me that he would pass him himself. (They had the power to override the decision of NCOs.) I begged the captain's pardon but told him Mr. Boccard would be even a poor company runner. The captain's face flushed. He dismissed me and sent Mr. Boccard on to Quantico. (In late 1945, when I reported to a provisional company to stand by for discharge, I ran into Boccard. I asked his status. "Company runner," he replied.)

I devised a plan. I would again go by the book—official Marine Corps policy. I would use it to train them, but I would supplement it with the kind of situations I knew they would run into in combat. I would leave the hatred for each of them to learn after his fashion. We jettisoned everything except the essentials, how to kill the enemy and keep oneself and one's command from being needlessly killed. We were supposed to be officers and gentlemen, but we had no time for the latter.

By and large I began to enjoy this OCA duty. We instructors got along well and worked together trying to break these men, especially the ones who seemed most cocky. We gave them nightmares of boot camp. We harassed them night and day with warnings about "Washing Machine Charlie" in his biplane. Write a good chit. Write a bad chit. If we pass you here, you can make it in Quantico. I treated my men as if they were to be combat lieutenants. Maj. Robert Rogers's best advice to his Rangers may have lain in an addendum to his rules, recommending vigilance and self-reliance because of "a thousand occurrences and circumstances which may happen that will make it necessary in some measure to depart from them and to put other arts and stratagems in practice; in which case every man's reason and judgment must be his guide." We were not teaching these future officers *rules*, because, as we learned on

Guadalcanal, the rules of how to fight one war may be useless in the next. Instead, we were trying to see that they kept "a firmness and presence of mind on every occasion," as Rogers puts it. What better few words of advice could you give to a fledgling lieutenant heading to Okinawa or Iwo Jima? Keep your head. Stay focused.

In general, the men acquitted themselves very well, and I came to be impressed by their commitment to the Corps. We had learned, and taught, one of the great lessons of the South Pacific, that each officer must be prepared to lead any kind of group, and to act on his own when necessary. That's the bottom line for a Marine.

As I suggested previously, we are always fighting the last war. As we taught these young kids the lessons we learned in the South Pacific, we also tried to instill in them the idea that every battle is different. Some SOCS graduates "had questions as to whether their training in the traditional small-unit fire and maneuver tactics really prepared them for what they encountered with the interconnecting bunkers, caves, and tunnels on Iwo and Okinawa."[10] Of course it didn't, any more than the lessons from the trenches of World War I prepared us for the jungle. What did help, I believe, was learning about our very singular enemy, the Japanese, from those who had gone into battle against him.

The Marine Corps wanted us to pass on our stories, our experience, our resourcefulness, the bitter truths we might distill from our time in the jungle. I learned later that the same was not true on the Japanese side. Akio Tana, one of the "Pistol Pete" artillery men on Guadalcanal, returned to Japan and taught at an elite military school, where, unlike at my own OCA, "nobody wished to hear about what we Guadalcanal veterans had been through. They avoided us at school . . . They could not really comprehend what we had been through and they did not want to try."[11] Years later, Tana himself would be welcomed at Marine Corps reunions and recognized as an honorable soldier for his country. Still, the two nations' concepts of honor were very different. We would never leave a buddy behind if there was hope for saving him, even if it put our own lives at stake. For the Japanese, surrender was the height of dishonor; better to be killed, even by intentional friendly fire. The Bushido warrior code of the Japanese was very different. On Attu Island, for example—in the Aleutians, and the only World War II battle to take place in incorporated U.S. territory—the Japanese sent grenades into the sick bays of their own troops just before their final banzai charge. Back in Japan their loved ones were informed they died in the honorable Japanese tradition of suicide.[12]

Meanwhile, Recie and I had come to enjoy our married life, finding mutual interests and more friends. We played horseshoes, cards, and other games for long hours in the evenings. On the day President Franklin D. Roosevelt visited Camp Lejeune I ordered my OCA charges to take the day off. I told Recie the president was coming and she could catch the bus to see him in person, which she did. That day we were told to return to our home or barracks and be ready to fall out at 1200 hours to stand honor guard for the president. I hailed a navy friend in the shore patrol, and he took me to the trailer park where Recie and I lived and I quickly pressed my uniform; after all, this was a once-in-a-lifetime event. We were three companies strong, all potential officers of the Corps.

Naturally I was proud of the men. Finally the president's motorcade arrived. He came within about 20 feet of me. I took a good long look. He wore a black robe, a custom I never saw in any other president. The thing I remember most is his top hat, which we normally associate with Abraham Lincoln. Roosevelt was impressive looking and carried himself with such authority that all who looked at him knew they were looking at history.

The malaria bug took over me again. The attacks worsened and began to sap my strength until it became a burden just to live. My yellow color from the atabrine faded, but the pain and chills were almost unbearable at times. I would recover from one attack, report for duty for a time, and be stricken again. Each time, a little more life seemed to run out of me.

During a lull in the sickness we left base for the weekend. We were in a restaurant in Winston-Salem, North Carolina, just waiting for our meal. I noticed a man in another booth staring at me. I paid him little attention, for the country was spotted with marines who had served in the Pacific. Our skin was pallid and yellow, and our looks were no doubt startling or repulsive to some. I kept feeling him staring at me. Recie was carrying our first child, and I began to grow nervous. I told her, "There's a man over there with something on his mind. If I point away from here, you move, and move fast."

When I looked up from my plate he was standing there, staring down at me. Too late for Recie to leave. Maybe I could reason with him, beg if I must, for him to leave us alone. A prayer welled up from deep inside me: *Please, God, not here of all places. I don't want to kill ever again.* Still no movement from the stranger. He was just standing there, looking.

I looked at him more closely. They were not the eyes of trouble but the misty eyes of compassion. Light tears formed on his cheeks. Slowly, he extended an open hand. His only words were "Thank you, son," and with that the stranger strode out into the street without even a backward glance. I sat there a long time, speechless, amazed, and ashamed that I had misjudged him. What had been his inspiration? The Guadalcanal patch? The Southern Cross insignia? Or was it simply compassion for the way I looked? Here was a grateful citizen who had chosen to personally thank one who had done his best.

This one man did as much to make me feel the job had been worthwhile as anything the government ever did. It was a mental citation and the only one the citizen had to give.

I had passed the exam for first sergeant and as of February 1945 was on track for the promotion. I was named acting first sergeant, with more administrative duties at OCA, but remained technically a gunny, eventually discharged as "qualified for first sergeant." I would have filled that role eventually, although I would always consider myself a gunny. In the summer of 1945 I received orders to make ready to ship out once again. I got all my shots for overseas duty—cowpox, typhoid and paratyphoid, yellow fever, tetanus. My wife was packed to go home to Otsego. Everything was in place so I could leave in very short order, back to the fray. The 1st Marine Division was busy in Okinawa, where I probably would have been sent, then on to invade mainland Japan. Japan had been bloodied by air raids and bombings, but knowing the fierceness of Japanese soldiers, a ground war on their turf was likely to be protracted and ruth-less and would cost many American lives.

It was not to be. On July 24 President Harry S. Truman had "casually mentioned to Stalin that we had a new weapon of unusual destructive force."[13] Only a handful of Americans could know what an understatement that was. Two weeks later, on August 6, a B-29 named *Enola Gay* dropped a bomb di-rectly on the Japanese city of Hiroshima, an industrial, ship-building city with an army headquarters. We dropped leaflets urging the city's residents to evacuate, and a hundred thousand did. The newspapers described the bomb as 20 megatons. They said it had leveled the entire city; eighty thousand were killed immediately, and thousands more succumbed to radiation poi-soning either acutely or as a result of cancer in the years that followed. Three days later a second bomb was dropped on Na-gasaki, with similar destruction.

The awakened giant of America had perfected the ultimate weapon. I read of this destruction and death with a knot in the pit of my stomach. *My God, what have we done? What does it mean to "split an atom"?* I had thought that the war could not be more devastating—the worst damage that humans could inflict on each other. Now we had found the means to erase the human race from the face of the earth. I recalled the words of Jesus: *I am come to send fire on the earth; and what will I, if it be already kindled?*[14] Five days after the bomb code-named "Fat Man" destroyed Nagasaki, the Japanese accepted our uncondi-tional terms of surrender.

On battlefields around the world guns fell silent, heads bowed in prayer, commanders breathed a sigh of relief at not having to order more men into the breach to be killed or maimed. Mothers stole away to secret prayers of thanks; wives anxiously clutched a picture of their loved ones and wondered. Our fighting men straggled home in much the same way they had come to the war. A lone soldier walked home to his father's farm, a sailor back to the factory, a marine to the coal fields of Appalachia. There was no fanfare for most of us, and none was expected.

In short order, I was transferred to a casual outfit to stand by for discharge. The Corps let me keep my uniform, belt, underclothes, and so on, as we had few civvies to wear.

Recie and I were going home.

10

INTO THE MINE

"Do you have any problems, son?"

RECIE AND I MOVED BACK to Otsego, where I began to look for work, with little success. The country was full of veterans looking for the same thing. Over and over I was asked, "What can you do? What are your skills?" Of course I could not answer honestly—"I'm a trained killer."

As indeed I was. Whatever our profession, it's not unreasonable for us to expect to be paid for services rendered. Those who have chosen a profession expect to be compensated for years of preparing for the job. As I looked back on my war service, I decided to figure my base pay for the four months I spent on Guadalcanal. Needless to say, the time spent was based on a twenty-four-hour day. There was no place to retire to at day's end except our foxholes. There were, of course, no timekeepers, no stopwatches to see how proficient we were. We already knew we were experts in our field. Our preparation for the job at hand had been refined and refined again to the point where our performance was automatic. Our responsibilities did not allow for a second opinion or time to reevaluate what must be done. Our own individual initiative had to be employed, and it was our job as individuals to act in teamwork with others who were similarly employed by the citizens of the United States. So I figured up my wages for my time on the Island of Death: a little less than nine cents per hour.

Now, I needed money, real money. I would soon have a child, and my health was unstable; my dream of attending college would have to wait. We were living in a borrowed trailer, and Recie was sick; the doctor bumped his head on the ceiling as he walked in. "You better get the hell out of here before the baby comes," he said. I would try anything, take any job, but in West Virginia there was only one job: coal mining. This paid better than Guadalcanal, but I would be trading the armed forces for the most dangerous occupation in America. I remembered visiting a mine just after I'd joined the Corps. I had watched the men come out with their black faces, as black as the coal they mined. You couldn't tell the color of a man's skin beneath the coal dust. I had looked down at the perfect crease in my marine uniform and saw the sun glinting off my spit-shined shoes and thought to myself of coal miners, *How and why in the hell do they do it?*

Cave-ins were frequent, and the families of men who were hurt or killed on the job were often left destitute. Before mechanization, when there was a big roof fall in the mine, the first question asked by the bosses was "Did any mules get hurt?"[1] Mules were expensive; another miner could always be hired. The miners were machines, and when they broke down they could be replaced by another young man hungry for decent pay.

Many thousands of West Virginians left the state in the decades after the war, finding well-paid work in factories in faraway places like Michigan, California, and Florida. I considered doing the same, but I didn't want to leave my parents and the rest of the family behind, nor could I envision abandoning our green hills.

If you are at all claustrophobic you should not be in the mines, for mining "rooms" converge at times to a coffinlike confinement, with too little space to stand erect or stretch; the work can be backbreaking, the air a haze of dust and choking silt, and the threat of cave-in or explosion constant. Miners' families would dread the siren that told them there was a problem at the mine, for it often meant someone's father or husband or son was dead. In Otsego, as in every coal-mining town, the families of the miners "had all experienced that unexplainable empty and scared feeling when the mine whistle would not stop blowing . . . Almost without exception every mine disaster meant death."[2]

I joined the United Mine Workers of America (UMWA), requiring that I pay my dues of thirty-five cents and swear an oath—"the obligation"—not to reveal the names of any other union members, because in the earlier days a man could be fired for even breathing the word "union." Before the coming of the UMWA, boys as young as nine or ten worked in the mines for long hours, and injured miners, or those whose lungs had clogged with coal dust and silica were simply let go, to recover, or not, on their own. Miners were paid in private company money, called "scrip," redeemable only at a company-owned store, into the 1950s.

My brother Huey went with me to the mine that first day. I

was afraid before we even got to the portal. I got my lamp and brass check—the piece of numbered metal that would identify my body if I should die in the mine—and walked over close to the mouth of the mine. The whistle sounded. Huey showed me how to get on the conveyor belt for the long ride down, and I crawled on behind him, the black hole in the mountain growing before me. My heartbeat quickened and darkness engulfed me, and I felt the same stab of fear I had felt when I landed on the Canal. The weight of the mountain seemed to settle down upon me. I had thought there could be no darkness deeper than the jungle on a rainy, moonless night, but I was wrong. If you turn off your headlamp in a mine the darkness actually hurts your eyes; nothing on the surface can prepare you for it. At times I would come to think a seam of coal beautiful; I was the first and perhaps the only human to see ancient fossils in the bituminous as the dynamite brought down great black sheets, before it was carried out on the conveyor belt. As I descended into the mine for my first day on the job, however, all I could think of was the wide, sunny hills I roamed as a youth, now a mile above my head.

I got a job cleaning the belt deep in the mine, a hard and dirty task I knew I'd never get used to. Many days in the mine brought the same feeling I had endured in the jungle, always on edge, listening, feeling my way. Cave-ins were a regular occurrence, and I would gradually learn to read the mountain and tell by a barely audible low rumble that it was about to fall in. I developed habits similar to those of our scouts on Guadalcanal, walking slowly and listening for the telltale groan of the timbers that supported the roof and the fall of a bit of dust from a crack, the low rumble of shifting rock that sounded like faint thunder. In one mine the roof had slowly settled to the point that there was barely room to crawl in and out of the section between all the timbers set to support the roof, and there were only a few inches between the roof and a man lying on the belt to ride to the surface. In another mine I was working on a piece of machinery and just happened to look up to see a light mist of dust spurt from a crevice. I immediately yelled to my buddy to run. We cleared the machine we were working on by about 12 feet before a huge rock fell on it. The pressure of the mountain would cause water to come out of any little fissure, rendering the floor of the mine a quagmire. In winter, by the time we arrived at the bathhouse at the end of the day our clothes would be frozen solid. The pressure in some mines forced methane gas out of the coal with such force it sounded like a thousand swarms of bees all buzzing together. In any mine, the danger of an explosion is always present, and if the explosion doesn't kill you the smoke or even the concussion might—in the closed space of the mine an explosion could drive the impact for a mile or more.

This type of work fed my terrors, and the thick dust and backbreaking labor ate away at my already compromised body. The heavy shoveling and lifting soon began to take its toll. It tore away at my insides, and I began to weaken. The malaria, the stomach sickness, and the memory of war began their pounding. I came home exhausted and slept fitfully, my old dreams and new now commingled in a common darkness. One night, mired deep in a nightmare, I almost twisted Recie's arm off when she tried to wake me, as my marine training engaged my dream enemy. Today they might refer to my condition as post-traumatic stress disorder, or back then perhaps as

"Guadalcanal neurosis," even though I was years removed from that island. It was the illness, fatigue, and the inability to eat well that drove me down and down.

One day as I shoveled coal the old chill began to shake me, and the sweat stood out on my forehead. The black coal dust mingled with the salty taste, and I wiped my face with a dirty glove. I glanced over at the moving belt and began to hallucinate. I blinked my eyes and shook my head to clear it, but the vision continued. A dead Japanese soldier rode by on the belt. The South Pacific sun burst through the coconut palms. The dampness of the mine evaporated, and the wind blew breakers upon the beach. A lump of coal rolled off the belt. A Japanese Zero strafed the beach.

I grabbed a timber, shook myself, and began to count silently. One, two, three, four, five, six. More bodies rolled by on the belt. Again I blinked, shook myself, and began repeating, "I am here. I am here." The miner part of me knew that I had to return to the surface. I climbed on the belt behind the last of the bodies and began the long ride up. As the daylight slowly approached, the specters began to fade, one by one. The belt stopped, and I rolled off. I only vaguely remember arriving home, and I still don't remember if I walked or rode.

This attack prompted me to go to the Veterans Hospital in Huntington. I was there twenty days. It marked the beginning of a new kind of war. I needed no guns for this war, but the enemy was as formidable as the previous one. I must fight it or die.

For about ten years after returning home I was torn between a desire to end it all or fight it out. Thanks be to God I chose to fight it to the last ditch. Still, during this period I sank to the lowest depths of despair before rising once again. Surety of remembrance follows any war. Nightmares would take me back to battle, and I would watch Tully again hide his wedding band. I would see Beltrami's gear laid out for inspection and the colonel asking where his razor was. I would hear Gargano back from liberty. "T.I., I got married!" The sparkle in his eyes was real. The darkness I hid in was the rain forest of New Britain. The nightmares brought with them the realization that I had one choice to make: My life could be fruitful or futile, and the chances of futility were directly related to my resolve. I must live to see my child born, to love it, to hold it in my arms, to let its love help to heal my heart.

The Marine Corps was my family during the most formative years of my young adulthood, and one very true motto of the Corps is "Once a marine, always a marine." Nevertheless, in these dark times of my life I wondered whether the price of admission to this family was more than I could bear. There are no ex-marines, though; we carry the Corps with us wherever we go. Counterbalancing the hard work of being a soldier is the humor that arises among those who have served in the armed forces, even in the most unlikely situations, and my visit to the VA Hospital had been no exception. It was also a constant reminder that it had been a hell of a war. Another veteran there was a living reminder of those days of combat. He had been shot through the throat and couldn't speak more than four or five words without stopping and going "ruff, ruff." One day his girlfriend visited him. He met her with "Honey, do you (ruff, ruff) love me like you (ruff, ruff) used to?" We all laughed, including him, but every time the man spoke it reminded me of that day in the rain forest in New Britain and Sergeant

Thompson's dying. His fatal wounding had also been through the throat, and I see him still, and hear him, in my dreams.

April 1, 1946, brought the end of our United Mine Workers contract with the mine, and at the time the rule was "No contract, no work." We went on strike. Many men my age migrated to the northern cities or textile factories in North Carolina. I couldn't do so and didn't want to do so; I had two parents and a sister to support, and in any event this was my home, and after the war I loved it more than ever. The same day I was thrown out of work by the end of our contract, my first son, Gilbert, was born, 8½ pounds of two-toned baby. He was partly brown and dark with the typical Miller/Cherokee/Melungeon coloration, and partly yellow, I guess from the atabrine. Responsibility caught up with me. The baby crying, my wife sick, money running out, and me unsure of myself in my new role as father. I fell into despair. The job I had been doing had not prepared me for the preservation of life, only its destruction. Recie was my rock, carrying even more of a burden than that of a typical miner's family, which was already fraught with the knowledge that death could arrive quickly and without warning.

When the long strike was settled I went back to work, but the malaria bug soon returned, and I was idle for a long time. I walked about the community some days hardly knowing what I was doing. One day as I walked the path between our house and Recie's parents' house I was confronted by a woman who lived nearby. Her question was valid, "Why don't you go to work and take care of your wife and baby?" I could offer no reply. God, the cost of war. The little malaria bug was a formidable foe; I had no defense against it. I had no book, no format. I turned around slowly and returned to my wife and child, where I knew I would find understanding. I would try to work in the mine again. The next day I trod the same path. The same woman confronted me again. Try as I might, I could not meet her gaze. This time she made no comment about my not working. There was only painful silence until I looked in her eyes. I read no contempt there. She spoke softly and tenderly. "I'm sorry, Thurman. I didn't know." My cousin Minnie had told her of my situation. I touched her briefly on the shoulder and told her it was all right. This dear lady remained a staunch friend of mine until the day she died.

My next bout of malaria lasted so long the company terminated my employment entirely. I tried to find any kind of work other than mining. I dug ditches and applied to many businesses for steady work, with no success. Again it became painfully evident that mining would be my lot if I stayed in West Virginia. I asked for work at another mine and was hired. This time the shaft bottom of the mountain was near my home, and I could walk to work. I was assigned to the midnight shift, midnight to 8:00 A.M., and therefore I had the advantage of working alongside my brothers Buck and Lee, who understood what I had been through and who were a great help to me. With the help of my brother Huey I gathered the necessary clothes and doctor's report and went to the mines.

My wife had decided to be baptized, and her immersion would be in Slab Creek, behind the company store, that Sunday. I went with the church crowd and stood on the bank of the river and watched them go one by one into the water. When it came time for Recie to go into the water, I watched as she waded into the stream. My heart quickened. I wished I were there with her, but I wasn't ready.

Then everyone disappeared. I stood alone in the sand, barefoot, my tommy gun hanging loosely at my side, the calm South Pacific shimmering in the morning sun. The chaplain said the words as he baptized the men, one by one. I spat on the sand, sneered at them, and called it "foxhole religion." I vowed I would not impose on God where the bullets were flying.

Someone shook my arm, and I stared back at him. Everyone was leaving Slab Creek.

My emotions were still far off center, and I sometimes still felt like a trained killer. In the mine where my brothers and I worked there was a huge man everyone called "Big 'Un" because that's what he was, 6' 7" and about 300 pounds. For one reason or another he'd chosen to pick on Lee and me, although we had done nothing to him. We hardly knew him. Each night he would seek us out and belittle us in front of the rest of the men. Lee and I talked about what we could do to put a stop to it, and we came up with a plan. Judge me if you want to.

Big 'Un would always go to the end of the entry belt and unload the supplies. Either Lee or I would load the outgoing material onto the belt, and afterward we would all three stay on the section and push the pans out of the worked-out rooms. This was the plan: On the way back Lee or I would get off the belt and find a belt roller or other suitable piece of iron. Whoever was in the lead was to fake tripping and come up with a handful of dust and throw it in Big 'Un's eyes and blind him. The other was to hit him in the head with the iron and knock him out. Then we would pull him into the worked-out room and pull rock down on him. We would go to the phone and call the boss and report the "accident" after having assured ourselves that he was truly dead.

However, providence was in control. The day before we were to do the deed they had cleaned up all the pieces of metal lying around, and by the time we got off the belt that day Big 'Un was gone. I remember being glad he wasn't there. Chance had spared me taking another life.

My next job was not as bad as the belt-cleaning job, and even though it was on the midnight shift—the "hoot owl"—I liked it much better. I was never alone, and my spirits began a slight upward trend. Then, coming home one morning, I suddenly felt the old bug coming on. One minute I was okay and the next I was shaking like a sarvis leaf in a storm. This attack was not as bad as some I'd had but was severe enough to keep me from working. There was a company rule that if you were off work for two or more days you must present a doctor's slip. I reasoned that since I personally knew men who would be off more than a week drunk without bringing a slip, surely they would not bother asking me for a slip since I was actually sick and they knew it. Not so. When I reported back to work the boss waited until just before work time to ask me for my slip. "I don't have any," I said. "You have to have one before I can let you work." "What about those men off drunk?" "I don't make the rules," he replied.

At about this time my relief valve was on a low setting. I blew up in his face, calling him all the names I'd learned in the Corps and in the slop chutes of the different liberty ports I'd seen. This was an impressive range of profanity. I went in to put my lamp away and found the general mine foreman was there, so I proceeded to curse him out, too. After I had blown off enough steam at the mine I went home and continued cursing until 3:00 A.M. Shortly after I'd arrived home I'd heard the sound of footsteps coming up the hill. It was my brother Lee, and he said that since I'd cussed them out so well he thought he'd make them even more short-handed.

The next day I went to see Dr. Byron W. Steele. The mining companies controlled every aspect of our lives, and he was the "company" doctor. I asked him for a doctor's slip. "How do I know you've been sick?" he asked. "You haven't been to see me." He proceeded to tell me he was going to put a stop to these people laying off drunk. That started me up again. I threw him a few well-rounded words of profanity and told him he was not the only doctor in town. I left and was almost down the stairs when a gruff voice caught me. "Come back up here, boy." Something in his tone of voice and facial expression caused me to walk back up the stairs and into his waiting room and through it, past many prying eyes, directly back into his office.

He sat and just stared at me for a few moments and then said he wasn't accusing me of being a drunkard. "I know where you've been." After that we were not only patient and doctor but also friends. He gave me the work slip, and the next night I did not present it to the foreman in private but waited for him to ask for it in front of the rest of the men.

I continued to work at the mine and began to slowly improve. The Veterans Administration had wondered why I was receiving 50 percent disability on malaria. This didn't represent a great deal of money, but given the unsteadiness of mining work and my record of hospitalization it was essential to keeping food on our table. The VA said I must have caught the disability rating board in a good mood. They then sent for my records, which showed twelve official attacks of the bug. What they didn't know was that I had had many more attacks that I did not report—the pharmacy in Mullens would sometimes give me the quinine for free. They called me back to Huntington and cut the disability rating to 30 percent because I had gone a full year without a major attack.

Although the malaria had subsided somewhat, it had left something wrong inside me. As I pushed the heavy pans and lifted the heavy timbers, the pain in my sides and stomach would sometimes cause me to crawl like a wounded dog out of the way of the rest of the men. I was ashamed of myself, but Lee and Buck understood, even if the rest of the men didn't. I began to eliminate foods from my diet as I saw they triggered my stomach pains. For about five years I ate no meat, and as time went by I kept eliminating the things that hurt me. Eventually I could eat nothing but dry toast, oatmeal, and skim milk.

In the latter part of the 1940s the VA canceled my disability entirely on the grounds that I had gone one year without an actual attack. My illness had become chronic rather than acute. When I reported in to the doctor in charge he asked a few pertinent questions.

"Good morning, son."

"Good morning, sir."

"Do you have any problems, son?"

"Yes, sir."

"What kind?"

"My stomach and side, sir."

"Are you a doctor?"

"No, sir."

"Where do you hurt?"

"Right here, sir."

"What is it that hurts?"

"My gall bladder, sir."

"I thought you just told me you were not a doctor."

"Sir, I have some letters from my family doctor and one in the hospital at Beckley."

"What kind?"

I laid them on the desk in front of him. He picked them up and threw them back into my chest. What I said to him is not worth relating here, for he accused me of trying to come up with a scheme to live off the government. I felt my face beginning to color, nerves expanding, the heat of battle coming up. I turned with much effort and left, in even more despair.

I didn't go home that night, for I didn't know where my anger might lead me. I remembered how Recie's screams had awakened me that morning I had her arm in my grasp and was perfectly capable of breaking it. Instead I stayed alone in a roach-ridden hotel in Logan until my anger subsided.

When I returned home and then to the mine I fell into a routine. I would come in from work, take a couple of knockout pills, sleep all night, and eat a couple of pieces of toast. I'd take skim milk in my lunch bucket the next day and repeat the whole process. The nausea and pain became the background for everything I did, but I found a way to keep working.

I kept few reminders of my time at war but hung them on the wall of a small room in our house and would look at them from time to time, wondering how the journey I had been on could be contained in such a small display. A yellow and blue crescent, a purple and blue medal and ribbon above it. A good conduct medal, thanks to Colonel Edson. Campaign medals. In the center a red, white, and blue diamond-shaped shoulder patch, a gift from the Australian people, designed by General Vandegrift, with a huge numeral 1 denoting the 1st Marine Division, flanked by the Southern Cross. I looked at the ribbons naming the weapons in which I was proficient—the Springfield rifle, the hand grenade, the pistol, the bayonet. My dog tags, with the same piece of string given to me in September of 1940. So much effort, so much killing, contained in a few pieces of paper and cloth. Three-quarters of a century fades to the recesses of the historian's page, a sepia photo tucked away in the Song of Solomon, a brown newspaper clipping in a dusty scrapbook.

Mining is a cyclical industry, and mines close and reopen. Now, fifteen years since I had walked out of Cedar Creek and hitchhiked to the recruiting depot in Charleston, I was laid off again—and I wasn't anxious to go back. I was able to work, but my home was not under the earth. I decided to spend the summer working hard in the sun. I wanted to use my hands and the simple tools I remembered from my childhood. I took a medium-weight double-bit ax and walked a half mile up Cedar Creek to a plot of ground I had remembered, where we had raised sugarcane to make molasses and we children played in the crushed cane.

I stepped into the creek bed and stood still, listening to the chatter of the water as it ran over the rocks. I recalled standing in exactly this same spot as a boy with my brother Buck when the sky had grown black and the wind stiffened and turned the leaves inside out and the lightning chased us home. Standing now at the same creek bed I thought of that storm and the rain forests of New Britain where the lightning and wind brought huge giants down all around us. I stood a long time at the creek, thinking of the past and all I'd seen. At last a bird's song brought me back to the present. The morning sun glinted off my ax, reminding me that I'd come here to do a job. I had no tool except the ax, and I was determined to cut down a big oak and carve it into fence posts, so I could reclaim the field.

The ax and I would do it all, and if my stamina allowed me to perform this task then truly I was home. I chose the trees carefully to avoid knots that would make them hard to split. I swung the ax evenly, in rhythm. The tree fell, and I began stripping off the limbs and cutting the trunk into short lengths. I made a maul from a white oak, and from a hickory I formed a glut with which to split the tree. Each section I cut yielded four fence posts, and with a posthole digger I dug out the holes and carried the posts until I had half an acre laid out. I placed the posts and strung barbed wire between them. I cleaned out the underbrush and readied the plot for plowing, which I hired, done by a man up the hollow who had his own mare and plow.

I came back and worked that field every day that summer, going home in the evening bone tired, but a good kind of tired; not the work of combat but the peaceful work of my hands striving to bring forth from the earth the kind of food I had yearned for while starving on captured rice and stale green hardtack. I tended my large crop of corn and potatoes, and when I hoed the corn the second time I planted field beans in each hill.

This was the prescription I needed. In the sun my skin returned to its natural dark brown except where the scars of malnutrition had permanently whitened it. The sparkle returned to my eyes, and my muscles gathered strength from the fresh air. At day's end I would have loved some cows to drive home, as when I was a boy. We had plenty of corn on the cob, and Recie canned up a lot of beans, and that summer and fall we truly enjoyed the fruits of our labor. My children needed new clothes, and I would return to work in the mines—but for the first time since the war, I felt whole again.

Epilogue

Mo stayed in the Corps through Peleliu, losing fingers but gaining a Bronze Star, and after the war he became a police chief, fire chief, and gentleman farmer back in Georgia. Scoop made a career of the military, retiring as a lieutenant colonel, and a fine one, no doubt. After recovering from malaria he served on the USS *Tennessee* back in the South Pacific. He was on the bridge when a kamikaze dived, depositing shrapnel in his leg. Again he recovered and was bounced around by the Corps, as career officers are expected to be—San Diego, Maryland, back to Camp Lejeune, then Quantico and Pearl Harbor, Camp Pendleton, and Okinawa before retiring to the Seattle area.

Jim also stayed in the Corps through Peleliu and then returned to New York to work a variety of jobs, from carpentry to automobiles; I spoke with him by telephone frequently, until his recent death, and I still chat frequently with Slim Somerville.

Captain Haldane—who would always be "Close Crop" to me—took a sniper's bullet on Peleliu, a respected leader and an experienced old marine, dead at the age of twenty-seven. Eugene Sledge wrote that Haldane "commanded our individual destinies under the most trying conditions with the utmost compassion. We knew he could never be replaced. He was the finest Marine officer I ever knew . . . To all of us the loss of our company commander at Peleliu was like losing a parent we depended upon for security—not our physical security, because we knew that was a commodity beyond our reach in combat, but our mental security . . . We had lost our leader and our friend."[1] I'm fortunate to have fought alongside him.

Young Lieutenant Bowerschmidt went on to be killed on Pelileu. Monk Arndt stayed in the marines into the 1960s, earning the Silver Star in Korea; he returned home to a peaceful life in Mississippi and died in 2008.

Pop Haney stayed with K/3/5 into the Peleliu battle, then asked to be rotated home. The Corps obliged him, and I think all agreed he had served his time in hell.

I fought malaria to a stalemate but never did conquer the fungus that invaded my body in the jungle, and to this day I have only slivers of fingernails and toenails, despite trying many treatments.

I gave the gold watch to my oldest son, as I promised myself I would.

I always regretted that I never went back for Tully's ring.

After my summer in the fields I returned to the mines, but on my own terms. I went to an electrical school in Chicago and got a much better job. Though I would work underground for twenty-five years before working aboveground, I became a electrician and mechanic, a position much like being a gunnery sergeant; I was a union man, the infantry of working life, but unless my team and I did our job no one else could do theirs. I built my own home and installed electrical power in it, and recalling our wire adventures in Guadalcanal I installed an antenna on a mountaintop and ran wire down to our little home, pulling in the first television images we'd seen in our narrow valleys.

Few of us mountain folk owned our land; much of West Virginia is owned by out-of-state mineral and timber interests, and we leased it from them on a short-term basis. In 1956 the timber company that owned the land near Otsego we had lived on all our lives forced us off the leasehold with only thirty days' notice. It was hard finding housing not only for Recie and me and two children, and another on the way, but also for my mother and father and sister Kathy, who had nowhere else to go. However, I was able to find two houses close to each other in the small coal camp of Helen, about 10 miles north of Otsego. I would live there for the next fifty years.

It was a hard adjustment. Instead of our farm there were houses on both sides of the road and a set of train tracks on either side of us. Instead of a clear mountain stream a coal-choked creek ran behind our house. The house we moved into had no insulation, and you could see through the cracks around the windows. It had formerly been a chicken coop. Again. We moved in in the fall of 1956 and were lucky it was a mild winter.

Coal companies built, maintained, and controlled life in a coal camp. We were paid in scrip, redeemable at the company store—at inflated prices. The company deducted your rent, equipment, and more against your wages. Yet there were many good qualities to living in Helen. Many coal camps had been built to attract good, steady workers during the coal-bloom years in the 1920s, and Helen, just a couple of miles south of Tams, one of the more famous coal camps, had a clubhouse, community church, movie theater, post office, boardinghouse for single men, and more.[2] Helen, Tams, and many other small towns in southern West Virginia benefited from this model-town initiative. Helen had an ethnically diverse population, left over from its development earlier in the century. Blacks, Italians, Canadians, Croatians, English, Greeks, Hungarians, Irish, and more populated a typical coal camp alongside native whites of varying heritage. Of these immigrants, Maj. W. P. Tams, wrote that "hard as life might be in the mills and mines, it was generally far easier than it had been in their home land."[3] There were different sections of town for whites, blacks, and ethnic immigrants, but miners all worked under the same conditions; after a shift, you couldn't tell a man's skin color. As a result our area was free of much of the racial tension that accompanied desegregation in much of the rest of the country.

After the war I did not stay in contact with my service mates, for lack of time, lack of money, and a fear of revisiting those days. Mo Darsey attended 1st Marine Division reunions well before I did, and on his way back to Georgia from Boston he decided to drive through West Virginia on one more patrol: *Find T.I.* Which he did. We shook hands, and I barely noticed his missing fingers. As soon as he grasped my hand the war years flooded back in an instant. Here was my brother. While I am in this world, Mo will always be in my heart. He was right. "Because of the hell we went through on Guadalcanal, there is a bond that doesn't exist between any other people."[4] Mo's visit made me realize I had to renew these acquaintances, and I decided to attend a Marine Corps reunion in Milwaukee with him. Recie and I were apprehensive at first, for we had no idea how my old friends and their wives would react after so many years. As it turned out, those with whom I had fought on Guadalcanal that August of 1942 remembered me quite well. We heard stories new and old, mostly not of conflict but of the love found in the hearts of our wives and children. I reconnected with R. V. Burgin and many other reserves who joined us in Australia and didn't share our Guadalcanal experience but represented the 1st Division so well at New Britain, Peleliu, and beyond. Even newer acquaintances seemed like old friends; Eugene Sledge always greeted me with "Whaddaya say, Gunny?" even though our South Pacific battles didn't overlap.

I would return once each to Parris Island and Camp Lejeune, as a guest. New recruits marched onto the parade ground in perfect unison to graduate from their boot training, with only their qualifying medals on their chests, no promotion stripes, no multicolored ribbons, no hash marks. A group of young women in ROTC training sat with us. The men of the 1st Division came away with the feeling that our country was still in good hands. My grandson served in the Marine Corps and was also stationed at Camp Lejeune, at the same spot where our tent city stood. He served in Okinawa, and I gave him one of the emblems I had carried on Guadalcanal and asked him to carry it with him. Thus, a part of me would ultimately reach the place where I would have eventually fought had the war lasted. I was proud Jeffrey completed the journey for me, with the Globe, Eagle, and Anchor.

As I write this, my last few nights have been filled with dreams. I see the faces of so many who have gone on before me. Many lie buried in the South Pacific—Dutch, Gargano, Thompson, Tully. Others came home and built the lives and careers we'd dreamed of as young men, and now they're gone as well. We were referred to as the Greatest Generation, and truly our generation was called on to do the impossible with the unavailable, to go to the unknown and perform tasks never before asked of a people. We answered the call, we went, we conquered; we came home and rebuilt a nation and contributed to rebuilding a world.

New and unforeseeable challenges await. We leave it in the hands of our youth, and I ask, Are you ready? Are you willing?

When my youngest son returned from summer camp one year he brought with him a close friend he'd made that summer, a Japanese boy. Neither knew much about the war then, nor could they know that I might have killed his father, or his father might have come close to killing me. Such is war. As I looked at the boys I felt no malice, no weight still left from those years, only hope and optimism for the future. The hatred I gained in the Solomons for an entire race of people was gone; I didn't need it any longer.

Appendix A

Original Sailing Roster of the USS *Wakefield*, May 20, 1942,
K Company, 3rd Battalion, 5th Marines (K/3/5),
1st Marine Division

U.S. MARINES (REGULARS)

*"KIA" and "WIA" refer to marines killed and wounded in action,
respectively*

Captain
Patterson, Lawrence V.   *Malaria, transferred to States*

Gunnery Sergeant
Cassel, John S.   *Malaria, transferred to States*

Platoon Sergeants
Haney, St. Elmo M.   *Malaria, rejoined company*
Minahan, Patrick J.
Rose, George H.
Wing, Robert W.   *Malaria, transferred to States;
                                         commissioned*

Sergeants
Gargano, Louis   *KIA, short round of 105 mm,
                                         Silver Star*

Kelley, John E.	WIA, left leg; commissioned
Miller, Thurman I.	
Owens, Homer L.	Silver Star; died

Mess Sergeant
Britt, Robert L.

Corporals

Barrett, John E.	
Beltrami, Charles	KIA, head
Hurst, Herman	WIA, left arm; KIA, Gilbert Islands
Kling, Lawrence	WIA, shoulder and side, Bronze Star
McEnery, James G.	
Mersky, Arnold	Malaria, transferred to States
Powell, William J.	WIA, neck
Powers, Ishmael	Malaria, transferred to States
Rader, Harry J.	Died November 9, 1978—Heart attack
Rose, Ralph L.	WIA, head
Schwerdel, John G.	
Suess, Carl A.	KIA, head and leg
Wingate, Leavelle W.	
Yanochko, Michael Jr.	

Privates First Class

Barrett, William H.	
Berry, Leroy F.	Malaria, transferred to States
Blakesley, Kenneth N.	WIA, right shoulder
Borgomainerio, Russell J.	Malaria, transferred to States; WIA, Korea
Cafarelli, Frank A.	Two Silver Stars
Clements, Robert L.	
Clinton, Lewis F., Jr.	KIA, abdomen
Crumbacker, Jesse L., Jr.	
Culler, Rufus F.	

Cunningham, Rinsley H.	*Malaria, transferred to States*
Dexlerow, Joseph W.	
DeLong, Weldon F.	*KIA, heart, Navy Cross (destroyer escort named after him)*
Dessel, Julius	*Malaria, transferred to States*
Detmer, Edwin C.	*WIA, stomach*
Fasimpaur, Edward F.	*WIA, left leg*
Gerlich, Alert R.	*WIA, left shoulder*
Gibson, Matthew B.	*Malaria, transferred to States*
Godwin, Horace E.	*KIA, chest*
Googe, Jessie L., Jr.	
Gwazdauskas, Charles G.	*Silver Star*
Heywood, Jack H.	*Malaria, transferred to States*
Higgins, Richard D.	
Himes, Carman A.	
Jackson, Harry E.	*Malaria, transferred to States*
Jackson, Richard	
Kelly, David Jr.	
Klobas, Joseph W.	*WIA, neck; second time WIA, shoulder*
March, Carl L.	
Marmet, John W.	
Matheney, Thomas M.	
May, Ralph A.	*WIA, left leg*
McAuliff, Kenneth S.	*KIA, head*
McCurley, Dewey M.	*WIA, left hand; died 1959 in Athens, Georgia*
Meyer, Keith E.	*WIA, left arm*
Melton, Robert L.	*Malaria, transferred to States*
Mettendorfer, Jacob S.	
Moss, Robert J.	*Malaria, transferred to States; WIA, Canal*
Mullen, Richard F.	
Newman, James H.	*Silver Star; malaria, transferred to States*
Palmore, James K.	*KIA, hip*
Parker, Wilson W.	*WIA, right shoulder*

Ray, William M.
Remaly, Edward H.   *WIA, left shoulder; second time*
                                          WIA right shoulder

Richardson, Charles E., Jr.   *WIA, leg*
Shaw, Albert V., Jr.
Shipman, Charles E.
Sumner, James E.   *WIA, abdomen*
Tant, Leonard E.   *WIA, both hands; second time*
                                          WIA, hands and arm

Toth, John J.   *KIA, head*
Walker, Joseph F.   *Malaria, transferred to States*
Whittington, Lonie W.   *WIA, left arm*
Zebic Frank J.

Assistant Cook
Whittemore, Warren L.

Privates
Abraszek, Thaddeus G.   *WIA, back*
Ardire, Anthony A.
Bors, Louis E.   *WIA, right leg*
Brown, William
Cook, Linton W.   *WIA, knee*
Da Silver, Joseph P.   *WIA, neck; Silver Star*
Daugherty, Burkett
De Fusco, Bernard J.   *KIA, head*
English, Daniel J.
Fahrenwald, Frank L.   *KIA, head*
Gunter, Paul C.   *KIA, bayonet*
Heller, Paul   *KIA, face*
Hoppa, Francis L.   *WIA, chest*
Howard, Joseph R.
Ingalls, Phillip G.
Jones, James F., Jr.   *Malaria, transferred to States*
Karlon, John P.   *KIA, head*
Lawton, John K.   *WIA, shoulder*

Lodeski, Alphonso T.   *Malaria, transferred to States*

Malinaro, Carmen A.

Massey, David K.   *Malaria, died of heart attack*

Michael, Theodore M.

Morse, Everett L.   *Malaria, transferred to States*

Murray, William   *WIA, hand*

Musto, William J.   *WIA, right arm*

Newcomb, Ray   *WIA, right knee*

Norman, Richard C.   *WIA, leg*

Ricketts, Edward   *KIA, head and abdomen*

Rua, Abel

Schantzenbach, Norman R.   *WIA, multiple; KIA short round
                                 of 105 mm on Cape Gloucester;
                                 Silver Star*

Schipski, Richard C.

Shute, David G.   *KIA, face*

Snodgrass, James A.   *KIA, chest*

Somerville, Charles F.

Stewart, George A.   *WIA, right leg; second time WIA,
                                 right arm*

Stewart, Howard F.   *Malaria, transferred to States*

Stovenken, John L., Jr.   *Malaria, transferred to States*

Studesbaker, Wilbur E.

Student, Emil S.   *KIA, abdomen*

Summers, William J.   *Malaria, transferred to States*

Teskevich, John E.   *WIA, left leg; second time KIA,
                                 stomach*

Turk, Robert H.

Tweedie, Richard D.   *WIA, right shoulder; second time
                                 WIA, stomach*

Vastinar, Peter J.

Wagner, Robert M.   *KIA, head*

Weaver, Harry F.

Weidman, Richard B.

Weiss, Dale H.   *WIA, shoulder*

Wilson, Philip A., Jr.   *WIA, right leg*

Wodinsky, Sidney D.

Zadroga, Stanley F.   *WIA, right shoulder; second time*
                                   WIA, left hand and right shoulder

Zaengle, John W.

Field Music
Williams, Harold J.

U.S. MARINES (RESERVES)

Sergeants
Andriolo, Anthony P.   *WIA, right hand—thumb*
                                  amputated

Darsey, Maurice O.   *WIA, hand*

Second Lieutenants
Adams, Arthur L.   *Malaria, transferred to States*
Carnwath, Samuel W.   *Malaria, transferred to States*
Davies, John H.   *Transferred to 7th Marines*

Sergeants
O'Neill, Thomas E.   *Commissioned*

Privates First Class
Bosanac, Paul   *Malaria, transferred to States*
Chudy, Michael   *WIA, canister—multiple*
Dimick, Arthur J.   *WIA, right side; Silver Star*
Flowers, Leroy L.
Hogg, James F.   *KIA*
Landrum, William J.   *KIA, abdomen*
McNulty, Robert J.   *WIA, head*
Shivek, Steven   *Malaria, transferred to States*
Williamson, Charles B.   *WIA, left arm and hand*
Zebley, Frank   *Malaria, transferred to States*

Privates
Brown, James C.   *WIA, left leg*

Comer, Avis O.	*KIA, head*
Conners, Jerome P.	
Duda, Paul P.	*WIA, leg*
Gavin, Joseph K.	*WIA, back*
Hanby, Charles E.	*WIA*
Justus, James F.	*KIA, chest*
Kemp, Clifton E.	
Knickerbocker, Henry C.	
Lanier, Fred L., Jr.	
Liazos, Arthur S.	
Malover, John W.	
Matte, William J.	
Phillips, Ralph W.	
Pressley, Vance M.	*KIA, right side*
Riegel, Charles W.	*Falling tree, broken legs*
Runnells, Perley E.	*WIA*
Scarpelli, Peter	
Shields, Robert G.	*Malaria, transferred to States*
Smith, Guy H.	*Died in fall in Melbourne*
Spence, William N.	
Sullivan, Gerald P.	
Thomas, David W.	*WIA, multiple back and shoulders*
Timmons, Winfred E.	
Turner, William W.	*KIA, head and back*
Twohill, Edward F.	
Uhl, Richard E.	*WIA, shoulder*
Woods, Robert J.	*WIA, chest and multiple leg*

Appendix B

These are the ships on which I sailed:

USS *Henderson,* AP-1, from Charleston, SC, on December 18, 1940, arriving in Guantánamo Bay, Cuba, on December 23

USS *McCawley,* APA-4, from Guantánamo Bay on April 3, 1941, sailing on April 4 for the Naval Operating Base, Norfolk, VA, arriving on April 8

USS *Wakefield,* AP-21, at First Base Depot in Norfolk on May 17, 1942, sailing from there on May 20, disembarking at Wellington, New Zealand, on June 18

USS *Fuller,* APA-7, from Wellington on July 2, stopping at Suva Bay in the Fiji Islands before combat landing on Guadalcanal in the British Solomon Islands on August 7, 1942

USS *President Jackson,* APA-18, from Guadalcanal on December 9 to Brisbane, Australia, arriving December 14

USS *West Point,* AP-23, from Brisbane on January 7, 1943, to Melbourne, Australia, arriving January 12

British SS *B. F. Shaw,* from Melbourne on September 26 to Milne Bay, New Guinea, arriving October 11

SS *Noel Palmer,* from Milne Bay on Christmas Eve 1943 to Oro Bay, New Guinea, arriving December 26

USS *LST-204,* from Oro Bay on December 28 to Cape Gloucester, New Britain, arriving on New Year's Day 1944

USS *Elmore,* APA-42, from Cape Gloucester on May 4 to Pavuvu, in the Russell Islands, arriving May 8

USS *General John Pope,* AP-110, from Pavuvu on June 24, 1944, crossing the equator on July 1, landing in San Diego July 7

ACKNOWLEDGMENTS

I am fortunate beyond words to have had the support and encouragement of many, many people in putting this book together. My beloved wife, Recie, listened to me work through early versions of this material, while helping me recover from the ravages of war. My son David, though he never served in the military, has been my trusted lieutenant throughout—editing, researching, organizing fragments into a true narrative, conducting interviews with surviving K Company members, and so much more. This book would not exist without him.

My daughter, Gloria, and son Gilbert have always encouraged my writing and provided their mother and me with a large and loving family of children and grandchildren.

Katie Hall helped shape this final version into a much better book than it could otherwise have been.

James Stone and the other men of the West Virginia chapter of the 1st Marine Division welcomed me into a close-knit fraternity who knew the cost of war, just what I needed at that point in my life. Dr. Joanna Roberts not only helped me recover much of my health over her four decades of care but encouraged me to tell these stories as part of my recovery.

In more recent years I've had the kindness and help of others too numerous to list in full, but special thanks go to my agent, Scott Miller of Trident Media; Bob Makos and the entire Makos family of Valor Studios; Gen. William Kirk and the great staff of the Eglin Air Force Association; Ted Corcoran and the Fort Walton Beach Chamber of Commerce; Jo-Ann Adams and John and Terry Adams Dawson; the Marine Corps Historical Association; author Lynn Walters; Christy Bailey and Rachel Booth of the Coal Heritage Authority; and historian Lori Copeland. Australians Rob Crawford, John Innes, and Peter Flahavin shared their research and many photos from their visits to present-day Guadalcanal. Doug Drumheller of Greatest Generation MIA Recoveries provided background on recent attempts to recover evidence of the Goettge patrol. My grandson Sgt. Jeffrey Castle also provided very helpful comments on earlier drafts of this book. I also received invaluable research help from many military men and women, both active and retired, including Lt. Col. Dick Renfro, U.S. Army, Ret.; Major Jeffrey Landis; Kara Newcomer of the United States Marine Corps History Division; and Joan Thomas of the National Museum of the Marine Corps.

My greatest thanks must be reserved for the men of K Company, those who came home and whose lifelong friendship I cherished, and those who did not return from those jungles. Those who did return were unfailingly helpful in researching this book. Charles "Slim" Somerville, Jerry Conners, and Jesse

Goodge all shared their memories with me and commented on early drafts of this material. Jim McEnery provided a copy of the map of Guadalcanal given to squad leaders just before our landing, as well as a wealth of other detail. Taped conversations among Scoop, Mo, and other members of K Company were invaluable, and many provided separate interviews, letters, and telephone calls.

Notes

1. WEST VIRGINIA, AMERICA, 1940

1. This family history is covered in various sections of Mary Bowman, *Reference Book of Wyoming County History* (Parsons, WV: McClain, 1965).
2. This lease living would come to an abrupt end after I came home from the war when strip miners bought the rights to the numerous coal seams in the area where we lived. Those rights gave them the authority to evict all of us with just thirty days' notice. The mountaintops above my family's farm are now being blasted away as the degradation of mountaintop removal scars my beautiful hills, the valleys full of fill dirt and rock and the streams clogged with silt and runoff.
3. James Webb, *Born Fighting: How the Scots-Irish Shaped America* (New York: Broadway Books, 2005).
4. See Lori Copeland, "Project 100,000: Harvesting Poverty's Labor Force for War" (master's thesis, University of Kentucky, 2008), for a long and interesting consideration of the relationship between the military and Appalachia.

2. THE UNITED STATES MARINE CORPS

1. Norman Dickenson, *We Few: The Marine Corps 400 in the War Against Japan* (Annapolis, MD: Naval Institute Press, 2001), 46.

2. I hadn't thought about the unlikelihood of that kind of duty, but years later 2nd Lt. Norman Elliott of the 4th Division would recall that "in the 1920's there was a rash of railroad mail car robberies and mail car clerks who were getting shot. The Commandant of the Marine Corps volunteered the marines as a policing agency to help with this national problem. Suddenly the robberies stopped." Gail Chatfield, *By Dammit, We're Marines! Veterans' Stories of Heroism, Horror, and Humor in World War II on the Pacific Front* (Paragould, AR: Wyndham House, 2008), 45 (Nook ed.).

3. Copeland, "Project 100,000," 39–40.

4. Article of War 44.

5. A. A. Vandegrift as told to Robert B. Asprey, *Once a Marine: The Memoirs of General A. A. Vandegrift*, United States Marine Corps (New York: Norton, 1964), 61.

6. See George McMillan, *The Old Breed: A History of the First Marine Division in World War II* (Washington: Infantry Journal Press, 1949) for an in-depth look at the Old Breed.

7. Eugene Sledge, *With the Old Breed At Peleliu and Okinawa* (Novato, Calif.: Presidio Press, 1981), 43, describes Haney as teaching school after World War I; Asa Bordages, in "Suicide Creek," pt. 2, *Collier's Weekly*, June 2, 1945, 32, reports him as selling vacuum cleaners.

8. Sledge, *With the Old Breed*, 21, quoting an unnamed private.

9. Interview with Mo's son Donald Darsey.

10. Gen H. M. Smith, *Coral and Brass* (New York: Charles Scribner's Sons, 1949), 72.

11. Stephen E. Ambrose, *D-Day, June 6, 1944: The Climactic Battle of World War II* (New York: Simon & Schuster, 1994), 45.

12. This may be apocryphal; the source is "Who's Afraid of the Big Bad Wolf? Who's Afraid of the Men of Higgins? No One Less than Adolf Hitler Himself!" *Eureka News Bulletin*, Aug. 1943, an official publication of Higgins Industries.

13. Jonathon R. B. Halbesleben, "The Man Who Won WWII: Andrew Jackson Higgins and the management of Higgins Industries,"

Management & Organizational History 1, no. 3 (Aug. 2006): 311–323, 313.

14. Interview with Billy Arthur, http://www.lejeune.usmc.mil/emd/Cultural/oralhistory/arthur.pdf, accessed Feb. 5, 2012.

15. Vandegrift, *Once a Marine*, 96.

16. Ibid., 99.

17. Ibid., 98.

18. *Charleston* (WV) *Gazette*, Dec. 7, 1941, 6.

3. K/3/5

1. Samuel B. Griffith, *The Battle for Guadalcanal* (1963; Urbana and Chicago: University of Illinois Press, 2000), 23–24.

2. The ship had an interesting history. According to Marine Corps documents supplied with the author's service record, the *Manhattan* departed New York City on August 10, 1932, for her maiden Atlantic crossing. "Arriving at Hamburg ten days later, she made the return voyage to New York in five days, fourteen hours and twenty-eight minutes—a record for passenger liners. Proudly carrying the title of 'The Fastest Cabin Ship in the World,' the liner continued to ply the North Atlantic from New York to Hamburg, via Ireland, England, and France into the late 1930s."

3. Interview with the author.

4. Richard B. Frank, *Guadalcanal: The Definitive Account of the Landmark Battle* (New York: Penguin, 1992), 6–21.

5. Vandegrift, *Once a Marine*, 110.

6. R. R. Keene, "'Pistol Pete': Akio Tani, the 'Mantis,' Sent Marines Scrambling," *Leatherneck*, Oct. 1992, 20.

7. Sister Mary Theresa, writing in *Guadalcanal Echoes*, Spring 2005, 4.

8. For a detailed account of the Koro preparation and landing, see William H. Bartsch, "What Went Wrong at Koro?" *Naval History Magazine* 23, no. 4 (Aug. 2009):58–64.

9. In fact, author William H. Bartsch titled a 2002 article in the *Journal of Military History* "Operation Dovetail: Bungled Guadalcanal Rehearsal, July 1942."

10. Richard Tregaskis, *Guadalcanal Diary* (New York: Random House, 1943).

11. Bartsch, "What Went Wrong at Koro?"
12. Vandegrift, *Once a Marine,* 122.

4. GUADALCANAL

1. Quoted in *Leatherneck,* July 1992, 36.
2. Eric Hammel, *Guadalcanal: Starvation Island* (New York: Crown, 1987), 34–35.
3. Henry I. Shaw Jr., *First Offensive: The Marine Campaign for Guadalcanal,* (Washington: Marine Corps Historical Center, 1992), available at http://www.ibiblio.org/hyperwar/USMC/USMC-C-Guadalcanal/index.html, acccessed Feb. 21, 2012.
4. Hough, Lt. Col. Frank O., Maj. Verle E. Ludwig, and Henry I. Shaw Jr. *History of U.S. Marine Corps Operations in World War II,* vol. 1, *Pearl Harbor to Guadalcanal,* pt. 6, "The Turning Point: Guadalcanal" (Washington: U.S. Government Printing Office, 1958), 254.
5. Letter to the author.
6. H. L. Merillat, quoted in George C. Dyer, *The Amphibians Came to Conquer,* http://www.ibiblio.org/hyperwar/USN/ACTC/actc-9.html#fn16.
7. Letter to the author.
8. The author is indebted to Australian researcher John Innes for background on the village. Innes has made numerous trips to Guadalcanal and leads tours of the area. He also interviewed some of the villagers as well as marines who were involved in searching for the remains of the Goettge patrol. In addition to e-mails to the author, Innes has summarized his research at http://www.pacificwrecks.com/people/visitors/innes/the_village/index.html, accessed May 1, 2012.
9. Frank, *Guadalcanal,* 62.
10. Quoted in John B. Lundstrom, *The First Team and the Guadalcanal Campaign: Naval Fighter Combat from August to November 1942* (Annapolis, MD: Naval Institute Press, 1994), 81.
11. For an interesting and detailed record of how Fletcher came to make the decision to withdraw, and an argument that he was correct to do so, see Scott T. Farr, "The Historical Record, Strategic

Decision Making, and Carrier Support to Operation Watchtower"
(master's thesis, U.S. Army Command and General Staff College,
2003), http://www.dtic.mil/cgi-bin/GetTRDoc?AD=ADA416432,
accessed March 1, 2012.

12. Eric Hammel, "October on Guadalcanal," *Leatherneck*, August 1992,
27.

13. McMillan, *The Old Breed,* 45.

14. Frank, *Guadalcanal,* 127.

15. Japanese naval leaders "tended to be less doctrinaire and some, by
Japanese standards, were quite liberal. One reason for these attitudes was that more naval officers had traveled and seen other nations firsthand, whereas very few of the army's senior commanders
had had the same opportunities. Army leaders were therefore more
given to underestimating the strength of a potential enemy." Harry
Gailey, *War in the Pacific: From Pearl Harbor to Tokyo Bay* (Novato,
CA: Presidio Press, 1995), 59 (Nook ed.).

16. Interrogation of Vice Adm. Shigeru Fukudome, reprinted at http://
www.ibiblio.org/hyperwar/AAF/USSBS/IJO/IJO-115.html, accessed
February 1, 2012.

17. Genjirou Inui, "My Guadalcanal," http://www.nettally.com/jrube/
genjirou/genjirou.htm, accessed January 15, 2012.

18. Statement of Platoon Sgt. Frank L. Few, quoted in First Marine
Division combat correspondent James Hurlbut's August 14, 1943
dispatch, http://www.usni.org/sites/default/files/magazine_uploads
/uploads/Canal%20Dispatch.pdf

19. Per John Innes, "The Japanese who told where they had their
trenches and where they buried the Patrol certainly would not have
mentioned any 'nasties.' Cutting arms, legs and heads off would not
have been something they would have talked about in their 1982
description of events" (e-mail to the author). The author is also
deeply indebted to historian Peter Flahavin for numerous photos of
Guadalcanal then and now as well as a wealth of information about
the island in general.

20. R. R. Keene, "The Goettge Patrol: Searching for Answers," *Leatherneck*, Aug. 1992, 29.

21. James McEnery, letter to the author.

22. FMFRP (Fleet Marine Force Reference Publication) 12-110, *Fighting on Guadalcanal* (Washington: Dept. of the Navy, 1943, released 1991), 48–49. Hereafter cited as FMFRP.

23. Macmillan, *The Old Breed*, 52.

24. J. Hammel, *Guadalcanal: Starvation Island*, 143.

25. Ore J. Marion with Thomas Cuddihy and Edward Cuddihy, *On the Canal: The Marines of L-3-5 on Guadalcanal, 1942* (Mechanicsburg, PA: Stackpole Books, 2004), 93–94.

26. Sledge, *With the Old Breed*, 33.

27. Letter from Thomas Holcomb to Florence Page Goettge, Sept. 2, 1942, *Thomas Holcomb, 1879–1965, Register of His Personal Papers*, Historical Division, USMC.

28. E.g., Lee Hadden, "The Geology of Guadalcanal: A Selected Bibliography of the Geology, Natural History, and the History of Guadalcanal," September 2007, Topographic Engineering Center, Engineer Research and Development Center, U.S. Army Corps of Engineers ("bibliography on the geographical, water and geological information of Guadalcanal was begun to fill a request for current information needed for the forensics recovery of the bodies of the US Marines of the Lt Col. Frank B. Goettge Reconnaissance patrol"); C. Boyd and D. C. Boyd, "Theory and the Scientific Basis for Forensic Anthropology," *Journal of Forensic Sciences* 56, no. 6 (Nov. 2011): 1407–15, DOI: 10.1111/j.1556-4029.2011.01852.x (a case study involving the search for the Goettge patrol).

29. Professor Donna Boyd, quoted in Tim Thornton, "Searching for Fallen Marines," *Roanoke (VA) Times*, Oct. 12, 2008, http://www.roanoke.com/news/nrv/wb/180137, accessed Feb. 25, 2012.

30. Cover, *Life* magazine, May 22, 1944.

31. Mark Shulman, "Why Men Fight," *Airpower Journal*, Fall 1996, 95, 96.

32. Quoted in Keene, " 'Pistol Pete' " 20.

5. BATTLE

1. For a fascinating diary kept by one of his men, see Genjirou Inui, "My Guadalcanal," http://www.nettally.com/jrube/genjirou/genjirou.htm, accessed Jan. 15, 2012.

2. Richard Tregaskis, *Guadalcanal Diary* (New York: Random House Modern Library paperback ed., 2000), 125.

3. However, many Japanese state that Ichiki was killed in battle; see Michael T. Smith, *Bloody Ridge: The Battle That Saved Guadalcanal* (New York: Pocket Books, 2003), 95.

4. Don Richter, *Where the Sun Stood Still* (Tawe, CA: Toucan Publishing, 1992), 380.

5. K Company reunion recording.

6. Quoted in R. R. Keene, "The Mop Up Begins," *Leatherneck*, Dec. 1992, 15.

7. Akio Tani quoted in Keene, "'Pistol Pete,'" 20.

8. Michael Finkel, "Malaria: Stopping a Global Killer," *National Geographic Magazine,* July 2007, http://ngm.nationalgeographic.com/2007/07/malaria/finkel-text, accessed February 25, 2012.

9. Jackson, Ralph Neal "Life in Hell: A Brief Sketch of the Living Conditions on Guadalcanal as Experienced by a United States Marine in World War II (student essay, unpublished, 1991).

10. Michael C. Capraro, quoted in Kathellen D. Valenzi, "Scouting Guadalcanal," *Military History,* Aug. 1995, 54–60.

11. K Company reunion recording.

12. Ibid.

13. Wayne R. Austerman, "Springfield—Ordnance Oddity Served Pacific War Soldiers," *World War II,* Feb. 2004.

14. FMFRP, 19.

15. Letter to the author.

16. FMFRP, 47.

17. William Breuer, *The Spy Who Spent the War in Bed: And Other Bizarre Tales from World War II* (Hoboken, NJ: John Wiley & Sons, 2003), 71.

18. K Company reunion recording.

6. THE MATANIKAU

1. Inui, "My Guadalcanal."
2. FMFRP, 1.
3. FMFRP, 52.
4. FMFRP, 13.

5. FMFRP, 25.

6. Ibid.

7. Sister Mary Theresa, writing in *Guadalcanal Echoes*, Spring 2005, 7.

8. Jackson, interview with Mo Darsey.

9. Jane Stafford, "Unique in Medical History—'Guadalcanal Neurosis' Plagues Invalids Returning from Fighting in South Pacific," *Pittsburgh Press*, May 23, 1943, sec. 3, 1.

10. "Q. Why were the reinforcements of Guadalcanal sent down in small units instead of one mass attack? A. Didn't have enough landing barges to make a landing. The main point of difficulty in our landing operations was the lack of landing barges. Boats and destroyers were used for landings. But we didn't have enough barges to begin with. Had plenty of big ships but not enough landing craft. Damage from American planes made it worse." Interrogation of Cmdr. Masatake Okumiya, reprinted at http://www.ibiblio.org/hyperwar/AAF/USSBS/IJO/IJO-16.html, accessed January 22, 2012.

11. Akio Tani quoted in Keene, " 'Pistol Pete'," 20.

12. K Company reunion recording.

13. Ibid.

14. Robert Leckie, *Helmet for My Pillow* (1957; New York: Bantam, 2010), 73.

15. Interrogation of Vice Adm. Paul H. Weneker, reprinted at http://www.ibiblio.org/hyperwar/AAF/USSBS/IJO/IJO-70.html (accessed February 2, 2012).

16. Gailey, *War in the Pacific,* 175 (Nook ed.).

17. FMFRP, 64.

18. Jackson, interview with Mo Darsey.

7. REPRIEVE

1. FMFRP, 30.

2. Interrogation of Adm. Soemu Toyoda, reprinted at http://www.ibiblio.org/hyperwar/AAF/USSBS/IJO/IJO-75.html, accessed Feb. 19, 2012.

3. Donald Keene, *So Lovely a Country Will Never Perish: Wartime Diaries of Japanese Writers*, Asia Perspectives: History, Society, and Culture (New York: Columbia University Press, 2010), 31.

4. Lt. Comdr. E. Rogers Smith, "Neuroses Resulting from Combat," *American Journal of Psychiatry,* 1943; 100: 94–95.

5. Stafford, "Unique in Medical History."

6. Ibid.

7. Ibid.

8. These are the figures cited in Richard Frank's exhaustive history *Guadalcanal: The Definitive Account of the Landmark Battle* (New York: Random House, 1990), 522.

9. William Johnson, *The Pacific Campaign in World War II: From Pearl Harbor to Guadalcanal* (New York: Rutledge, 2006), 286.

10. FMFRP Introductory Foreword.

11. FMFRP, Document Foreword.

12. FMFRP, v.

13. Kenneth Roberts, *Northwest Passage* (New York: Doubleday, Doran, 1937).

14. Quoted in Keene, " 'Pistol Pete'," *Leatherneck,* Oct. 1992, 23.

15. Interrogation of Vice Adm. Paul H. Weneker, reprinted at http://www.ibiblio.org/hyperwar/AAF/USSBS/IJO/IJO-70.html.

16. FMFRP, 29.

17. FMFRP, 33.

18. Vandegrift, *Once a Marine,* 207.

19. Letter to the author.

8. NEW BRITAIN: SUICIDE CREEK AND WALT'S RIDGE

1. *USMC Special Action Report, Cape Gloucester Operation, First Marine Division 1943–194,* N-7443-A (unpaginated), available at http://www.scribd.com/doc/45586358/WWII-1st-Marines-Division, accessed Feb. 26, 2012.

2. Lt. Col. Frank O. Hough, "Some Explanation in Regard to Place Names," in *The Campaign on New Britain* (Washington: Historical Branch, HQ, USMC, 1952), 196–97. retrieved from http://www.ibiblio.org/hyperwar/USMC/USMC-M-NBrit/USMC-M-NBrit-III.html, accessed Feb. 25, 2012.

3. *USMC Special Action Report.*

4. Ibid.

5. Ibid.

6. Asa Bordages, "Suicide Creek," pt. 1, *Collier's Weekly*, May 26, 1945, 12.

7. Ibid., 11.

8. Asa Bordages, "Suicide Creek," pt. 2, *Collier's Weekly*, June 2, 1945, 21.

9. Bordages, "Suicide Creek," pt. 1, 30.

10. Bordages, "Suicide Creek," pt. 2, 32.

11. Steve Solloway, "Haldane's Spirit Lives Among Us," *Portland Press Herald,* March 14, 2010, http://www.pressherald.com/sports/haldanes-spirit-lives-among-us_2010-03-13.html, accessed May 23, 2012.

12. K Company reunion recording.

13. Brig. Gen. Robert H. Williams, *The Old Corps* (Annapolis, MD: Naval Institute Press, 1982), quoted at http://www.angelfire.com/ca/dickg/oldcorps.html, accessed Febr. 7, 2012.

14. Hough, "Some Explanation in Regard to Place Names," 196.

16. Interrogation of Cmdr. Masatake Okumiya, reprinted at http://www.ibiblio.org/hyperwar/AAF/USSBS/IJO/IJO-16.html, accessed January 22, 2012.

17. Dell Comics' *War Heroes* no. 10 was published in late 1944 and included the story *"Peace Patrol"* specifically about the Goettge patrol, featuring a (fictional) Captain Edelstein and mentioning Arndt (but not Goettge) by name. The comic takes great liberty with the facts, but it ends with the basic lesson of the "last 'peace patrol' the marines will ever send": "Bitter knowledge struck Edelstein's men as they gazed at their dead buddies. Treachery and fiendish cruelty are the Jap code!" However, since I saw Arndt reading his comic in early 1943, it must have been a different one.

18. *Fortitudine: Bulletin of the Marine Corps Historical Program* 22, no. 1 (Summer 1992): 13.

19. R. V. Burgin with Bill Marvell, *Islands of the Damned: A Marine at War in the Pacific* (New York: New American Library, 2010).

9. CAMP LEJEUNE

1. For the story of the Royal Dutch Marines training at Lejeune, see e.g. http://theindoproject.org/site/www/dutch-marines-to-east-indies-train-at-camp-lejeune.

2. Technically this was the Fleet Marine Force Training Command; its name has changed slightly over the years, as military names do, but we always referred to it colloquially as OCA. See Kenneth Condit, Gerald Diamond, and Edwin Turnbladh, *Marine Corps Ground Training in World War II* (Washington: Historical Branch, G-3 Division, HQ, USMC, 1956) for a complete look at the various efforts the Corps made to get qualified officers into the field as quickly as possible.

3. Bernard C. Nalty and Lt. Col. Ralph F. Moody, (*A Brief History of U.S. Marine Corps Officer Procurement*, 1775–1969, rev. ed. Washington: USMC Historical Division Headquarters, 1970): "The anticipated officer shortage, however, failed to develop; and by August 1 [1943] in spite of the fact that voluntary enlistment for candidate training no longer was permitted, there was an overabundance of second lieutenants. Standards therefore, were raised until only noncommissioned officers with two years of college and a high degree of natural aptitude were eligible for the classes. A further obstacle placed in the path of the officer candidate occurred when the Commandant in April 1943 established Candidates' Detachments at Camp Elliott and Camp Lejeune for the further screening of potential platoon leaders. To earn his appointment, the noncommissioned officer was required to survive two rigorous courses of instruction, the Pre-Officer Candidate School (as the Candidates' Detachments were called after their consolidation at Camp Lejeune) and the Officer Candidates' School itself" [footnotes omitted].

4. Dickenson, *We Few*, 58.

5. For an excellent account of this remarkable first class, a cohesive bunch who kept in contact over the years and still does, see Dickenson, *We Few*.

6. John C. Shively, *The Last Lieutenant: A Foxhole View of the Epic Battle for Iwo Jima* (Bloomington: Indiana University Press, 2006), 24.

7. FMFRP, 60. Emphasis in original.

8. Cpl. Fred Carter, Company I, Fifth Marines, ibid., 10.
9. Ibid., 20.
10. Dickenson, *We Few,* 65.
11. Quoted in Keene, " 'Pistol Pete,' " 23.
12. As described in Keene, *So Lovely a Country,* 34.
13. Harry S. Truman, *1945: Year of Decisions* (Garden City, NY: Doubleday, 1955), 416.
14. Luke 12:49, *Holy Bible,* American King James version.

10. INTO THE MINE

1. Former United Mine Workers of America President Arnold Miller quoted in "Growing Up on Cabin Creek," http://www.wvgenweb.org/wvcoal/miller3.html, accessed Feb. 20, 2012.
2. David Halsey, "Otsego: Remembering a Wyoming County Coal Camp," *Goldenseal,* Fall 2000, 27.

EPILOGUE

1. Sledge, *With the Old Breed,* 140–41.
2. See Robert F. Munn, "The Development of Model Towns in the Bituminous Coal Fields," *West Virginia History* 40, no. 3 (Spring 1979): 243–51, for an excellent account of how and why such model towns came to be.
3. Tams, Maj. W. P., Jr. *The Smokeless Coal Fields of West Virginia* (Morgantown: West Virginia University Press, 1983), 61.
4. Jackson, interview with Mo Darsey.

Selected Bibliography

Ambrose, Hugh. *The Pacific*. New York: Penguin Group (USA), 2010.

Bordages, Asa. "Suicide Creek," pts. 1 and 2. *Collier's Weekly*, May 26, June 2, 1945.

Bowman, Mary. *Reference Book of Wyoming County History*. Parsons, WV: McClain, 1965.

Brokaw, Tom. *The Greatest Generation*. New York: Random House, 1998. Good coverage of Europe but very little about the South Pacific campaign.

Burdette, Cody. "Recalling the Great Depression: Hard Times on a Hillside Farm. *Goldenseal*, Winter 1993.

Burgin, R. V., with Bill Marvel. *Islands of the Damned: A Marine at War in the Pacific*. New York: New American Library, 2010.

Cameron, Craig. *American Samurai: Myth and Imagination in the Conduct of Battle in the First Marine Division, 1941–1951*. Cambridge: Cambridge University Press, 1994.

Chatfield, Gail. *By Dammit, We're Marines! Veterans' Stories of Heroism, Horror, and Humor in World War II on the Pacific Front*. Paragould, AR: Wyndham House, 2008.

Clemens, Martin. *Alone on Guadalcanal: A Coastwatcher's Story*. Annapolis, MD: Naval Institute Press, 1998.

Cohen, Stan. *King Coal: A Pictorial Heritage of West Virginia Coal Mining*. Charleston, WV: Quarrier Press, 1984.

Condit, Kenneth, Gerald Diamond, and Edwin Turnbladh. *Marine Corps Ground Training in World War II*. Washington: Division, HQ, USMC, Historical Branch, G-3 Division, 1956.

Cook, Charles. *The Battle of Cape Esperance: Encounter at Guadalcanal*. Annapolis, MD: Naval Institute Press, 1992).

Coombe, Jack D. *Derailing the Tokyo Express: The Naval Battles for the Solomon Islands That Sealed Japan's Fate*. Harrisburg, PA: Stackpole Books, 1991.

Crenshaw, Russell Sydnor. *South Pacific Destroyer: The Battle for the Solomons from Savo Island to Vella Gulf*. Annapolis, MD: Naval Institute Press, 1998.

Corbin, David. *Life, Work, and Rebellion in the Coal Fields: The Southern West Virginia Miners, 1880–1922* Urbana: University of Illinois Press, 1981.

Davis, Burke. *Marine! The Life of Lieutenant General Lewis B. (Chesty) Puller*. Boston: Little, Brown, 1962.

Dickenson, Norman. *We Few: The Marine Corps 400 in the War Against Japan*. Annapolis, MD: Naval Institute Press, 2001.

Dillon, Lacy A. *They Died in the Darkness*. Parsons, WV: McClain, 1976.

Dixon, Thomas W., Jr. *Appalachian Coal Mines and Railroads*. Lynchburg, VA: TLC, 1994. Lib. of Cong.

Feuer, A. B., ed. *Coast Watching in the Solomon Islands: The Bougainville Reports, December 1941–July 1943*. Westport, CT: Praeger, 1992.

FMFRP (Fleet Marine Force Reference Publication) 12–110. *Fighting on Guadalcanal*. Washington: Dept. of the Navy, 1943; released 1991.

Fortitudine: Bulletin of the Marine Corps Historical Program 22, no. 1 (Summer 1992).

Frank, Richard B. *Guadalcanal: The Definitive Account of the Landmark Battle*. 1990; New York: Penguin, 1992. An excellent, exhaustive history of the battle.

Gailey, Harry. *War in the Pacific: From Pearl Harbor to Tokyo Bay.* Novato, CA: Presidio Press, 1995.

Garand, George, and Truman Strobridge. *History of U.S. Marine Corps Operations in World War II*, vol. 4, *Western Pacific Operations.* Washington: Historical Branch, G-3 Division, HQ, USMC, 1971.

Giesen, Carol. *Coal Miners' Wives: Portraits of Endurance.* Lexington: University of Kentucky Press, 1995.

Gillespie, Oliver A. *The Pacific*, in *The Official History of New Zealand in the Second World War, 1939–1945.* http://www.nzetc.org/tm/scholarly /tei-WH2Paci.html.

Goralski, Robert. *World War II Almanac*, 1931–1945. New York: Bonanza Books, 1981.

Gordon, Ian. *Comic Strips and Consumer Culture,* 1890–1945. Washington and London: Smithsonian Institution Press, 1998.

Grace, James W. *Naval Battle of Guadalcanal: Night Action, 13 November 1942.* Annapolis, MD: Naval Institute Press, 1999.

Haga, Pauline. "Looking Back at Helen." *Beckley* (WV) *Raleigh Register/ Post-Herald,* Jan. 11, 1996.

Hallas, James H. *The Devil's Anvil: The Assault on Peleliu Island.* Westport, CT: Praeger, 1994.

Halsey, David. "Otsego: Remembering a Wyoming County Coal Camp." *Goldenseal,* Summer 2000.

Hammel, Eric. *Guadalcanal: Starvation Island.* New York: Crown, 1987.

———. *Guadalcanal: The Carrier Battles: Carrier Operations in the Solomons, August–October 1942.* New York: Crown, 1987.

Hickam, Homer. *Rocket Boys.* New York: Delacorte Press, 1998.

Hometown Heroes. Maurice O. "Mo" Darsey page, July 8, 2010. http:// dublinlaurenshometownheroes.blogspot.com/2010/07/maurice-o -mo-darsey.html. Retrieved Feb. 5, 2012.

Hough, Lt. Col. Frank O., and Maj. John A. Crown. *The Campaign on New Britain.* Washington: Historical Branch, HQ, USMC, 1952, available at http://www.ibiblio.org/hyperwar/USMC/USMC-M -NBrit/index.html.

Hough, Lt. Col. Frank O., Maj. Verle E. Ludwig, and Henry I. Shaw Jr. *History of U.S. Marine Corps Operations in World War II*, vol. 1, *Pearl*

Harbor to Guadalcanal, pt. 6, "The Turning Point: Guadalcanal" (Washington: U.S. Government Printing Office, 1958).

Hoyt, Edwin P. *The Glory of the Solomons*. New York: Stein & Day, 1983.

———. *Guadalcanal*. New York: Stein & Day, 1981.

Hunt, George P. *Coral Comes High*. New York: Harper & Brothers, 1946.

Inui, Genjirou. "My Guadalcanal." http://www.nettally.com/jrube/gen jirou/genjirou.htm, accessed January 15, 2012.

Jackson, Ralph Neal. "Life in Hell: A Brief Sketch of the Living Conditions on Guadalcanal as Experienced by a United States Marine in World War II." Student essay, unpublished, 1991.

Keene, Donald. *So Lovely a Country Will Never Perish: Wartime Diaries of Japanese Writers*. Asia Perspectives: History, Society, and Culture. New York: Columbia University Press, 2010.

Keene, R. R. "'Pistol Pete': Akio Tani, the 'Mantis,' Sent Marines Scrambling." *Leatherneck*, Oct. 1992.

Keeney, L. Douglas. *This Is Guadalcanal: The Original Combat Photography*. New York: Quill, 1999.

Kimmel, Eric. *Starvation Island: Guadalcanal* New York: Cone, 1987.

Koburger, Charles W. *Pacific Turning Point: The Solomons Campaign, 1942–1943*. (Westport, CT: Praeger, 1995.

Leckie, Robert. *Challenge for the Pacific: The Bloody Six-Month Battle of Guadalcanal*. Garden City, NY: Doubleday, 1965.

———. *Helmet for My Pillow*. New York: Random House, 1957; New York: Bantam, 2010.

———. *Strong Men Armed*. New York: Random House, 1962.

Lee, Howard B. *The Burning Springs and Other Tales of the Little Kanawha*. Morgantown: West Virginia University Press, 1968.

Lunt, Richard D. *Law and Order vs. the Miners: West Virginia, 1907–1933*. Charleston, WV: Appalachian Editions, 1992.

McGee, William. *The Solomons Campaigns, 1942–1943: From Guadalcanal to Bougainville—Pacific War Turning Point*. Tiburon, CA: BMC Publications, 2007.

McMillan, George. *The Old Breed: A History of the First Marine Division in World War II*. Washington: Infantry Journal Press, 1949.

Meader, Michael. "The Redneck War of 1921." *Goldenseal*, April–June 1981.

Means, Lawrence. *The "Raggedy Assed" Marines Are on Parade*. North Bend, OR: Wildwood Publishing, 1995.

Miller, Danny L. *The Miller Families of Ashe County, NC*. Privately published, undated.

Miller, James Edward. *My Autobiography*. Unpublished, 1990.

Miller, John, Jr. *Guadalcanal: The First Offensive*. Washington: Historical Division, Dept. of the Army, 1949.

Munn, Robert F. "The Development of Model Towns in the Bituminous Coal Fields." *West Virginia History*, 40, no. 3 (Spring 1979): 243–51.

Nalty, Bernard C., and Lt. Col. Ralph F. Moody. *A Brief History of U.S. Marine Corps Officer Procurement, 1775–1969*. Rev. ed. Washington: USMC Historical Division Headquarters, 1970.

Richter, Don. *Where the Sun Stood Still*. (Tawe, CA: Toucan Publishing, 1992.

Savage, Lon. *Thunder in the Mountains: The West Virginia Mine War, 1920–21*. Pittsburgh: University of Pittsburgh Press, 1990.

Sledge, Eugene B. *With the Old Breed at Peleliu and Okinawa*. Novato, CA: Presidio Press, 1981.

Stafford, Jane. "Unique in Medical History—'Guadalcanal Neurosis' Plagues Invalids Returning from Fighting in South Pacific." *Pittsburgh Press*, May 23, 1943, sec. 3, 1.

Stevenson, Mary Legg, *Coal Towns of West Virginia* Charleston, WV: Quarrier Press, 1998.

Sullivan, Ken, ed. *Goldenseal Book of the West Virginia Mine Wars*. Charleston, WV: Pictorial Histories, 1991.

Tams, Maj. W. P., Jr. *The Smokeless Coal Fields of West Virginia*. Morgantown: West Virginia University Press, 1983.

Toland, John. *The Rising Sun: The Decline and Fall of the Japanese Empire, 1936–1945*. New York: Random House, 1970.

Tregaskis, Richard. *Guadalcanal Diary*. New York: Random House, 1943; Random House Modern Library paperback ed., 2000.

USMC Special Action Report, Cape Gloucester Operation, First Marine Division 1943–1944, N-7443-A (unpaginated), available at http://www

.scribd.com/doc/45586358/WWII-1st-Marines-Division, accessed Feb. 26, 2012.

Vandegrift, Gen. A. A., as told to Robert B. Asprey. *Once a Marine: The Memoirs of General A. A. Vandergrift, United States Marine Corps.* New York: Norton, 1964.

Zimmerman, Major John L. *The Guadalcanal Campaign.* Washington: Historical Division, HQ, USMC, 1949, available at http://www.ibiblio .org/hyperwar/USMC/USMC-M-Guadalcanal.html.

Index